Kosovo Immigration Laws and Regulations Handbook: Strategic Information and Basic Laws

Just The facts101 Textbook Key Facts

by cram101

Textbook NOT Included

Table of Contents

Title Page

Copyright

Foundations of Business

Management

Business law

Finance

Human resource management

Information systems

Marketing

Manufacturing

Commerce

Business ethics

Accounting

Index: Answers

Just The Facts101

Exam Prep for

Kosovo Immigration Laws and Regulations Handbook: Strategic Information and Basic Laws

Just The Facts101 Exam Prep is your link from
the textbook and lecture to your exams.

**Just The Facts101 Exam Preps are unauthorized and comprehensive reviews
of your textbooks.**

All material provided by CTI Publications (c) 2019

Textbook publishers and textbook authors do not participate in or contribute to these reviews.

Just The Facts101 Exam Prep

Copyright © 2019 by CTI Publications. All rights reserved.

eAIN 438779

Foundations of Business

A business, also known as an enterprise, agency or a firm, is an entity involved in the provision of goods and/or services to consumers. Businesses are prevalent in capitalist economies, where most of them are privately owned and provide goods and services to customers in exchange for other goods, services, or money.

_____ is a means of protection from financial loss. It is a form of risk management, primarily used to hedge against the risk of a contingent or uncertain loss

Exam Probability: **Medium**

1. *Answer choices:*

(see index for correct answer)

- a. Insurance
- b. empathy
- c. corporate values
- d. cultural

Guidance: level 1

:: ::

Competition arises whenever at least two parties strive for a goal which cannot be shared: where one's gain is the other's loss.

Exam Probability: **Low**

2. *Answer choices:*

(see index for correct answer)

- a. imperative
- b. surface-level diversity
- c. Character
- d. hierarchical

Guidance: level 1

:: Television commercials ::

_____ is a characteristic that distinguishes physical entities that have biological processes, such as signaling and self-sustaining processes, from those that do not, either because such functions have ceased, or because they never had such functions and are classified as inanimate. Various forms of _____ exist, such as plants, animals, fungi, protists, archaea, and bacteria. The criteria can at times be ambiguous and may or may not define viruses, viroids, or potential synthetic _____ as "living". Biology is the science concerned with the study of _____ .

Exam Probability: **Low**

3. *Answer choices:*
(see index for correct answer)

- a. Birds
- b. Reassuringly Expensive
- c. Old Lions
- d. The LeBrons

Guidance: level 1

:: E-commerce ::

_____ is the activity of buying or selling of products on online services or over the Internet. Electronic commerce draws on technologies such as mobile commerce, electronic funds transfer, supply chain management, Internet marketing, online transaction processing, electronic data interchange , inventory management systems, and automated data collection systems.

Exam Probability: **High**

4. *Answer choices:*

(see index for correct answer)

- a. Online insurance
- b. Cooling-off period
- c. Address Verification System
- d. E-commerce

Guidance: level 1

:: Business ::

_____ is a trade policy that does not restrict imports or exports; it can also be understood as the free market idea applied to international trade. In government, _____ is predominantly advocated by political parties that hold liberal economic positions while economically left-wing and nationalist political parties generally support protectionism, the opposite of _____ .

Exam Probability: **Medium**

5. *Answer choices:*

(see index for correct answer)

- a. Free trade
- b. Business analysis
- c. Cognitive inertia
- d. Operating subsidiary

Guidance: level 1

:: Management occupations ::

_____ ship is the process of designing, launching and running a new business, which is often initially a small business. The people who create these businesses are called _____ s.

Exam Probability: **Low**

6. *Answer choices:*

(see index for correct answer)

- a. Corporate trainer
- b. Faculty consulting
- c. Legislator
- d. Councillor

Guidance: level 1

:: Management ::

_____ is the process of thinking about the activities required to achieve a desired goal. It is the first and foremost activity to achieve desired results. It involves the creation and maintenance of a plan, such as psychological aspects that require conceptual skills. There are even a couple of tests to measure someone's capability of _____ well. As such, _____ is a fundamental property of intelligent behavior. An important further meaning, often just called " _____ " is the legal context of permitted building developments.

Exam Probability: **Low**

7. *Answer choices:*

(see index for correct answer)

- a. Certified Energy Manager
- b. Total security management
- c. Dominant design

- d. Wireless informatics

Guidance: level 1

:: Problem solving ::

In other words, _____ is a situation where a group of people meet to generate new ideas and solutions around a specific domain of interest by removing inhibitions. People are able to think more freely and they suggest as many spontaneous new ideas as possible. All the ideas are noted down and those ideas are not criticized and after _____ session the ideas are evaluated. The term was popularized by Alex Faickney Osborn in the 1953 book Applied Imagination.

Exam Probability: **Medium**

8. *Answer choices:*
(see index for correct answer)

- a. Cognitive acceleration
- b. Trizics
- c. Lateral computing
- d. Heuristic

Guidance: level 1

:: ::

_____ is a marketing communication that employs an openly sponsored, non-personal message to promote or sell a product, service or idea. Sponsors of _____ are typically businesses wishing to promote their products or services. _____ is differentiated from public relations in that an advertiser pays for and has control over the message. It differs from personal selling in that the message is non-personal, i.e., not directed to a particular individual. _____ is communicated through various mass media, including traditional media such as newspapers, magazines, television, radio, outdoor _____ or direct mail; and new media such as search results, blogs, social media, websites or text messages. The actual presentation of the message in a medium is referred to as an advertisement, or "ad" or advert for short.

Exam Probability: **High**

9. *Answer choices:*

(see index for correct answer)

- a. corporate values
- b. surface-level diversity
- c. interpersonal communication
- d. Advertising

Guidance: level 1

:: Mereology ::

_____, in the abstract, is what belongs to or with something, whether as an attribute or as a component of said thing. In the context of this article, it is one or more components, whether physical or incorporeal, of a person's estate; or so belonging to, as in being owned by, a person or jointly a group of people or a legal entity like a corporation or even a society. Depending on the nature of the _____, an owner of _____ has the right to consume, alter, share, redefine, rent, mortgage, pawn, sell, exchange, transfer, give away or destroy it, or to exclude others from doing these things, as well as to perhaps abandon it; whereas regardless of the nature of the _____, the owner thereof has the right to properly use it, or at the very least exclusively keep it.

Exam Probability: **Medium**

10. *Answer choices:*
(see index for correct answer)

- a. Mereotopology
- b. Mereology
- c. Property
- d. Gunk

Guidance: level 1

:: Management ::

A _____ is when two or more people come together to discuss one or more topics, often in a formal or business setting, but _____ s also occur in a variety of other environments. Many various types of _____ s exist.

Exam Probability: **High**

11. *Answer choices:*

(see index for correct answer)

- a. Context analysis
- b. Industrial forensics
- c. Meeting
- d. Vasa syndrome

Guidance: level 1

:: ::

_____ is the collection of mechanisms, processes and relations by which corporations are controlled and operated. Governance structures and principles identify the distribution of rights and responsibilities among different participants in the corporation and include the rules and procedures for making decisions in corporate affairs. _____ is necessary because of the possibility of conflicts of interests between stakeholders, primarily between shareholders and upper management or among shareholders.

Exam Probability: **High**

12. *Answer choices:*

(see index for correct answer)

- a. information systems assessment

- b. Corporate governance
- c. functional perspective
- d. personal values

Guidance: level 1

:: Customs duties ::

A _____ is a tax on imports or exports between sovereign states. It is a form of regulation of foreign trade and a policy that taxes foreign products to encourage or safeguard domestic industry. _____ s are the simplest and oldest instrument of trade policy. Traditionally, states have used them as a source of income. Now, they are among the most widely used instruments of protection, along with import and export quotas.

Exam Probability: **High**

13. *Answer choices:*

(see index for correct answer)

- a. Immigration tariff
- b. Duty-free shop
- c. Specific rate duty
- d. Customs area

Guidance: level 1

:: Logistics ::

_____ is generally the detailed organization and implementation of a complex operation. In a general business sense, _____ is the management of the flow of things between the point of origin and the point of consumption in order to meet requirements of customers or corporations. The resources managed in _____ may include tangible goods such as materials, equipment, and supplies, as well as food and other consumable items. The _____ of physical items usually involves the integration of information flow, materials handling, production, packaging, inventory, transportation, warehousing, and often security.

Exam Probability: **Low**

14. *Answer choices:*

(see index for correct answer)

- a. Logistics
- b. Low Altitude Parachute Extraction System
- c. E2e Supply Chain Management
- d. Tracking number

Guidance: level 1

:: Financial crises ::

A _____ is any of a broad variety of situations in which some financial assets suddenly lose a large part of their nominal value. In the 19th and early 20th centuries, many financial crises were associated with banking panics, and many recessions coincided with these panics. Other situations that are often called financial crises include stock market crashes and the bursting of other financial bubbles, currency crises, and sovereign defaults. Financial crises directly result in a loss of paper wealth but do not necessarily result in significant changes in the real economy .

Exam Probability: **High**

15. *Answer choices:*

(see index for correct answer)

- a. Panic of 1825
- b. Financial crisis
- c. Kibbutz crisis
- d. Twin crises

Guidance: level 1

:: Employment ::

_____ is a relationship between two parties, usually based on a contract where work is paid for, where one party, which may be a corporation, for profit, not-for-profit organization, co-operative or other entity is the employer and the other is the employee. Employees work in return for payment, which may be in the form of an hourly wage, by piecework or an annual salary, depending on the type of work an employee does or which sector she or he is working in. Employees in some fields or sectors may receive gratuities, bonus payment or stock options. In some types of _____ , employees may receive benefits in addition to payment. Benefits can include health insurance, housing, disability insurance or use of a gym. _____ is typically governed by _____ laws, regulations or legal contracts.

Exam Probability: **Low**

16. *Answer choices:*

(see index for correct answer)

- a. Forced retention
- b. Employment
- c. EuroMayDay
- d. Nominative determinism

Guidance: level 1

:: Business process ::

A _____ or business method is a collection of related, structured activities or tasks by people or equipment which in a specific sequence produce a service or product for a particular customer or customers. _____ es occur at all organizational levels and may or may not be visible to the customers. A _____ may often be visualized as a flowchart of a sequence of activities with interleaving decision points or as a process matrix of a sequence of activities with relevance rules based on data in the process. The benefits of using _____ es include improved customer satisfaction and improved agility for reacting to rapid market change. Process-oriented organizations break down the barriers of structural departments and try to avoid functional silos.

Exam Probability: **Medium**

17. *Answer choices:*

(see index for correct answer)

- a. Process-centered design
- b. ProcessEdge
- c. Business process
- d. Business logic

Guidance: level 1

:: Marketing techniques ::

_____ is the activity of dividing a broad consumer or business market, normally consisting of existing and potential customers, into sub-groups of consumers based on some type of shared characteristics. In dividing or segmenting markets, researchers typically look for common characteristics such as shared needs, common interests, similar lifestyles or even similar demographic profiles. The overall aim of segmentation is to identify high yield segments – that is, those segments that are likely to be the most profitable or that have growth potential – so that these can be selected for special attention.

Exam Probability: **High**

18. *Answer choices:*

(see index for correct answer)

- a. Market segmentation
- b. SONCAS
- c. Relevant space
- d. Horizontal marketing system

Guidance: level 1

:: Packaging ::

In work place, _____ or job _____ means good ranking with the hypothesized conception of requirements of a role. There are two types of job _____ s: contextual and task. Task _____ is related to cognitive ability while contextual _____ is dependent upon personality. Task _____ are behavioral roles that are recognized in job descriptions and by remuneration systems, they are directly related to organizational _____, whereas, contextual _____ are value based and additional behavioral roles that are not recognized in job descriptions and covered by compensation; they are extra roles that are indirectly related to organizational _____. Citizenship _____ like contextual _____ means a set of individual activity/contribution that supports the organizational culture.

Exam Probability: **Low**

19. *Answer choices:*

(see index for correct answer)

- a. Logoplaste
- b. Tamper-evident band
- c. Performance
- d. Bag-in-box

Guidance: level 1

:: Stock market ::

The _____ of a corporation is all of the shares into which ownership of the corporation is divided. In American English, the shares are commonly known as "_____s". A single share of the _____ represents fractional ownership of the corporation in proportion to the total number of shares. This typically entitles the _____ holder to that fraction of the company's earnings, proceeds from liquidation of assets, or voting power, often dividing these up in proportion to the amount of money each _____ holder has invested. Not all _____ is necessarily equal, as certain classes of _____ may be issued for example without voting rights, with enhanced voting rights, or with a certain priority to receive profits or liquidation proceeds before or after other classes of shareholders.

Exam Probability: **High**

20. *Answer choices:*

(see index for correct answer)

- a. Event-driven investing
- b. Stock
- c. International Retail Service
- d. Abnormal return

Guidance: level 1

:: Labour relations ::

_____ is a field of study that can have different meanings depending on the context in which it is used. In an international context, it is a subfield of labor history that studies the human relations with regard to work – in its broadest sense – and how this connects to questions of social inequality. It explicitly encompasses unregulated, historical, and non-Western forms of labor. Here, _____ define "for or with whom one works and under what rules. These rules determine the type of work, type and amount of remuneration, working hours, degrees of physical and psychological strain, as well as the degree of freedom and autonomy associated with the work."

Exam Probability: **High**

21. *Answer choices:*

(see index for correct answer)

- a. Review Body
- b. Negotiated cartelism
- c. Broad left
- d. Global union federation

Guidance: level 1

:: Marketing analytics ::

_____ is a long-term, forward-looking approach to planning with the fundamental goal of achieving a sustainable competitive advantage. Strategic planning involves an analysis of the company's strategic initial situation prior to the formulation, evaluation and selection of market-oriented competitive position that contributes to the company's goals and marketing objectives.

Exam Probability: **High**

22. *Answer choices:*

(see index for correct answer)

- a. Marketing accountability
- b. Marketing strategy
- c. Marketing performance measurement and management
- d. marketing dashboard

Guidance: level 1

:: Foreign direct investment ::

A _____ is an investment in the form of a controlling ownership in a business in one country by an entity based in another country. It is thus distinguished from a foreign portfolio investment by a notion of direct control.

Exam Probability: **High**

23. Answer choices:

(see index for correct answer)

- a. EB-5 visa
- b. Diamond model
- c. Dutch disease
- d. FDI stock

Guidance: level 1

:: Stock market ::

_____ is a form of corporate equity ownership, a type of security. The terms voting share and ordinary share are also used frequently in other parts of the world; "_____" being primarily used in the United States. They are known as Equity shares or Ordinary shares in the UK and other Commonwealth realms. This type of share gives the stockholder the right to share in the profits of the company, and to vote on matters of corporate policy and the composition of the members of the board of directors.

Exam Probability: **Low**

24. Answer choices:

(see index for correct answer)

- a. Stock split
- b. PLUS Markets Group
- c. Bear raid

- d. Common stock

Guidance: level 1

:: Information science ::

A _____ is a written, drawn, presented, or memorialized representation of thought. a _____ is a form, or written piece that trains a line of thought or as in history, a significant event. The word originates from the Latin _____ um, which denotes a "teaching" or "lesson": the verb doceo denotes "to teach". In the past, the word was usually used to denote a written proof useful as evidence of a truth or fact. In the computer age, "_____" usually denotes a primarily textual computer file, including its structure and format, e.g. fonts, colors, and images. Contemporarily, "_____" is not defined by its transmission medium, e.g., paper, given the existence of electronic _____ s. "_____ ation" is distinct because it has more denotations than "_____". _____ s are also distinguished from "realia", which are three-dimensional objects that would otherwise satisfy the definition of "_____" because they memorialize or represent thought; _____ s are considered more as 2 dimensional representations. While _____ s are able to have large varieties of customization, all _____ s are able to be shared freely, and have the right to do so, creativity can be represented by _____ s, also. History, events, examples, opinion, etc. all can be expressed in _____ s.

Exam Probability: **Medium**

25. *Answer choices:*

(see index for correct answer)

- a. Secondary source

- b. Information: The New Language of Science
- c. Information Rules
- d. Legal informatics

Guidance: level 1

:: Cash flow ::

_____ s are narrowly interconnected with the concepts of value, interest rate and liquidity. A _____ that shall happen on a future day tN can be transformed into a _____ of the same value in t0.

Exam Probability: **Low**

26. *Answer choices:*

(see index for correct answer)

- a. Free cash flow
- b. Discounted cash flow
- c. Propequity
- d. Cash carrier

Guidance: level 1

:: Debt ::

_____ , in finance and economics, is payment from a borrower or deposit-taking financial institution to a lender or depositor of an amount above repayment of the principal sum , at a particular rate. It is distinct from a fee which the borrower may pay the lender or some third party. It is also distinct from dividend which is paid by a company to its shareholders from its profit or reserve, but not at a particular rate decided beforehand, rather on a pro rata basis as a share in the reward gained by risk taking entrepreneurs when the revenue earned exceeds the total costs.

Exam Probability: **High**

27. *Answer choices:*

(see index for correct answer)

- a. Museum of Foreign Debt
- b. Sum certain
- c. Interest
- d. Phantom debt

Guidance: level 1

:: Project management ::

Some scenarios associate "this kind of planning" with learning "life skills". _____ s are necessary, or at least useful, in situations where individuals need to know what time they must be at a specific location to receive a specific service, and where people need to accomplish a set of goals within a set time period.

Exam Probability: **High**

28. *Answer choices:*

(see index for correct answer)

- a. ISO 21500
- b. LibrePlan
- c. Schedule
- d. PRINCE2

Guidance: level 1

:: Export and import control ::

"_____" means the Government Service which is responsible for the administration of _____ law and the collection of duties and taxes and which also has the responsibility for the application of other laws and regulations relating to the importation, exportation, movement or storage of goods.

Exam Probability: **High**

29. *Answer choices:*

(see index for correct answer)

- a. Customs
- b. CoCom

- c. Wassenaar Arrangement
- d. VNIIS Exemption Letter

Guidance: level 1

:: ::

In regulatory jurisdictions that provide for it, _____ is a group of laws and organizations designed to ensure the rights of consumers as well as fair trade, competition and accurate information in the marketplace. The laws are designed to prevent the businesses that engage in fraud or specified unfair practices from gaining an advantage over competitors. They may also provides additional protection for those most vulnerable in society. _____ laws are a form of government regulation that aim to protect the rights of consumers. For example, a government may require businesses to disclose detailed information about products—particularly in areas where safety or public health is an issue, such as food.

Exam Probability: **Medium**

30. *Answer choices:*
(see index for correct answer)

- a. hierarchical perspective
- b. deep-level diversity
- c. cultural
- d. corporate values

Guidance: level 1

:: Interest rates ::

An _____ is the amount of interest due per period, as a proportion of the amount lent, deposited or borrowed. The total interest on an amount lent or borrowed depends on the principal sum, the _____ , the compounding frequency, and the length of time over which it is lent, deposited or borrowed.

Exam Probability: **Medium**

31. *Answer choices:*

(see index for correct answer)

- a. Real interest rate
- b. Effective annual interest rate
- c. Official bank rate
- d. Official cash rate

Guidance: level 1

:: Market research ::

_____ is an organized effort to gather information about target markets or customers. It is a very important component of business strategy. The term is commonly interchanged with marketing research; however, expert practitioners may wish to draw a distinction, in that marketing research is concerned specifically about marketing processes, while _____ is concerned specifically with markets.

Exam Probability: **Low**

32. *Answer choices:*

(see index for correct answer)

- a. Worm
- b. Customer advisory council
- c. Brand elections
- d. Market research

Guidance: level 1

:: ::

A _____ is an organization, usually a group of people or a company, authorized to act as a single entity and recognized as such in law. Early incorporated entities were established by charter. Most jurisdictions now allow the creation of new _____ s through registration.

Exam Probability: **Low**

33. Answer choices:

(see index for correct answer)

- a. empathy
- b. surface-level diversity
- c. Corporation
- d. information systems assessment

Guidance: level 1

:: Production economics ::

In microeconomics, _____ are the cost advantages that enterprises obtain due to their scale of operation, with cost per unit of output decreasing with increasing scale.

Exam Probability: **Low**

34. Answer choices:

(see index for correct answer)

- a. Constant elasticity of transformation
- b. Economies of scale
- c. Peer production
- d. Production theory

Guidance: level 1

:: Real estate valuation ::

_____ or OMV is the price at which an asset would trade in a competitive auction setting. _____ is often used interchangeably with open _____, fair value or fair _____, although these terms have distinct definitions in different standards, and may or may not differ in some circumstances.

Exam Probability: **Medium**

35. *Answer choices:*

(see index for correct answer)

- a. Philip Michael Faraday
- b. Uniform Standards of Professional Appraisal Practice
- c. Market value
- d. Zillow

Guidance: level 1

:: Data management ::

_____ is a form of intellectual property that grants the creator of an original creative work an exclusive legal right to determine whether and under what conditions this original work may be copied and used by others, usually for a limited term of years. The exclusive rights are not absolute but limited by limitations and exceptions to _____ law, including fair use. A major limitation on _____ on ideas is that _____ protects only the original expression of ideas, and not the underlying ideas themselves.

Exam Probability: **Medium**

36. *Answer choices:*

(see index for correct answer)

- a. Copyright
- b. Client-side persistent data
- c. Virtual data room
- d. National Information Governance Board for Health and Social Care

Guidance: level 1

:: Organizational behavior ::

_____ is the state or fact of exclusive rights and control over property, which may be an object, land/real estate or intellectual property. _____ involves multiple rights, collectively referred to as title, which may be separated and held by different parties.

Exam Probability: **Medium**

37. *Answer choices:*

(see index for correct answer)

- a. Span of control
- b. Civic virtue
- c. Informal organization
- d. Organizational retaliatory behavior

Guidance: level 1

:: Statistical terminology ::

_____ es can be learned implicitly within cultural contexts. People may develop _____ es toward or against an individual, an ethnic group, a sexual or gender identity, a nation, a religion, a social class, a political party, theoretical paradigms and ideologies within academic domains, or a species. _____ ed means one-sided, lacking a neutral viewpoint, or not having an open mind. _____ can come in many forms and is related to prejudice and intuition.

Exam Probability: **High**

38. *Answer choices:*

(see index for correct answer)

- a. Kurtosis risk
- b. P-value
- c. Statistical epidemiology

- d. Iterated conditional modes

Guidance: level 1

:: Consumer theory ::

_____ is the quantity of a good that consumers are willing and able to purchase at various prices during a given period of time.

Exam Probability: **Medium**

39. *Answer choices:*

(see index for correct answer)

- a. Demand
- b. Time-based pricing
- c. Expenditure function
- d. Income effect

Guidance: level 1

:: Goods ::

In most contexts, the concept of _____ denotes the conduct that should be preferred when posed with a choice between possible actions. _____ is generally considered to be the opposite of evil, and is of interest in the study of morality, ethics, religion and philosophy. The specific meaning and etymology of the term and its associated translations among ancient and contemporary languages show substantial variation in its inflection and meaning depending on circumstances of place, history, religious, or philosophical context.

Exam Probability: **Medium**

40. *Answer choices:*

(see index for correct answer)

- a. Intermediate good
- b. Yellow goods
- c. Merit good
- d. Good

Guidance: level 1

:: International trade ::

_____ involves the transfer of goods or services from one person or entity to another, often in exchange for money. A system or network that allows _____ is called a market.

Exam Probability: **High**

41. *Answer choices:*

(see index for correct answer)

- a. Public international law
- b. Balanced trade
- c. Trade
- d. Agreement on Agriculture

Guidance: level 1

:: Scientific method ::

In the social sciences and life sciences, a _____ is a research method involving an up-close, in-depth, and detailed examination of a subject of study, as well as its related contextual conditions.

Exam Probability: **High**

42. *Answer choices:*

(see index for correct answer)

- a. Case study
- b. Causal research
- c. pilot project
- d. explanatory research

Guidance: level 1

:: Supply chain management ::

_____ is the process of finding and agreeing to terms, and acquiring goods, services, or works from an external source, often via a tendering or competitive bidding process. _____ is used to ensure the buyer receives goods, services, or works at the best possible price when aspects such as quality, quantity, time, and location are compared. Corporations and public bodies often define processes intended to promote fair and open competition for their business while minimizing risks such as exposure to fraud and collusion.

Exam Probability: **Medium**

43. *Answer choices:*

(see index for correct answer)

- a. Dynamic discounting
- b. LLamasoft
- c. Enterprise carbon accounting
- d. Symphony EYC

Guidance: level 1

:: Business terms ::

A _____ is a short statement of why an organization exists, what its overall goal is, identifying the goal of its operations: what kind of product or service it provides, its primary customers or market, and its geographical region of operation. It may include a short statement of such fundamental matters as the organization's values or philosophies, a business's main competitive advantages, or a desired future state—the "vision".

Exam Probability: **Medium**

44. *Answer choices:*
(see index for correct answer)

- a. front office
- b. operating cost
- c. granular
- d. strategic plan

Guidance: level 1

:: ::

Business is the activity of making one's living or making money by producing or buying and selling products. Simply put, it is "any activity or enterprise entered into for profit. It does not mean it is a company, a corporation, partnership, or have any such formal organization, but it can range from a street peddler to General Motors."

Exam Probability: **Low**

45. *Answer choices:*

(see index for correct answer)

- a. process perspective
- b. Firm
- c. cultural
- d. hierarchical perspective

Guidance: level 1

:: Stock market ::

A _____, equity market or share market is the aggregation of buyers and sellers of stocks , which represent ownership claims on businesses; these may include securities listed on a public stock exchange, as well as stock that is only traded privately. Examples of the latter include shares of private companies which are sold to investors through equity crowdfunding platforms. Stock exchanges list shares of common equity as well as other security types, e.g. corporate bonds and convertible bonds.

Exam Probability: **Low**

46. *Answer choices:*

(see index for correct answer)

- a. Relative valuation
- b. Piqqem
- c. Stock market

- d. Secondary shares

Guidance: level 1

:: Supply chain management terms ::

In business and finance, _____ is a system of organizations, people, activities, information, and resources involved in moving a product or service from supplier to customer. _____ activities involve the transformation of natural resources, raw materials, and components into a finished product that is delivered to the end customer. In sophisticated _____ systems, used products may re-enter the _____ at any point where residual value is recyclable. _____ s link value chains.

Exam Probability: **Medium**

47. *Answer choices:*

(see index for correct answer)

- a. Final assembly schedule
- b. Supply chain
- c. Most valuable customers
- d. Capital spare

Guidance: level 1

:: Economic globalization ::

_____ is an agreement in which one company hires another company to be responsible for a planned or existing activity that is or could be done internally, and sometimes involves transferring employees and assets from one firm to another.

Exam Probability: **Medium**

48. *Answer choices:*

(see index for correct answer)

- a. Outsourcing
- b. global financial

Guidance: level 1

:: Retailing ::

_____ is the process of selling consumer goods or services to customers through multiple channels of distribution to earn a profit. _____ ers satisfy demand identified through a supply chain. The term " _____ er" is typically applied where a service provider fills the small orders of a large number of individuals, who are end-users, rather than large orders of a small number of wholesale, corporate or government clientele. Shopping generally refers to the act of buying products. Sometimes this is done to obtain final goods, including necessities such as food and clothing; sometimes it takes place as a recreational activity. Recreational shopping often involves window shopping and browsing: it does not always result in a purchase.

Exam Probability: **Low**

49. Answer choices:

(see index for correct answer)

- a. Variety store
- b. Retail
- c. Shopping channel
- d. Garage sale

Guidance: level 1

:: Information science ::

_____ is the resolution of uncertainty; it is that which answers the question of "what an entity is" and thus defines both its essence and nature of its characteristics. _____ relates to both data and knowledge, as data is meaningful _____ representing values attributed to parameters, and knowledge signifies understanding of a concept. _____ is uncoupled from an observer, which is an entity that can access _____ and thus discern what it specifies; _____ exists beyond an event horizon for example. In the case of knowledge, the _____ itself requires a cognitive observer to be obtained.

Exam Probability: **Medium**

50. Answer choices:

(see index for correct answer)

- a. Data curation
- b. Information

- c. Hydroinformatics
- d. Overcategorization

Guidance: level 1

:: Stock market ::

A _____, securities exchange or bourse, is a facility where stock brokers and traders can buy and sell securities, such as shares of stock and bonds and other financial instruments. _____ s may also provide for facilities the issue and redemption of such securities and instruments and capital events including the payment of income and dividends. Securities traded on a _____ include stock issued by listed companies, unit trusts, derivatives, pooled investment products and bonds. _____ s often function as "continuous auction" markets with buyers and sellers consummating transactions via open outcry at a central location such as the floor of the exchange or by using an electronic trading platform.

Exam Probability: **Medium**

51. *Answer choices:*
(see index for correct answer)

- a. Short-term trading
- b. Stock exchange
- c. End of day
- d. International Retail Service

Guidance: level 1

:: Statistical terminology ::

_____ is the magnitude or dimensions of a thing. _____ can be measured as length, width, height, diameter, perimeter, area, volume, or mass.

Exam Probability: **Low**

52. *Answer choices:*

(see index for correct answer)

- a. Size
- b. Efficient estimator
- c. Iterated conditional modes
- d. Kurtosis risk

Guidance: level 1

:: Casting (manufacturing) ::

A _____ is a regularity in the world, man-made design, or abstract ideas. As such, the elements of a _____ repeat in a predictable manner. A geometric _____ is a kind of _____ formed of geometric shapes and typically repeated like a wallpaper design.

Exam Probability: **Low**

53. *Answer choices:*

(see index for correct answer)

- a. Pattern
- b. Permanent mold casting
- c. Evaporative-pattern casting
- d. Riser

Guidance: level 1

:: National accounts ::

_____ is a monetary measure of the market value of all the final goods and services produced in a period of time, often annually. GDP per capita does not, however, reflect differences in the cost of living and the inflation rates of the countries; therefore using a basis of GDP per capita at purchasing power parity is arguably more useful when comparing differences in living standards between nations.

Exam Probability: **Medium**

54. *Answer choices:*

(see index for correct answer)

- a. capital formation
- b. National Income
- c. Fixed capital

Guidance: level 1

:: Marketing ::

A _____ is an overall experience of a customer that distinguishes an organization or product from its rivals in the eyes of the customer. _____ s are used in business, marketing, and advertising. Name _____ s are sometimes distinguished from generic or store _____ s.

Exam Probability: **High**

55. *Answer choices:*

(see index for correct answer)

- a. Generic trademark
- b. Preference-rank translation
- c. Product churning
- d. Loyalty program

Guidance: level 1

:: Budgets ::

A _____ is a financial plan for a defined period, often one year. It may also include planned sales volumes and revenues, resource quantities, costs and expenses, assets, liabilities and cash flows. Companies, governments, families and other organizations use it to express strategic plans of activities or events in measurable terms.

Exam Probability: **Low**

56. *Answer choices:*

(see index for correct answer)

- a. Performance-based budgeting
- b. Budget
- c. Operating budget
- d. Participatory budgeting

Guidance: level 1

:: Costs ::

In microeconomic theory, the _____, or alternative cost, of making a particular choice is the value of the most valuable choice out of those that were not taken. In other words, opportunity that will require sacrifices.

Exam Probability: **Low**

57. *Answer choices:*

(see index for correct answer)

- a. Flyaway cost
- b. Sliding scale
- c. Cost of products sold
- d. Opportunity cost

Guidance: level 1

:: Business law ::

_____ is where a person's financial liability is limited to a fixed sum, most commonly the value of a person's investment in a company or partnership. If a company with _____ is sued, then the claimants are suing the company, not its owners or investors. A shareholder in a limited company is not personally liable for any of the debts of the company, other than for the amount already invested in the company and for any unpaid amount on the shares in the company, if any. The same is true for the members of a _____ partnership and the limited partners in a limited partnership. By contrast, sole proprietors and partners in general partnerships are each liable for all the debts of the business.

Exam Probability: **Low**

58. *Answer choices:*
(see index for correct answer)

- a. Statutory liability
- b. Time-and-a-half

- c. Fraudulent trading
- d. Business license

Guidance: level 1

:: Business models ::

A _____ is "an autonomous association of persons united voluntarily to meet their common economic, social, and cultural needs and aspirations through a jointly-owned and democratically-controlled enterprise". _____ s may include.

Exam Probability: **Low**

59. *Answer choices:*
(see index for correct answer)

- a. One stop shop
- b. Cooperative
- c. Subscription business model
- d. Product-service system

Guidance: level 1

Management

Management is the administration of an organization, whether it is a business, a not-for-profit organization, or government body. Management includes the activities of setting the strategy of an organization and coordinating the efforts of its employees (or of volunteers) to accomplish its objectives through the application of available resources, such as financial, natural, technological, and human resources.

:: Employment discrimination ::

A _____ is a metaphor used to represent an invisible barrier that keeps a given demographic from rising beyond a certain level in a hierarchy.

Exam Probability: **High**

1. *Answer choices:*

(see index for correct answer)

- a. MacBride Principles
- b. LGBT employment discrimination in the United States
- c. Employment discrimination
- d. New South Wales selection bias

Guidance: level 1

:: Employment ::

The _____ is an individual's metaphorical "journey" through learning, work and other aspects of life. There are a number of ways to define _____ and the term is used in a variety of ways.

Exam Probability: **Low**

2. *Answer choices:*

(see index for correct answer)

- a. Extreme Blue
- b. Career
- c. Personal chef
- d. Workhaven

Guidance: level 1

:: Management ::

In organizational studies, _____ is the efficient and effective development of an organization's resources when they are needed. Such resources may include financial resources, inventory, human skills, production resources, or information technology and natural resources.

Exam Probability: **High**

3. *Answer choices:*
(see index for correct answer)

- a. Competitive advantage
- b. manager's right to manage
- c. Resource management
- d. Fall guy

Guidance: level 1

:: Production and manufacturing ::

_____ is a theory of management that analyzes and synthesizes workflows. Its main objective is improving economic efficiency, especially labor productivity. It was one of the earliest attempts to apply science to the engineering of processes and to management. _____ is sometimes known as Taylorism after its founder, Frederick Winslow Taylor.

Exam Probability: **Low**

4. *Answer choices:*

(see index for correct answer)

- a. Predetermined motion time system
- b. Beltweigher
- c. Scientific management
- d. Low rate initial production

Guidance: level 1

:: Electronic feedback ::

_____ occurs when outputs of a system are routed back as inputs as part of a chain of cause-and-effect that forms a circuit or loop. The system can then be said to feed back into itself. The notion of cause-and-effect has to be handled carefully when applied to _____ systems.

Exam Probability: **High**

5. *Answer choices:*

(see index for correct answer)

- a. feedback loop
- b. Positive feedback

Guidance: level 1

:: Employee relations ::

_____ ownership, or employee share ownership, is an ownership interest in a company held by the company's workforce. The ownership interest may be facilitated by the company as part of employees' remuneration or incentive compensation for work performed, or the company itself may be employee owned.

Exam Probability: **Low**

6. *Answer choices:*

(see index for correct answer)

- a. Employee engagement
- b. Employee morale
- c. Employee handbook
- d. employee stock ownership

Guidance: level 1

:: Legal terms ::

_____ is a type of meaning in which a phrase, statement or resolution is not explicitly defined, making several interpretations plausible. A common aspect of _____ is uncertainty. It is thus an attribute of any idea or statement whose intended meaning cannot be definitively resolved according to a rule or process with a finite number of steps.

Exam Probability: **High**

7. *Answer choices:*

(see index for correct answer)

- a. Injunction
- b. Comity
- c. Plant variety
- d. Ambiguity

Guidance: level 1

A _____ is a leader's method of providing direction, implementing plans, and motivating people. Various authors have proposed identifying many different _____ s as exhibited by leaders in the political, business or other fields. Studies on _____ are conducted in the military field, expressing an approach that stresses a holistic view of leadership, including how a leader's physical presence determines how others perceive that leader. The factors of physical presence in this context include military bearing, physical fitness, confidence, and resilience. The leader's intellectual capacity helps to conceptualize solutions and to acquire knowledge to do the job. A leader's conceptual abilities apply agility, judgment, innovation, interpersonal tact, and domain knowledge. Domain knowledge encompasses tactical and technical knowledge as well as cultural and geopolitical awareness. Daniel Goleman in his article "Leadership that Gets Results" talks about six styles of leadership.

Exam Probability: **Medium**

8. *Answer choices:*

(see index for correct answer)

- a. functional perspective
- b. information systems assessment
- c. Leadership style
- d. co-culture

Guidance: level 1

:: Management ::

_____ is a method of quality control which employs statistical methods to monitor and control a process. This helps to ensure that the process operates efficiently, producing more specification-conforming products with less waste . SPC can be applied to any process where the "conforming product" output can be measured. Key tools used in SPC include run charts, control charts, a focus on continuous improvement, and the design of experiments. An example of a process where SPC is applied is manufacturing lines.

Exam Probability: **Medium**

9. *Answer choices:*

(see index for correct answer)

- a. Productive efficiency
- b. PhD in management
- c. Virtual customer environment
- d. Duality

Guidance: level 1

An _____ is a person temporarily or permanently residing in a country other than their native country. In common usage, the term often refers to professionals, skilled workers, or artists taking positions outside their home country, either independently or sent abroad by their employers, who can be companies, universities, governments, or non-governmental organisations. Effectively migrant workers, they usually earn more than they would at home, and less than local employees. However, the term ` _____ ` is also used for retirees and others who have chosen to live outside their native country. Historically, it has also referred to exiles.

Exam Probability: **High**

10. *Answer choices:*

(see index for correct answer)

- a. Sarbanes-Oxley act of 2002
- b. imperative
- c. empathy
- d. Expatriate

Guidance: level 1

:: Hospitality management ::

A _____ is an establishment that provides paid lodging on a short-term basis. Facilities provided may range from a modest-quality mattress in a small room to large suites with bigger, higher-quality beds, a dresser, a refrigerator and other kitchen facilities, upholstered chairs, a flat screen television, and en-suite bathrooms. Small, lower-priced _____ s may offer only the most basic guest services and facilities. Larger, higher-priced _____ s may provide additional guest facilities such as a swimming pool, business centre , childcare, conference and event facilities, tennis or basketball courts, gymnasium, restaurants, day spa, and social function services. _____ rooms are usually numbered to allow guests to identify their room. Some boutique, high-end _____ s have custom decorated rooms. Some _____ s offer meals as part of a room and board arrangement. In the United Kingdom, a _____ is required by law to serve food and drinks to all guests within certain stated hours. In Japan, capsule _____ s provide a tiny room suitable only for sleeping and shared bathroom facilities.

Exam Probability: **High**

11. *Answer choices:*

(see index for correct answer)

- a. BSc. HCM
- b. IHM Pusa
- c. Restaurant management
- d. Hotel

Guidance: level 1

:: ::

Some scenarios associate "this kind of planning" with learning "life skills". Schedules are necessary, or at least useful, in situations where individuals need to know what time they must be at a specific location to receive a specific service, and where people need to accomplish a set of goals within a set time period.

Exam Probability: **Low**

12. *Answer choices:*

(see index for correct answer)

- a. Sarbanes-Oxley act of 2002
- b. Scheduling
- c. cultural
- d. information systems assessment

Guidance: level 1

:: International trade ::

_____ involves the transfer of goods or services from one person or entity to another, often in exchange for money. A system or network that allows _____ is called a market.

Exam Probability: **Low**

13. *Answer choices:*

(see index for correct answer)

- a. Balassa index
- b. Autarky
- c. Trade
- d. Gravity model of trade

Guidance: level 1

:: Game theory ::

To _____ is to make a deal between different parties where each party gives up part of their demand. In arguments, _____ is a concept of finding agreement through communication, through a mutual acceptance of terms—often involving variations from an original goal or desires.

Exam Probability: **Low**

14. *Answer choices:*

(see index for correct answer)

- a. Uncorrelated asymmetry
- b. Theorycraft
- c. Compromise
- d. Divide and choose

Guidance: level 1

:: Customs duties ::

A _____ is a tax on imports or exports between sovereign states. It is a form of regulation of foreign trade and a policy that taxes foreign products to encourage or safeguard domestic industry. _____ s are the simplest and oldest instrument of trade policy. Traditionally, states have used them as a source of income. Now, they are among the most widely used instruments of protection, along with import and export quotas.

Exam Probability: **Low**

15. *Answer choices:*

(see index for correct answer)

- a. Court of Exchequer
- b. Customs bond
- c. Tariff-rate quota
- d. Tariff

Guidance: level 1

:: Production and manufacturing ::

An _____ is a manufacturing process in which parts are added as the semi-finished assembly moves from workstation to workstation where the parts are added in sequence until the final assembly is produced. By mechanically moving the parts to the assembly work and moving the semi-finished assembly from work station to work station, a finished product can be assembled faster and with less labor than by having workers carry parts to a stationary piece for assembly.

Exam Probability: **Medium**

16. *Answer choices:*

(see index for correct answer)

- a. Product data record
- b. Nondestructive testing
- c. Bill of resources
- d. Production equipment control

Guidance: level 1

:: ::

An _____ is a contingent motivator. Traditional _____ s are extrinsic motivators which reward actions to yield a desired outcome. The effectiveness of traditional _____ s has changed as the needs of Western society have evolved. While the traditional _____ model is effective when there is a defined procedure and goal for a task, Western society started to require a higher volume of critical thinkers, so the traditional model became less effective. Institutions are now following a trend in implementing strategies that rely on intrinsic motivations rather than the extrinsic motivations that the traditional _____ s foster.

Exam Probability: **Medium**

17. *Answer choices:*

(see index for correct answer)

- a. Incentive
- b. open system
- c. co-culture
- d. corporate values

Guidance: level 1

:: Life skills ::

_____ , emotional leadership , emotional quotient and _____ quotient , is the capability of individuals to recognize their own emotions and those of others, discern between different feelings and label them appropriately, use emotional information to guide thinking and behavior, and manage and/or adjust emotions to adapt to environments or achieve one's goal.

Exam Probability: **High**

18. *Answer choices:*

(see index for correct answer)

- a. emotion work
- b. Emotional intelligence
- c. coping mechanism
- d. multiple intelligence

Guidance: level 1

:: Leadership ::

_____ /Management is a part of a style of leadership that focuses on supervision, organization, and performance; it is an integral part of the Full Range Leadership Model. _____ is a style of leadership in which leaders promote compliance by followers through both rewards and punishments. Through a rewards and punishments system, transactional leaders are able to keep followers motivated for the short-term. Unlike transformational leaders, those using the transactional approach are not looking to change the future, they look to keep things the same. Leaders using _____ as a model pay attention to followers' work in order to find faults and deviations.

Exam Probability: **Low**

19. *Answer choices:*

(see index for correct answer)

- a. Meta-leadership
- b. Transactional leadership
- c. Ethical leadership
- d. Consideration and Initiating Structure

Guidance: level 1

:: Stochastic processes ::

_____ is a system of rules that are created and enforced through social or governmental institutions to regulate behavior. It has been defined both as "the Science of Justice" and "the Art of Justice". _____ is a system that regulates and ensures that individuals or a community adhere to the will of the state. State-enforced _____ s can be made by a collective legislature or by a single legislator, resulting in statutes, by the executive through decrees and regulations, or established by judges through precedent, normally in common _____ jurisdictions. Private individuals can create legally binding contracts, including arbitration agreements that may elect to accept alternative arbitration to the normal court process. The formation of _____ s themselves may be influenced by a constitution, written or tacit, and the rights encoded therein. The _____ shapes politics, economics, history and society in various ways and serves as a mediator of relations between people.

Exam Probability: **Medium**

20. *Answer choices:*
(see index for correct answer)

- a. Markov reward model

- b. Multiscale decision-making
- c. Bussgang theorem
- d. Law

Guidance: level 1

:: Social psychology ::

In social psychology, _____ is the phenomenon of a person exerting less effort to achieve a goal when he or she works in a group than when working alone. This is seen as one of the main reasons groups are sometimes less productive than the combined performance of their members working as individuals, but should be distinguished from the accidental coordination problems that groups sometimes experience.

Exam Probability: **Medium**

21. *Answer choices:*
(see index for correct answer)

- a. externalization
- b. Body language
- c. Social loafing
- d. Mind control

Guidance: level 1

:: Leadership ::

_____ is a theory of leadership where a leader works with teams to identify needed change, creating a vision to guide the change through inspiration, and executing the change in tandem with committed members of a group; it is an integral part of the Full Range Leadership Model. _____ serves to enhance the motivation, morale, and job performance of followers through a variety of mechanisms; these include connecting the follower's sense of identity and self to a project and to the collective identity of the organization; being a role model for followers in order to inspire them and to raise their interest in the project; challenging followers to take greater ownership for their work, and understanding the strengths and weaknesses of followers, allowing the leader to align followers with tasks that enhance their performance.

Exam Probability: **Low**

22. *Answer choices:*

(see index for correct answer)

- a. Inspired Leadership Award
- b. BTS Group
- c. Jewish leadership
- d. Tribal Leadership

Guidance: level 1

:: ::

_____ consists of using generic or ad hoc methods in an orderly manner to find solutions to problems. Some of the problem-solving techniques developed and used in philosophy, artificial intelligence, computer science, engineering, mathematics, or medicine are related to mental problem-solving techniques studied in psychology.

Exam Probability: **Medium**

23. *Answer choices:*
(see index for correct answer)

- a. hierarchical
- b. levels of analysis
- c. hierarchical perspective
- d. interpersonal communication

Guidance: level 1

:: Production economics ::

_____ is the joint use of a resource or space. It is also the process of dividing and distributing. In its narrow sense, it refers to joint or alternating use of inherently finite goods, such as a common pasture or a shared residence. Still more loosely, "_____" can actually mean giving something as an outright gift: for example, to "share" one's food really means to give some of it as a gift. _____ is a basic component of human interaction, and is responsible for strengthening social ties and ensuring a person's well-being.

Exam Probability: **High**

24. *Answer choices:*

(see index for correct answer)

- a. Returns to scale
- b. Sharing
- c. Robinson Crusoe economy
- d. Peer production

Guidance: level 1

:: Behavior modification ::

In psychotherapy and mental health, _____ has a positive sense of empowering individuals, or a negative sense of encouraging dysfunctional behavior.

Exam Probability: **High**

25. *Answer choices:*

(see index for correct answer)

- a. Enabling
- b. Thought stopping

Guidance: level 1

:: Human resource management ::

_____ is the strategic approach to the effective management of people in an organization so that they help the business to gain a competitive advantage. It is designed to maximize employee performance in service of an employer's strategic objectives. HR is primarily concerned with the management of people within organizations, focusing on policies and on systems. HR departments are responsible for overseeing employee-benefits design, employee recruitment, training and development, performance appraisal, and Reward management . HR also concerns itself with organizational change and industrial relations, that is, the balancing of organizational practices with requirements arising from collective bargaining and from governmental laws.

Exam Probability: **Low**

26. *Answer choices:*
(see index for correct answer)

- a. Human resource management
- b. ABC Consultants
- c. Corporate Equality Index
- d. Job description management

Guidance: level 1

:: Project management ::

A _____ is a team whose members usually belong to different groups, functions and are assigned to activities for the same project. A team can be divided into sub-teams according to need. Usually _____ s are only used for a defined period of time. They are disbanded after the project is deemed complete. Due to the nature of the specific formation and disbandment, _____ s are usually in organizations.

Exam Probability: **Low**

27. *Answer choices:*

(see index for correct answer)

- a. Code name
- b. Constructability
- c. Bottleneck
- d. Project team

Guidance: level 1

:: Human resource management ::

_____ expands the capacity of individuals to perform in leadership roles within organizations. Leadership roles are those that facilitate execution of a company's strategy through building alignment, winning mindshare and growing the capabilities of others. Leadership roles may be formal, with the corresponding authority to make decisions and take responsibility, or they may be informal roles with little official authority.

Exam Probability: **Low**

28. *Answer choices:*

(see index for correct answer)

- a. Leadership development
- b. Employee relationship management
- c. Continuing professional development
- d. Randstad Holding

Guidance: level 1

:: ::

In communications and information processing, _____ is a system of rules to convert information—such as a letter, word, sound, image, or gesture—into another form or representation, sometimes shortened or secret, for communication through a communication channel or storage in a storage medium. An early example is the invention of language, which enabled a person, through speech, to communicate what they saw, heard, felt, or thought to others. But speech limits the range of communication to the distance a voice can carry, and limits the audience to those present when the speech is uttered. The invention of writing, which converted spoken language into visual symbols, extended the range of communication across space and time.

Exam Probability: **Medium**

29. *Answer choices:*

(see index for correct answer)

- a. corporate values
- b. levels of analysis
- c. Code
- d. information systems assessment

Guidance: level 1

:: Decision theory ::

A _____ is a decision support tool that uses a tree-like model of decisions and their possible consequences, including chance event outcomes, resource costs, and utility. It is one way to display an algorithm that only contains conditional control statements.

Exam Probability: **Low**

30. *Answer choices:*

(see index for correct answer)

- a. Decision tree
- b. Taleb distribution
- c. Distinction bias
- d. Decision-making software

Guidance: level 1

:: Industrial Revolution ::

The _____ , now also known as the First _____ , was the transition to new manufacturing processes in Europe and the US, in the period from about 1760 to sometime between 1820 and 1840. This transition included going from hand production methods to machines, new chemical manufacturing and iron production processes, the increasing use of steam power and water power, the development of machine tools and the rise of the mechanized factory system. The _____ also led to an unprecedented rise in the rate of population growth.

Exam Probability: **Low**

31. *Answer choices:*

(see index for correct answer)

- a. Grubb Family Iron Dynasty
- b. Luddite
- c. Stocking frame
- d. Industrial Revolution

Guidance: level 1

:: Human resource management ::

An organizational chart is a diagram that shows the structure of an organization and the relationships and relative ranks of its parts and positions/jobs. The term is also used for similar diagrams, for example ones showing the different elements of a field of knowledge or a group of languages.

Exam Probability: **Low**

32. *Answer choices:*

(see index for correct answer)

- a. Lego Serious Play
- b. Individual development plan
- c. Job description management
- d. Organization chart

Guidance: level 1

:: Organizational behavior ::

In organizational behavior and industrial and organizational psychology, _____ is an individual's psychological attachment to the organization. The basis behind many of these studies was to find ways to improve how workers feel about their jobs so that these workers would become more committed to their organizations. _____ predicts work variables such as turnover, organizational citizenship behavior, and job performance. Some of the factors such as role stress, empowerment, job insecurity and employability, and distribution of leadership have been shown to be connected to a worker's sense of _____ .

Exam Probability: **Medium**

33. *Answer choices:*

(see index for correct answer)

- a. Organizational storytelling
- b. Organizational commitment
- c. Organizational justice
- d. Affective events theory

Guidance: level 1

:: Financial risk ::

_____ is a type of risk faced by investors, corporations, and governments that political decisions, events, or conditions will significantly affect the profitability of a business actor or the expected value of a given economic action. _____ can be understood and managed with reasoned foresight and investment.

Exam Probability: **Low**

34. *Answer choices:*

(see index for correct answer)

- a. Nine money personalities model
- b. Profit risk
- c. Political risk
- d. Distortion risk measure

Guidance: level 1

:: Management ::

_____ is the identification, evaluation, and prioritization of risks followed by coordinated and economical application of resources to minimize, monitor, and control the probability or impact of unfortunate events or to maximize the realization of opportunities.

Exam Probability: **Low**

35. *Answer choices:*

(see index for correct answer)

- a. Bed management
- b. Business relationship management
- c. Supply chain sustainability
- d. Risk management

Guidance: level 1

:: Organizational theory ::

_____ is the process of creating, retaining, and transferring knowledge within an organization. An organization improves over time as it gains experience. From this experience, it is able to create knowledge. This knowledge is broad, covering any topic that could better an organization. Examples may include ways to increase production efficiency or to develop beneficial investor relations. Knowledge is created at four different units: individual, group, organizational, and inter organizational.

Exam Probability: **High**

36. *Answer choices:*

(see index for correct answer)

- a. High reliability organization
- b. Resource dependence theory
- c. Organizational learning
- d. Organizational field

Guidance: level 1

:: Management ::

A _____ is a formal written document containing business goals, the methods on how these goals can be attained, and the time frame within which these goals need to be achieved. It also describes the nature of the business, background information on the organization, the organization's financial projections, and the strategies it intends to implement to achieve the stated targets. In its entirety, this document serves as a road map that provides direction to the business.

Exam Probability: **Low**

37. *Answer choices:*

(see index for correct answer)

- a. Planning

- b. Corporate recovery
- c. Meeting system
- d. Business plan

Guidance: level 1

:: Majority–minority relations ::

_____ , also known as reservation in India and Nepal, positive discrimination / action in the United Kingdom, and employment equity in Canada and South Africa, is the policy of promoting the education and employment of members of groups that are known to have previously suffered from discrimination. Historically and internationally, support for _____ has sought to achieve goals such as bridging inequalities in employment and pay, increasing access to education, promoting diversity, and redressing apparent past wrongs, harms, or hindrances.

Exam Probability: **Low**

38. *Answer choices:*

(see index for correct answer)

- a. positive discrimination
- b. Affirmative action
- c. cultural dissonance

Guidance: level 1

:: ::

A _____ or sample _____ is a single measure of some attribute of a sample. It is calculated by applying a function to the values of the items of the sample, which are known together as a set of data.

Exam Probability: **Low**

39. *Answer choices:*

(see index for correct answer)

- a. Statistic
- b. similarity-attraction theory
- c. information systems assessment
- d. co-culture

Guidance: level 1

:: Management ::

The term _____ refers to measures designed to increase the degree of autonomy and self-determination in people and in communities in order to enable them to represent their interests in a responsible and self-determined way, acting on their own authority. It is the process of becoming stronger and more confident, especially in controlling one's life and claiming one's rights. _____ as action refers both to the process of self-_____ and to professional support of people, which enables them to overcome their sense of powerlessness and lack of influence, and to recognize and use their resources. To do work with power.

Exam Probability: **High**

40. *Answer choices:*

(see index for correct answer)

- a. Competitive advantage
- b. Matrix management
- c. Complementary assets
- d. Empowerment

Guidance: level 1

:: Organizational behavior ::

_____ is the state or fact of exclusive rights and control over property, which may be an object, land/real estate or intellectual property. _____ involves multiple rights, collectively referred to as title, which may be separated and held by different parties.

Exam Probability: **Low**

41. *Answer choices:*

(see index for correct answer)

- a. Ownership
- b. Satisficing
- c. Burnout
- d. Affective events theory

Guidance: level 1

:: ::

A _____ is a research instrument consisting of a series of questions for the purpose of gathering information from respondents. The _____ was invented by the Statistical Society of London in 1838.

Exam Probability: **Medium**

42. *Answer choices:*

(see index for correct answer)

- a. empathy
- b. Questionnaire
- c. hierarchical
- d. Sarbanes-Oxley act of 2002

Guidance: level 1

:: Supply chain management ::

_____ is the process of finding and agreeing to terms, and acquiring goods, services, or works from an external source, often via a tendering or competitive bidding process. _____ is used to ensure the buyer receives goods, services, or works at the best possible price when aspects such as quality, quantity, time, and location are compared. Corporations and public bodies often define processes intended to promote fair and open competition for their business while minimizing risks such as exposure to fraud and collusion.

Exam Probability: **High**

43. *Answer choices:*

(see index for correct answer)

- a. Design for logistics
- b. Helveta
- c. Transportation management system
- d. Procurement

Guidance: level 1

:: Training ::

_____ is teaching, or developing in oneself or others, any skills and knowledge that relate to specific useful competencies. _____ has specific goals of improving one's capability, capacity, productivity and performance. It forms the core of apprenticeships and provides the backbone of content at institutes of technology. In addition to the basic _____ required for a trade, occupation or profession, observers of the labor-market recognize as of 2008 the need to continue _____ beyond initial qualifications: to maintain, upgrade and update skills throughout working life. People within many professions and occupations may refer to this sort of _____ as professional development.

Exam Probability: **Medium**

44. *Answer choices:*

(see index for correct answer)

- a. Jeff Phillips
- b. Training
- c. International Society for Performance Improvement
- d. Leonardo da Vinci programme

Guidance: level 1

:: International relations ::

A _____ is any event that is going to lead to an unstable and dangerous situation affecting an individual, group, community, or whole society. Crises are deemed to be negative changes in the security, economic, political, societal, or environmental affairs, especially when they occur abruptly, with little or no warning. More loosely, it is a term meaning "a testing time" or an "emergency event".

Exam Probability: **High**

45. *Answer choices:*

(see index for correct answer)

- a. Pact
- b. Crisis
- c. Next Eleven
- d. Centre of Excellence on Public Security

Guidance: level 1

:: Occupational safety and health ::

_____ is a chemical element with symbol Pb and atomic number 82. It is a heavy metal that is denser than most common materials. _____ is soft and malleable, and also has a relatively low melting point. When freshly cut, _____ is silvery with a hint of blue; it tarnishes to a dull gray color when exposed to air. _____ has the highest atomic number of any stable element and three of its isotopes are endpoints of major nuclear decay chains of heavier elements.

Exam Probability: **Medium**

46. *Answer choices:*

(see index for correct answer)

- a. Lead
- b. Risk Information Exchange
- c. Defensible space
- d. Prevention through design

Guidance: level 1

:: Television commercials ::

_____ is a phenomenon whereby something new and somehow valuable is formed. The created item may be intangible or a physical object.

Exam Probability: **Low**

47. *Answer choices:*

(see index for correct answer)

- a. Creativity
- b. Frozen Peas
- c. Blue Velvet
- d. An American Revolution

Guidance: level 1

:: ::

_____ involves decision making. It can include judging the merits of multiple options and selecting one or more of them. One can make a _____ between imagined options or between real options followed by the corresponding action. For example, a traveler might choose a route for a journey based on the preference of arriving at a given destination as soon as possible. The preferred route can then follow from information such as the length of each of the possible routes, traffic conditions, etc. The arrival at a _____ can include more complex motivators such as cognition, instinct, and feeling.

Exam Probability: **Low**

48. *Answer choices:*

(see index for correct answer)

- a. Choice
- b. Character
- c. imperative
- d. Sarbanes-Oxley act of 2002

Guidance: level 1

:: Human resource management ::

_____ means increasing the scope of a job through extending the range of its job duties and responsibilities generally within the same level and periphery. _____ involves combining various activities at the same level in the organization and adding them to the existing job. It is also called the horizontal expansion of job activities. This contradicts the principles of specialisation and the division of labour whereby work is divided into small units, each of which is performed repetitively by an individual worker and the responsibilities are always clear. Some motivational theories suggest that the boredom and alienation caused by the division of labour can actually cause efficiency to fall. Thus, _____ seeks to motivate workers through reversing the process of specialisation. A typical approach might be to replace assembly lines with modular work; instead of an employee repeating the same step on each product, they perform several tasks on a single item. In order for employees to be provided with _____ they will need to be retrained in new fields to understand how each field works.

Exam Probability: **Medium**

49. *Answer choices:*

(see index for correct answer)

- a. Employee exit management
- b. Job enlargement
- c. Management by observation
- d. Talent management

Guidance: level 1

_____ is the stock of habits, knowledge, social and personality attributes embodied in the ability to perform labor so as to produce economic value.

Exam Probability: **High**

50. *Answer choices:*

(see index for correct answer)

- a. process perspective
- b. functional perspective
- c. levels of analysis
- d. Human capital

Guidance: level 1

:: Market research ::

_____ is an organized effort to gather information about target markets or customers. It is a very important component of business strategy. The term is commonly interchanged with marketing research; however, expert practitioners may wish to draw a distinction, in that marketing research is concerned specifically about marketing processes, while _____ is concerned specifically with markets.

Exam Probability: **High**

51. *Answer choices:*

(see index for correct answer)

- a. Cogent Research
- b. Market research
- c. Automated Measurement of Lineups
- d. Cluster sampling

Guidance: level 1

:: ::

_____ is the exchange of capital, goods, and services across international borders or territories.

Exam Probability: **High**

52. *Answer choices:*

(see index for correct answer)

- a. co-culture
- b. Character
- c. interpersonal communication
- d. information systems assessment

Guidance: level 1

:: Workplace ::

A _____ is a process through which feedback from an employee's subordinates, colleagues, and supervisor, as well as a self-evaluation by the employee themselves is gathered. Such feedback can also include, when relevant, feedback from external sources who interact with the employee, such as customers and suppliers or other interested stakeholders. _____ is so named because it solicits feedback regarding an employee's behavior from a variety of points of view. It therefore may be contrasted with "downward feedback", or "upward feedback" delivered to supervisory or management employees by subordinates only.

Exam Probability: **Low**

53. *Answer choices:*
(see index for correct answer)

- a. Micromanagement
- b. Evaluation
- c. Hostile environment sexual harassment
- d. Workplace aggression

Guidance: level 1

:: ::

_____ Corporation was an American energy, commodities, and services company based in Houston, Texas. It was founded in 1985 as a merger between Houston Natural Gas and InterNorth, both relatively small regional companies. Before its bankruptcy on December 3, 2001, _____ employed approximately 29,000 staff and was a major electricity, natural gas, communications and pulp and paper company, with claimed revenues of nearly $101 billion during 2000. Fortune named _____ "America's Most Innovative Company" for six consecutive years.

Exam Probability: **Low**

54. *Answer choices:*

(see index for correct answer)

- a. hierarchical
- b. Enron
- c. corporate values
- d. information systems assessment

Guidance: level 1

:: Goods ::

In most contexts, the concept of _____ denotes the conduct that should be preferred when posed with a choice between possible actions. _____ is generally considered to be the opposite of evil, and is of interest in the study of morality, ethics, religion and philosophy. The specific meaning and etymology of the term and its associated translations among ancient and contemporary languages show substantial variation in its inflection and meaning depending on circumstances of place, history, religious, or philosophical context.

Exam Probability: **Low**

55. *Answer choices:*

(see index for correct answer)

- a. Good
- b. Private good
- c. Common good
- d. Durable good

Guidance: level 1

:: ::

In logic and philosophy, an _____ is a series of statements, called the premises or premisses, intended to determine the degree of truth of another statement, the conclusion. The logical form of an _____ in a natural language can be represented in a symbolic formal language, and independently of natural language formally defined " _____ s" can be made in math and computer science.

Exam Probability: **Low**

56. *Answer choices:*

(see index for correct answer)

- a. information systems assessment
- b. imperative
- c. Argument
- d. hierarchical perspective

Guidance: level 1

:: ::

A _____, or also known as foreman, overseer, facilitator, monitor, area coordinator, or sometimes gaffer, is the job title of a low level management position that is primarily based on authority over a worker or charge of a workplace. A _____ can also be one of the most senior in the staff at the place of work, such as a Professor who oversees a PhD dissertation. Supervision, on the other hand, can be performed by people without this formal title, for example by parents. The term _____ itself can be used to refer to any personnel who have this task as part of their job description.

Exam Probability: **Low**

57. *Answer choices:*

(see index for correct answer)

- a. Supervisor
- b. imperative
- c. interpersonal communication
- d. corporate values

Guidance: level 1

:: Production and manufacturing ::

_____ consists of organization-wide efforts to "install and make permanent climate where employees continuously improve their ability to provide on demand products and services that customers will find of particular value." "Total" emphasizes that departments in addition to production are obligated to improve their operations; "management" emphasizes that executives are obligated to actively manage quality through funding, training, staffing, and goal setting. While there is no widely agreed-upon approach, TQM efforts typically draw heavily on the previously developed tools and techniques of quality control. TQM enjoyed widespread attention during the late 1980s and early 1990s before being overshadowed by ISO 9000, Lean manufacturing, and Six Sigma.

Exam Probability: **Low**

58. *Answer choices:*

(see index for correct answer)

- a. Back-story
- b. Low rate initial production
- c. Memo motion
- d. Total quality management

Guidance: level 1

:: Management ::

_____ is a process by which entities review the quality of all factors involved in production. ISO 9000 defines _____ as "A part of quality management focused on fulfilling quality requirements".

Exam Probability: **High**

59. *Answer choices:*

(see index for correct answer)

- a. Product differentiation
- b. Logistics management
- c. Social risk management
- d. Intopia

Guidance: level 1

Business law

Corporate law (also known as business law) is the body of law governing the rights, relations, and conduct of persons, companies, organizations and businesses. It refers to the legal practice relating to, or the theory of corporations. Corporate law often describes the law relating to matters which derive directly from the life-cycle of a corporation. It thus encompasses the formation, funding, governance, and death of a corporation.

:: ::

_____s and acquisitions are transactions in which the ownership of companies, other business organizations, or their operating units are transferred or consolidated with other entities. As an aspect of strategic management, M&A can allow enterprises to grow or downsize, and change the nature of their business or competitive position.

Exam Probability: **High**

1. *Answer choices:*

(see index for correct answer)

- a. similarity-attraction theory
- b. Merger
- c. personal values
- d. process perspective

Guidance: level 1

:: ::

A _____ is an individual or institution that legally owns one or more shares of stock in a public or private corporation. _____ s may be referred to as members of a corporation. Legally, a person is not a _____ in a corporation until their name and other details are entered in the corporation's register of _____ s or members.

Exam Probability: **Medium**

2. *Answer choices:*

(see index for correct answer)

- a. empathy
- b. Shareholder
- c. imperative
- d. deep-level diversity

Guidance: level 1

:: ::

In law, a _____ is the formal finding of fact made by a jury on matters or questions submitted to the jury by a judge. In a bench trial, the judge's decision near the end of the trial is simply referred to as a finding. In England and Wales, a coroner's findings are called _____ s.

Exam Probability: **Medium**

3. *Answer choices:*

(see index for correct answer)

- a. co-culture
- b. hierarchical perspective
- c. functional perspective
- d. Verdict

Guidance: level 1

:: ::

The _____ is an intergovernmental organization that is concerned with the regulation of international trade between nations. The WTO officially commenced on 1 January 1995 under the Marrakesh Agreement, signed by 124 nations on 15 April 1994, replacing the General Agreement on Tariffs and Trade , which commenced in 1948. It is the largest international economic organization in the world.

Exam Probability: **High**

4. *Answer choices:*

(see index for correct answer)

- a. World Trade Organization
- b. co-culture
- c. Character
- d. surface-level diversity

Guidance: level 1

:: Legal procedure ::

_____ , adjective law, or rules of court comprises the rules by which a court hears and determines what happens in civil, lawsuit, criminal or administrative proceedings. The rules are designed to ensure a fair and consistent application of due process or fundamental justice to all cases that come before a court.

Exam Probability: **Medium**

5. Answer choices:

(see index for correct answer)

- a. civil procedure
- b. appellate
- c. Opening statement
- d. Closing argument

Guidance: level 1

:: ::

A _____ is a formal written enactment of a legislative authority that governs the legal entities of a city, state, or country by way of consent. Typically, _____ s command or prohibit something, or declare policy. _____ s are rules made by legislative bodies; they are distinguished from case law or precedent, which is decided by courts, and regulations issued by government agencies.

Exam Probability: **Medium**

6. Answer choices:

(see index for correct answer)

- a. open system
- b. Character
- c. Sarbanes-Oxley act of 2002
- d. deep-level diversity

Guidance: level 1

:: ::

Industrial espionage, _____ , corporate spying or corporate espionage is a form of espionage conducted for commercial purposes instead of purely national security. While _____ is conducted or orchestrated by governments and is international in scope, industrial or corporate espionage is more often national and occurs between companies or corporations.

Exam Probability: **High**

7. *Answer choices:*

(see index for correct answer)

- a. personal values
- b. process perspective
- c. Economic espionage
- d. deep-level diversity

Guidance: level 1

:: ::

_____, or auditory perception, is the ability to perceive sounds by detecting vibrations, changes in the pressure of the surrounding medium through time, through an organ such as the ear. The academic field concerned with _____ is auditory science.

Exam Probability: **Medium**

8. *Answer choices:*

(see index for correct answer)

- a. empathy
- b. Hearing
- c. levels of analysis
- d. cultural

Guidance: level 1

:: ::

The Sherman Antitrust Act of 1890 was a United States antitrust law that regulates competition among enterprises, which was passed by Congress under the presidency of Benjamin Harrison.

Exam Probability: **Low**

9. *Answer choices:*

(see index for correct answer)

- a. Sarbanes-Oxley act of 2002
- b. Sherman Act
- c. Character
- d. co-culture

Guidance: level 1

:: Business law ::

A _____ is an offer that will remain open for a certain period or until a certain time or occurrence of a certain event, during which it is incapable of being revoked. As a general rule, all offers are revocable at any time prior to acceptance, even those offers that purport to be irrevocable on their face.

Exam Probability: **Low**

10. *Answer choices:*
(see index for correct answer)

- a. Complex structured finance transactions
- b. Starting a Business Index
- c. Enhanced use lease
- d. Firm offer

Guidance: level 1

The _____ is the highest court within the hierarchy of courts in many legal jurisdictions. Other descriptions for such courts include court of last resort, apex court, and high court of appeal. Broadly speaking, the decisions of a _____ are not subject to further review by any other court. _____ s typically function primarily as appellate courts, hearing appeals from decisions of lower trial courts, or from intermediate-level appellate courts.

Exam Probability: **Low**

11. *Answer choices:*

(see index for correct answer)

- a. Supreme Court
- b. co-culture
- c. functional perspective
- d. similarity-attraction theory

Guidance: level 1

An _____, commonly called an appeals court, court of appeals, appeal court, court of second instance or second instance court, is any court of law that is empowered to hear an appeal of a trial court or other lower tribunal. In most jurisdictions, the court system is divided into at least three levels: the trial court, which initially hears cases and reviews evidence and testimony to determine the facts of the case; at least one intermediate _____; and a supreme court which primarily reviews the decisions of the intermediate courts. A jurisdiction's supreme court is that jurisdiction's highest _____. _____s nationwide can operate under varying rules.

Exam Probability: **High**

12. *Answer choices:*

(see index for correct answer)

- a. empathy
- b. hierarchical perspective
- c. co-culture
- d. corporate values

Guidance: level 1

:: ::

The _____ Act of 1890 was a United States antitrust law that regulates competition among enterprises, which was passed by Congress under the presidency of Benjamin Harrison.

Exam Probability: **High**

13. *Answer choices:*

(see index for correct answer)

- a. Sherman Antitrust
- b. cultural
- c. similarity-attraction theory
- d. personal values

Guidance: level 1

:: Abuse of the legal system ::

_____ occurs when a person is restricted in their personal movement within any area without justification or consent. Actual physical restraint is not necessary for _____ to occur. A _____ claim may be made based upon private acts, or upon wrongful governmental detention. For detention by the police, proof of _____ provides a basis to obtain a writ of habeas corpus.

Exam Probability: **High**

14. *Answer choices:*

(see index for correct answer)

- a. Obstruction of Justice
- b. False arrest

- c. False imprisonment

Guidance: level 1

:: ::

Competition law is a law that promotes or seeks to maintain market competition by regulating anti-competitive conduct by companies. Competition law is implemented through public and private enforcement. Competition law is known as "_____ law" in the United States for historical reasons, and as "anti-monopoly law" in China and Russia. In previous years it has been known as trade practices law in the United Kingdom and Australia. In the European Union, it is referred to as both _____ and competition law.

Exam Probability: **High**

15. *Answer choices:*
(see index for correct answer)

- a. personal values
- b. corporate values
- c. levels of analysis
- d. Antitrust

Guidance: level 1

:: ::

In law, an _____ is the process in which cases are reviewed, where parties request a formal change to an official decision. _____ s function both as a process for error correction as well as a process of clarifying and interpreting law. Although appellate courts have existed for thousands of years, common law countries did not incorporate an affirmative right to _____ into their jurisprudence until the 19th century.

Exam Probability: **High**

16. *Answer choices:*

(see index for correct answer)

- a. co-culture
- b. open system
- c. process perspective
- d. Appeal

Guidance: level 1

:: Legal doctrines and principles ::

The _____ rule is a rule in the Anglo-American common law that governs what kinds of evidence parties to a contract dispute can introduce when trying to determine the specific terms of a contract. The rule also prevents parties who have reduced their agreement to a final written document from later introducing other evidence, such as the content of oral discussions from earlier in the negotiation process, as evidence of a different intent as to the terms of the contract. The rule provides that "extrinsic evidence is inadmissible to vary a written contract". The term "parol" derives from the Anglo-Norman French parol or parole, meaning "word of mouth" or "verbal", and in medieval times referred to oral pleadings in a court case.

Exam Probability: **High**

17. *Answer choices:*

(see index for correct answer)

- a. Parol evidence
- b. unconscionable contract
- c. Nonacquiescence
- d. Eminent domain

Guidance: level 1

A _____, in law, is a set of facts sufficient to justify a right to sue to obtain money, property, or the enforcement of a right against another party. The term also refers to the legal theory upon which a plaintiff brings suit. The legal document which carries a claim is often called a 'statement of claim' in English law, or a 'complaint' in U.S. federal practice and in many U.S. states. It can be any communication notifying the party to whom it is addressed of an alleged fault which resulted in damages, often expressed in amount of money the receiving party should pay/reimburse.

Exam Probability: **Low**

18. *Answer choices:*

(see index for correct answer)

- a. surface-level diversity
- b. Cause of action
- c. functional perspective
- d. hierarchical perspective

Guidance: level 1

:: Business models ::

A _____ is "an autonomous association of persons united voluntarily to meet their common economic, social, and cultural needs and aspirations through a jointly-owned and democratically-controlled enterprise". _____ s may include.

Exam Probability: **Low**

19. *Answer choices:*

(see index for correct answer)

- a. Blended value
- b. Cooperative
- c. Free-to-play
- d. Fractional ownership

Guidance: level 1

:: ::

The words "_____" and "testify" both derive from the Latin word testis, referring to the notion of a disinterested third-party witness.

Exam Probability: **High**

20. *Answer choices:*

(see index for correct answer)

- a. Testimony
- b. imperative
- c. levels of analysis
- d. interpersonal communication

Guidance: level 1

:: ::

_____ is the assignment of any responsibility or authority to another person to carry out specific activities. It is one of the core concepts of management leadership. However, the person who delegated the work remains accountable for the outcome of the delegated work. _____ empowers a subordinate to make decisions, i.e. it is a shifting of decision-making authority from one organizational level to a lower one. _____ , if properly done, is not fabrication. The opposite of effective _____ is micromanagement, where a manager provides too much input, direction, and review of delegated work. In general, _____ is good and can save money and time, help in building skills, and motivate people. On the other hand, poor _____ might cause frustration and confusion to all the involved parties. Some agents, however, do not favour a _____ and consider the power of making a decision rather burdensome.

Exam Probability: **Low**

21. *Answer choices:*

(see index for correct answer)

- a. cultural
- b. functional perspective
- c. open system
- d. similarity-attraction theory

Guidance: level 1

:: Contract law ::

Offer and acceptance analysis is a traditional approach in contract law. The offer and acceptance formula, developed in the 19th century, identifies a moment of formation when the parties are of one mind. This classical approach to contract formation has been modified by developments in the law of estoppel, misleading conduct, misrepresentation and unjust enrichment.

Exam Probability: **Low**

22. *Answer choices:*

(see index for correct answer)

- a. Beneficial interest
- b. Postnuptial agreement
- c. Offeree
- d. Memorandum of understanding

Guidance: level 1

:: Contract law ::

A _____ is a legally-binding agreement which recognises and governs the rights and duties of the parties to the agreement. A _____ is legally enforceable because it meets the requirements and approval of the law. An agreement typically involves the exchange of goods, services, money, or promises of any of those. In the event of breach of _____ , the law awards the injured party access to legal remedies such as damages and cancellation.

Exam Probability: **Low**

23. *Answer choices:*

(see index for correct answer)

- a. Seal
- b. ConsensusDOCS
- c. Principles of European Contract Law
- d. Contract

Guidance: level 1

:: Generally Accepted Accounting Principles ::

In accounting, _____ is the income that a business have from its normal business activities, usually from the sale of goods and services to customers. _____ is also referred to as sales or turnover. Some companies receive _____ from interest, royalties, or other fees. _____ may refer to business income in general, or it may refer to the amount, in a monetary unit, earned during a period of time, as in "Last year, Company X had _____ of $42 million". Profits or net income generally imply total _____ minus total expenses in a given period. In accounting, in the balance statement it is a subsection of the Equity section and _____ increases equity, it is often referred to as the "top line" due to its position on the income statement at the very top. This is to be contrasted with the "bottom line" which denotes net income.

Exam Probability: **Medium**

24. Answer choices:

(see index for correct answer)

- a. Indian Accounting Standards
- b. Revenue
- c. Petty cash
- d. Earnings before interest, taxes and depreciation

Guidance: level 1

:: Sureties ::

In finance, a _____ , _____ bond or guaranty involves a promise by one party to assume responsibility for the debt obligation of a borrower if that borrower defaults. The person or company providing the promise is also known as a " _____ " or as a "guarantor".

Exam Probability: **High**

25. Answer choices:

(see index for correct answer)

- a. Peace bond
- b. Estreature
- c. Little Miller Act
- d. Supersedeas bond

Guidance: level 1

:: Contract law ::

_____ , in human interactions, is a sincere intention to be fair, open, and honest, regardless of the outcome of the interaction. While some Latin phrases lose their literal meaning over centuries, this is not the case with bona fides; it is still widely used and interchangeable with its generally accepted modern-day English translation of _____ . It is an important concept within law and business. The opposed concepts are bad faith, mala fides and perfidy . In contemporary English, the usage of bona fides is synonymous with credentials and identity. The phrase is sometimes used in job advertisements, and should not be confused with the bona fide occupational qualifications or the employer`s _____ effort, as described below.

Exam Probability: **High**

26. *Answer choices:*
(see index for correct answer)

- a. Contract price
- b. Letter of comfort
- c. Ticket cases
- d. Extended warranty

Guidance: level 1

:: Manufactured goods ::

A _____ or final good is any commodity that is produced or consumed by the consumer to satisfy current wants or needs. _____s are ultimately consumed, rather than used in the production of another good. For example, a microwave oven or a bicycle that is sold to a consumer is a final good or _____, but the components that are sold to be used in those goods are intermediate goods. For example, textiles or transistors can be used to make some further goods.

Exam Probability: **Low**

27. *Answer choices:*

(see index for correct answer)

- a. Bespoke
- b. Household goods
- c. Tarpaulin
- d. Consumer Good

Guidance: level 1

:: Business ::

An _____ is a key document used by limited liability companies to outline the business' financial and functional decisions including rules, regulations and provisions. The purpose of the document is to govern the internal operations of the business in a way that suits the specific needs of the business owners. Once the document is signed by the members of the limited liability company, it acts as an official contract binding them to its terms. _____ is mandatory as per laws only in 5 states - California, Delaware, Maine, Missouri, and New York LLCs operating without an _____ are governed by the state's default rules contained in the relevant statute and developed through state court decisions. An _____ is similar in function to corporate by-laws, or analogous to a partnership agreement in multi-member LLCs. In single-member LLCs, an _____ is a declaration of the structure that the member has chosen for the company and sometimes used to prove in court that the LLC structure is separate from that of the individual owner and thus necessary so that the owner has documentation to prove that he or she is indeed separate from the entity itself.

Exam Probability: **Low**

28. *Answer choices:*

(see index for correct answer)

- a. Absentee business owner
- b. Business interoperability interface
- c. Operating agreement
- d. OrderUp

Guidance: level 1

:: Fair use ::

_____ is a doctrine in the law of the United States that permits limited use of copyrighted material without having to first acquire permission from the copyright holder. _____ is one of the limitations to copyright intended to balance the interests of copyright holders with the public interest in the wider distribution and use of creative works by allowing as a defense to copyright infringement claims certain limited uses that might otherwise be considered infringement.

Exam Probability: **High**

29. *Answer choices:*

(see index for correct answer)

- a. Fair use
- b. Derivative work
- c. Fair Use: The Story of the Letter U and the Numeral 2
- d. FAIR USE Act

Guidance: level 1

:: Contract Clause case law ::

The _____ appears in the United States Constitution, Article I, section 10, clause 1. The clause prohibits a State from passing any law that "impairs the obligation of contracts" or "makes any thing but gold and silver coin a tender in payment of debts". It states.

Exam Probability: **High**

30. *Answer choices:*

(see index for correct answer)

- a. Contract Clause
- b. Smyth v. Ames
- c. Charles River Bridge v. Warren Bridge

Guidance: level 1

:: Legal doctrines and principles ::

In some common law jurisdictions, _____ is a defense to a tort claim based on negligence. If it is available, the defense completely bars plaintiffs from any recovery if they contribute to their own injury through their own negligence.

Exam Probability: **Medium**

31. *Answer choices:*

(see index for correct answer)

- a. compulsory purchase
- b. Mutual mistake
- c. Res ipsa loquitur
- d. Acquiescence

Guidance: level 1

:: ::

_____ is "property consisting of land and the buildings on it, along with its natural resources such as crops, minerals or water; immovable property of this nature; an interest vested in this an item of real property, buildings or housing in general. Also: the business of _____ ; the profession of buying, selling, or renting land, buildings, or housing." It is a legal term used in jurisdictions whose legal system is derived from English common law, such as India, England, Wales, Northern Ireland, United States, Canada, Pakistan, Australia, and New Zealand.

Exam Probability: **Low**

32. *Answer choices:*

(see index for correct answer)

- a. Character
- b. Sarbanes-Oxley act of 2002
- c. levels of analysis
- d. corporate values

Guidance: level 1

:: ::

A _____ is an organization, usually a group of people or a company, authorized to act as a single entity and recognized as such in law. Early incorporated entities were established by charter. Most jurisdictions now allow the creation of new _____ s through registration.

Exam Probability: **High**

33. *Answer choices:*

(see index for correct answer)

- a. Corporation
- b. personal values
- c. co-culture
- d. levels of analysis

Guidance: level 1

:: ::

_____, often abbreviated cert. in the United States, is a process for seeking judicial review and a writ issued by a court that agrees to review. A _____ is issued by a superior court, directing an inferior court, tribunal, or other public authority to send the record of a proceeding for review.

Exam Probability: **Medium**

34. *Answer choices:*

(see index for correct answer)

- a. deep-level diversity
- b. functional perspective
- c. Sarbanes-Oxley act of 2002
- d. information systems assessment

Guidance: level 1

:: Fraud ::

The _____ refers to the requirement that certain kinds of contracts be memorialized in writing, signed by the party to be charged, with sufficient content to evidence the contract.

Exam Probability: **Medium**

35. *Answer choices:*

(see index for correct answer)

- a. Control fraud
- b. Statute of frauds
- c. Shell corporation
- d. Plastic shaman

Guidance: level 1

:: Fraud ::

_____ is the deliberate use of someone else's identity, usually as a method to gain a financial advantage or obtain credit and other benefits in the other person's name, and perhaps to the other person's disadvantage or loss. The person whose identity has been assumed may suffer adverse consequences, especially if they are held responsible for the perpetrator's actions. _____ occurs when someone uses another's personally identifying information, like their name, identifying number, or credit card number, without their permission, to commit fraud or other crimes. The term _____ was coined in 1964. Since that time, the definition of _____ has been statutorily prescribed throughout both the U.K. and the United States as the theft of personally identifying information, generally including a person's name, date of birth, social security number, driver's license number, bank account or credit card numbers, PIN numbers, electronic signatures, fingerprints, passwords, or any other information that can be used to access a person's financial resources.

Exam Probability: **High**

36. *Answer choices:*
(see index for correct answer)

- a. Transcript fraud
- b. Identity theft
- c. Corporate scandal
- d. Tunneling

Guidance: level 1

:: False advertising law ::

> The Lanham Act is the primary federal trademark statute of law in the United States. The Act prohibits a number of activities, including trademark infringement, trademark dilution, and false advertising.

Exam Probability: **High**

37. *Answer choices:*

(see index for correct answer)

- a. POM Wonderful LLC v. Coca-Cola Co.
- b. Rebecca Tushnet

Guidance: level 1

:: Contract law ::

> _____ are damages whose amount the parties designate during the formation of a contract for the injured party to collect as compensation upon a specific breach.

Exam Probability: **Low**

38. *Answer choices:*

(see index for correct answer)

- a. Liquidated damages
- b. Nudum pactum
- c. Unconscionability
- d. Subcontractor

Guidance: level 1

:: Commercial item transport and distribution ::

A _____ in common law countries is a person or company that transports goods or people for any person or company and that is responsible for any possible loss of the goods during transport. A _____ offers its services to the general public under license or authority provided by a regulatory body. The regulatory body has usually been granted "ministerial authority" by the legislation that created it. The regulatory body may create, interpret, and enforce its regulations upon the _____ with independence and finality, as long as it acts within the bounds of the enabling legislation.

Exam Probability: **Medium**

39. *Answer choices:*

(see index for correct answer)

- a. Toll Global Forwarding
- b. Euro container
- c. Common carrier
- d. Refrigerator truck

Guidance: level 1

:: Statutory law ::

_____ is a principal's approval of an act of its agent that lacked the authority to bind the principal legally. _____ defines the international act in which a state indicates its consent to be bound to a treaty if the parties intended to show their consent by such an act. In the case of bilateral treaties, _____ is usually accomplished by exchanging the requisite instruments, and in the case of multilateral treaties, the usual procedure is for the depositary to collect the _____ s of all states, keeping all parties informed of the situation.

Exam Probability: **Medium**

40. *Answer choices:*
(see index for correct answer)

- a. Ratification
- b. incorporation by reference
- c. statute law
- d. Statute of repose

Guidance: level 1

:: Industrial agreements ::

_____ is a process of negotiation between employers and a group of employees aimed at agreements to regulate working salaries, working conditions, benefits, and other aspects of workers' compensation and rights for workers. The interests of the employees are commonly presented by representatives of a trade union to which the employees belong. The collective agreements reached by these negotiations usually set out wage scales, working hours, training, health and safety, overtime, grievance mechanisms, and rights to participate in workplace or company affairs.

Exam Probability: **Low**

41. *Answer choices:*

(see index for correct answer)

- a. Collective bargaining
- b. Collaborative bargaining
- c. Mutual gains bargaining
- d. Industrial Disputes Act 1947

Guidance: level 1

:: ::

_____ is a legal term which, in its broadest sense, is a synonym for anyone in a position of trust and so can refer to any person who holds property, authority, or a position of trust or responsibility for the benefit of another. A _____ can also refer to a person who is allowed to do certain tasks but not able to gain income. Although in the strictest sense of the term a _____ is the holder of property on behalf of a beneficiary, the more expansive sense encompasses persons who serve, for example, on the board of _____ s of an institution that operates for a charity, for the benefit of the general public, or a person in the local government.

Exam Probability: **High**

42. *Answer choices:*

(see index for correct answer)

- a. empathy
- b. Sarbanes-Oxley act of 2002
- c. Trustee
- d. similarity-attraction theory

Guidance: level 1

:: Business law ::

A _____, also known as the sole trader, individual entrepreneurship or proprietorship, is a type of enterprise that is owned and run by one person and in which there is no legal distinction between the owner and the business entity. A sole trader does not necessarily work 'alone'—it is possible for the sole trader to employ other people.

Exam Probability: **Medium**

43. *Answer choices:*

(see index for correct answer)

- a. Legal tender
- b. Trading while insolvent
- c. Lien
- d. Sole proprietorship

Guidance: level 1

:: ::

An _____ is the production of goods or related services within an economy. The major source of revenue of a group or company is the indicator of its relevant _____ . When a large group has multiple sources of revenue generation, it is considered to be working in different industries. Manufacturing _____ became a key sector of production and labour in European and North American countries during the Industrial Revolution, upsetting previous mercantile and feudal economies. This came through many successive rapid advances in technology, such as the production of steel and coal.

Exam Probability: **Low**

44. *Answer choices:*

(see index for correct answer)

- a. Sarbanes-Oxley act of 2002
- b. Industry
- c. process perspective
- d. functional perspective

Guidance: level 1

:: Real property law ::

_____ , sometimes colloquially described as 'squatter's rights', is a legal principle under which a person who does not have legal title to a piece of property—usually land—acquires legal ownership based on continuous possession or occupation of the land without the permission of its legal owner.

Exam Probability: **Low**

45. *Answer choices:*

(see index for correct answer)

- a. United States Court of Private Land Claims
- b. Adverse possession
- c. Good guy clause
- d. Customary freehold

Guidance: level 1

:: Law ::

_____ is a body of law which defines the role, powers, and structure of different entities within a state, namely, the executive, the parliament or legislature, and the judiciary; as well as the basic rights of citizens and, in federal countries such as the United States and Canada, the relationship between the central government and state, provincial, or territorial governments.

Exam Probability: **Low**

46. *Answer choices:*

(see index for correct answer)

- a. Comparative law
- b. Legal case

Guidance: level 1

:: Notes (finance) ::

A _____ , sometimes referred to as a note payable, is a legal instrument , in which one party promises in writing to pay a determinate sum of money to the other , either at a fixed or determinable future time or on demand of the payee, under specific terms.

Exam Probability: **Medium**

47. *Answer choices:*

(see index for correct answer)

- a. Note issuance facility
- b. Large-sized note
- c. Promissory note
- d. Treasury Note

Guidance: level 1

:: Contract law ::

Generally, a _____ is a loan or a credit transaction in which the lender acquires a security interest in collateral owned by the borrower and is entitled to foreclose on or repossess the collateral in the event of the borrower's default. The terms of the relationship are governed by a contract, or security agreement. A common example would be a consumer who purchases a car on credit. If the consumer fails to make the payments on time, the lender will take the car and resell it, applying the proceeds of the sale toward the loan. Mortgages and deeds of trust are another example. In the United States, _____ s in personal property are governed by Article 9 of the Uniform Commercial Code .

Exam Probability: **Medium**

48. *Answer choices:*

(see index for correct answer)

- a. Capacity

- b. Culpa in contrahendo
- c. Impracticability
- d. Warranty tolling

Guidance: level 1

:: Legal doctrines and principles ::

_____ is a defense in the law of torts, which bars or reduces a plaintiff's right to recovery against a negligent tortfeasor if the defendant can demonstrate that the plaintiff voluntarily and knowingly assumed the risks at issue inherent to the dangerous activity in which he was participating at the time of his or her injury.

Exam Probability: **High**

49. *Answer choices:*

(see index for correct answer)

- a. Mutual assent
- b. compulsory acquisition
- c. Assumption of risk
- d. Attractive nuisance doctrine

Guidance: level 1

:: Employment discrimination ::

_____ is a form of discrimination based on race, gender, religion, national origin, physical or mental disability, age, sexual orientation, and gender identity by employers. Earnings differentials or occupational differentiation—where differences in pay come from differences in qualifications or responsibilities—should not be confused with _____. Discrimination can be intended and involve disparate treatment of a group or be unintended, yet create disparate impact for a group.

Exam Probability: **Low**

50. *Answer choices:*
(see index for correct answer)

- a. United Kingdom employment equality law
- b. Employment Non-Discrimination Act
- c. Employment discrimination
- d. MacBride Principles

Guidance: level 1

:: Contract law ::

Offer and acceptance analysis is a traditional approach in contract law. The offer and acceptance formula, developed in the 19th century, identifies a moment of formation when the parties are of one mind. This classical approach to contract formation has been modified by developments in the law of estoppel, misleading conduct, misrepresentation and unjust enrichment.

Exam Probability: **Low**

51. *Answer choices:*

(see index for correct answer)

- a. Contract
- b. Terms of service
- c. Memorandum of understanding
- d. Interlineation

Guidance: level 1

:: Marketing ::

_____ or stock is the goods and materials that a business holds for the ultimate goal of resale.

Exam Probability: **Low**

52. *Answer choices:*

(see index for correct answer)

- a. Movie gimmick
- b. Cola Wars
- c. Processing fluency theory of aesthetic pleasure
- d. Inventory

Guidance: level 1

:: ::

A federation is a political entity characterized by a union of partially self-governing provinces, states, or other regions under a central _____. In a federation, the self-governing status of the component states, as well as the division of power between them and the central government, is typically constitutionally entrenched and may not be altered by a unilateral decision of either party, the states or the federal political body. Alternatively, federation is a form of government in which sovereign power is formally divided between a central authority and a number of constituent regions so that each region retains some degree of control over its internal affairs. It is often argued that federal states where the central government has the constitutional authority to suspend a constituent state's government by invoking gross mismanagement or civil unrest, or to adopt national legislation that overrides or infringe on the constituent states' powers by invoking the central government's constitutional authority to ensure "peace and good government" or to implement obligations contracted under an international treaty, are not truly federal states.

Exam Probability: **High**

53. *Answer choices:*

(see index for correct answer)

- a. functional perspective
- b. cultural
- c. corporate values
- d. Federal government

Guidance: level 1

:: ::

_____ is a concept of English common law and is a necessity for simple contracts but not for special contracts . The concept has been adopted by other common law jurisdictions, including the US.

Exam Probability: **High**

54. *Answer choices:*

(see index for correct answer)

- a. Consideration
- b. Character
- c. hierarchical
- d. corporate values

Guidance: level 1

:: Negotiable instrument law ::

In the United States, The Preservation of Consumers' Claims and Defenses [_____ Rule], formally known as the "Trade Regulation Rule Concerning Preservation of Consumers' Claims and Defenses," protects consumers when merchants sell a consumer's credit contracts to other lenders. Specifically, it preserves consumers' right to assert the same legal claims and defenses against anyone who purchases the credit contract, as they would have against the seller who originally provided the credit. [16 Code of Federal Regulations Part 433]

Exam Probability: **High**

55. *Answer choices:*
(see index for correct answer)

- a. Negotiable Instruments Act, 1881
- b. Real defense
- c. holder in due course doctrine
- d. Gold v. Eddy

Guidance: level 1

:: ::

_____ is the act or practice of forbidding something by law; more particularly the term refers to the banning of the manufacture, storage, transportation, sale, possession, and consumption of alcoholic beverages. The word is also used to refer to a period of time during which such bans are enforced.

Exam Probability: **Medium**

56. *Answer choices:*

(see index for correct answer)

- a. imperative
- b. process perspective
- c. levels of analysis
- d. Prohibition

Guidance: level 1

:: ::

_____ is a type of government support for the citizens of that society. _____ may be provided to people of any income level, as with social security , but it is usually intended to ensure that the poor can meet their basic human needs such as food and shelter. _____ attempts to provide poor people with a minimal level of well-being, usually either a free- or a subsidized-supply of certain goods and social services, such as healthcare, education, and vocational training.

Exam Probability: **Medium**

57. *Answer choices:*

(see index for correct answer)

- a. co-culture

- b. Sarbanes-Oxley act of 2002
- c. Welfare
- d. surface-level diversity

Guidance: level 1

:: Trade secrets ::

The _____ of 1996 was a 6 title Act of Congress dealing with a wide range of issues, including not only industrial espionage, but the insanity defense, matters regarding the Boys & Girls Clubs of America, requirements for presentence investigation reports, and the United States Sentencing Commission reports regarding encryption or scrambling technology, and other technical and minor amendments.

Exam Probability: **Medium**

58. *Answer choices:*
(see index for correct answer)

- a. Kayfabe
- b. Old Bay Seasoning
- c. Apple v. Does
- d. Economic Espionage Act

Guidance: level 1

:: Debt ::

_____ is the trust which allows one party to provide money or resources to another party wherein the second party does not reimburse the first party immediately, but promises either to repay or return those resources at a later date. In other words, _____ is a method of making reciprocity formal, legally enforceable, and extensible to a large group of unrelated people.

Exam Probability: **Medium**

59. *Answer choices:*
(see index for correct answer)

- a. Credit
- b. Credit cycle
- c. Phantom debt
- d. Christians Against Poverty

Guidance: level 1

Finance

Finance is a field that is concerned with the allocation (investment) of assets and liabilities over space and time, often under conditions of risk or uncertainty. Finance can also be defined as the science of money management. Participants in the market aim to price assets based on their risk level, fundamental value, and their expected rate of return. Finance can be split into three sub-categories: public finance, corporate finance and personal finance.

An _____ is an asset that lacks physical substance. It is defined in opposition to physical assets such as machinery and buildings. An _____ is usually very hard to evaluate. Patents, copyrights, franchises, goodwill, trademarks, and trade names. The general interpretation also includes software and other intangible computer based assets are all examples of _____s. _____s generally—though not necessarily—suffer from typical market failures of non-rivalry and non-excludability.

Exam Probability: **Low**

1. *Answer choices:*

(see index for correct answer)

- a. Intangible asset
- b. corporate values
- c. co-culture
- d. information systems assessment

Guidance: level 1

:: Data management ::

_____ is a form of intellectual property that grants the creator of an original creative work an exclusive legal right to determine whether and under what conditions this original work may be copied and used by others, usually for a limited term of years. The exclusive rights are not absolute but limited by limitations and exceptions to _____ law, including fair use. A major limitation on _____ on ideas is that _____ protects only the original expression of ideas, and not the underlying ideas themselves.

Exam Probability: **Low**

2. *Answer choices:*

(see index for correct answer)

- a. H-Store
- b. Copyright
- c. Core data integration
- d. Enterprise information system

Guidance: level 1

:: Fundamental analysis ::

_____ is the monetary value of earnings per outstanding share of common stock for a company.

Exam Probability: **High**

3. *Answer choices:*

(see index for correct answer)

- a. Earnings per share
- b. Economic Value Added
- c. Restricted stock
- d. Market value added

Guidance: level 1

:: Management accounting ::

_____ is a managerial accounting cost concept. Under this method, manufacturing overhead is incurred in the period that a product is produced. This addresses the issue of absorption costing that allows income to rise as production rises. Under an absorption cost method, management can push forward costs to the next period when products are sold. This artificially inflates profits in the period of production by incurring less cost than would be incurred under a _____ system. _____ is generally not used for external reporting purposes. Under the Tax Reform Act of 1986, income statements must use absorption costing to comply with GAAP.

Exam Probability: **High**

4. *Answer choices:*

(see index for correct answer)

- a. Variable Costing
- b. Institute of Certified Management Accountants
- c. Bridge life-cycle cost analysis
- d. Direct material usage variance

Guidance: level 1

:: Stock market ::

_____ is a form of stock which may have any combination of features not possessed by common stock including properties of both an equity and a debt instrument, and is generally considered a hybrid instrument. _____ s are senior to common stock, but subordinate to bonds in terms of claim and may have priority over common stock in the payment of dividends and upon liquidation. Terms of the _____ are described in the issuing company's articles of association or articles of incorporation.

Exam Probability: **High**

5. *Answer choices:*

(see index for correct answer)

- a. Preferred stock
- b. Super-majority amendment
- c. Correlation trading
- d. Slippage

Guidance: level 1

:: Insolvency ::

_____ is the process in accounting by which a company is brought to an end in the United Kingdom, Republic of Ireland and United States. The assets and property of the company are redistributed. _____ is also sometimes referred to as winding-up or dissolution, although dissolution technically refers to the last stage of _____ . The process of _____ also arises when customs, an authority or agency in a country responsible for collecting and safeguarding customs duties, determines the final computation or ascertainment of the duties or drawback accruing on an entry.

Exam Probability: **Low**

6. *Answer choices:*

(see index for correct answer)

- a. Insolvency law of Russia
- b. Preferential creditor
- c. George Samuel Ford
- d. Liquidation

Guidance: level 1

:: Business law ::

A _____ , also known as the sole trader, individual entrepreneurship or proprietorship, is a type of enterprise that is owned and run by one person and in which there is no legal distinction between the owner and the business entity. A sole trader does not necessarily work 'alone'—it is possible for the sole trader to employ other people.

Exam Probability: **High**

7. *Answer choices:*

(see index for correct answer)

- a. Sole proprietorship
- b. Commercial law
- c. Principal
- d. Bulk transfer

Guidance: level 1

:: Financial ratios ::

_____ or asset turns is a financial ratio that measures the efficiency of a company's use of its assets in generating sales revenue or sales income to the company.

Exam Probability: **Low**

8. *Answer choices:*

(see index for correct answer)

- a. Return on capital
- b. Asset turnover
- c. Bias ratio
- d. Debtor collection period

Guidance: level 1

:: Business ::

The seller, or the provider of the goods or services, completes a sale in response to an acquisition, appropriation, requisition or a direct interaction with the buyer at the point of sale. There is a passing of title of the item, and the settlement of a price, in which agreement is reached on a price for which transfer of ownership of the item will occur. The seller, not the purchaser typically executes the sale and it may be completed prior to the obligation of payment. In the case of indirect interaction, a person who sells goods or service on behalf of the owner is known as a _____ man or _____ woman or _____ person, but this often refers to someone selling goods in a store/shop, in which case other terms are also common, including _____ clerk, shop assistant, and retail clerk.

Exam Probability: **Medium**

9. *Answer choices:*
(see index for correct answer)

- a. Open-book contract
- b. Joint employment
- c. Vladislav Doronin
- d. Ian McLeod

Guidance: level 1

:: Asset ::

_____ s, also known as tangible assets or property, plant and equipment, is a term used in accounting for assets and property that cannot easily be converted into cash. This can be compared with current assets such as cash or bank accounts, described as liquid assets. In most cases, only tangible assets are referred to as fixed. IAS 16 defines _____ s as assets whose future economic benefit is probable to flow into the entity, whose cost can be measured reliably. _____ s belong to one of 2 types:"Freehold Assets" – assets which are purchased with legal right of ownership and used, and "Leasehold Assets" – assets used by owner without legal right for a particular period of time.

Exam Probability: **Medium**

10. *Answer choices:*

(see index for correct answer)

- a. Asset
- b. Current asset

Guidance: level 1

:: Financial markets ::

As money became a commodity, the _____ became a component of the financial market for assets involved in short-term borrowing, lending, buying and selling with original maturities of one year or less. Trading in _____ s is done over the counter and is wholesale.

Exam Probability: **Medium**

11. *Answer choices:*

(see index for correct answer)

- a. Power Plus Pro
- b. Money market
- c. Financial instrument
- d. Odd lot

Guidance: level 1

:: ::

In financial markets, a share is a unit used as mutual funds, limited partnerships, and real estate investment trusts. The owner of _____ in the corporation/company is a shareholder of the corporation. A share is an indivisible unit of capital, expressing the ownership relationship between the company and the shareholder. The denominated value of a share is its face value, and the total of the face value of issued _____ represent the capital of a company, which may not reflect the market value of those _____ .

Exam Probability: **High**

12. *Answer choices:*

(see index for correct answer)

- a. similarity-attraction theory
- b. Shares
- c. corporate values
- d. functional perspective

Guidance: level 1

:: Generally Accepted Accounting Principles ::

A _____ , in accrual accounting, is any account where the asset or liability is not realized until a future date , e.g. annuities, charges, taxes, income, etc. The deferred item may be carried, dependent on type of _____ , as either an asset or liability. See also accrual.

Exam Probability: **Low**

13. *Answer choices:*

(see index for correct answer)

- a. Operating income
- b. Operating income before depreciation and amortization
- c. French generally accepted accounting principles
- d. Contributed capital

Guidance: level 1

:: Accounting terminology ::

_____ or capital expense is the money a company spends to buy, maintain, or improve its fixed assets, such as buildings, vehicles, equipment, or land. It is considered a _____ when the asset is newly purchased or when money is used towards extending the useful life of an existing asset, such as repairing the roof.

Exam Probability: **High**

14. *Answer choices:*

(see index for correct answer)

- a. Mark-to-market
- b. Impairment cost
- c. Capital expenditure
- d. Accrual

Guidance: level 1

:: Contract law ::

A _____ is a legally-binding agreement which recognises and governs the rights and duties of the parties to the agreement. A _____ is legally enforceable because it meets the requirements and approval of the law. An agreement typically involves the exchange of goods, services, money, or promises of any of those. In the event of breach of _____ , the law awards the injured party access to legal remedies such as damages and cancellation.

Exam Probability: **Low**

15. *Answer choices:*

(see index for correct answer)

- a. Beneficial interest
- b. Drop dead date
- c. Firm commitment
- d. Right of first refusal

Guidance: level 1

:: ::

Business is the activity of making one's living or making money by producing or buying and selling products . Simply put, it is "any activity or enterprise entered into for profit. It does not mean it is a company, a corporation, partnership, or have any such formal organization, but it can range from a street peddler to General Motors."

Exam Probability: **Low**

16. *Answer choices:*

(see index for correct answer)

- a. empathy
- b. corporate values

- c. Character
- d. Firm

Guidance: level 1

:: Public finance ::

_____ is the process by which the monetary authority of a country, typically the central bank or currency board, controls either the cost of very short-term borrowing or the money supply, often targeting inflation rate or interest rate to ensure price stability and general trust in the currency.

Exam Probability: **High**

17. *Answer choices:*

(see index for correct answer)

- a. Monetary policy
- b. Budget Code of Russia
- c. California Municipal Treasurers Association
- d. Fiscal incidence

Guidance: level 1

:: Financial markets ::

The _____ , also called the aftermarket and follow on public offering is the financial market in which previously issued financial instruments such as stock, bonds, options, and futures are bought and sold. Another frequent usage of " _____ " is to refer to loans which are sold by a mortgage bank to investors such as Fannie Mae and Freddie Mac.

Exam Probability: **Low**

18. *Answer choices:*

(see index for correct answer)

- a. National best bid and offer
- b. Secondary market
- c. Internal financing
- d. Fution

Guidance: level 1

:: International trade ::

_____ involves the transfer of goods or services from one person or entity to another, often in exchange for money. A system or network that allows _____ is called a market.

Exam Probability: **Medium**

19. *Answer choices:*

(see index for correct answer)

- a. Public international law
- b. Trade
- c. Nanban trade
- d. European Customs Information Portal

Guidance: level 1

:: Financial accounting ::

In accounting, _____ is the value of an asset according to its balance sheet account balance. For assets, the value is based on the original cost of the asset less any depreciation, amortization or impairment costs made against the asset. Traditionally, a company's _____ is its total assets minus intangible assets and liabilities. However, in practice, depending on the source of the calculation, _____ may variably include goodwill, intangible assets, or both. The value inherent in its workforce, part of the intellectual capital of a company, is always ignored. When intangible assets and goodwill are explicitly excluded, the metric is often specified to be "tangible _____ ".

Exam Probability: **Medium**

20. *Answer choices:*
(see index for correct answer)

- a. Working capital
- b. Convenience translation

- c. Book value
- d. Money measurement

Guidance: level 1

:: Fraud ::

In law, _____ is intentional deception to secure unfair or unlawful gain, or to deprive a victim of a legal right. _____ can violate civil law, a criminal law, or it may cause no loss of money, property or legal right but still be an element of another civil or criminal wrong. The purpose of _____ may be monetary gain or other benefits, for example by obtaining a passport, travel document, or driver's license, or mortgage _____, where the perpetrator may attempt to qualify for a mortgage by way of false statements.

Exam Probability: **Medium**

21. *Answer choices:*

(see index for correct answer)

- a. Fraud
- b. Medicare fraud
- c. Drug fraud
- d. Lebanese loop

Guidance: level 1

:: Asset ::

In accounting, a _____ is any asset which can reasonably be expected to be sold, consumed, or exhausted through the normal operations of a business within the current fiscal year or operating cycle. Typical _____ s include cash, cash equivalents, short-term investments, accounts receivable, stock inventory, supplies, and the portion of prepaid liabilities which will be paid within a year. In simple words, assets which are held for a short period are known as _____ s. Such assets are expected to be realised in cash or consumed during the normal operating cycle of the business.

Exam Probability: **Medium**

22. *Answer choices:*

(see index for correct answer)

- a. Current asset
- b. Fixed asset

Guidance: level 1

:: Costs ::

In economics, _____ is the total economic cost of production and is made up of variable cost, which varies according to the quantity of a good produced and includes inputs such as labour and raw materials, plus fixed cost, which is independent of the quantity of a good produced and includes inputs that cannot be varied in the short term: fixed costs such as buildings and machinery, including sunk costs if any. Since cost is measured per unit of time, it is a flow variable.

Exam Probability: **High**

23. *Answer choices:*

(see index for correct answer)

- a. Prospective costs
- b. Total cost
- c. Implicit cost
- d. Cost of products sold

Guidance: level 1

:: Bonds (finance) ::

A _____ is a type of bond that allows the issuer of the bond to retain the privilege of redeeming the bond at some point before the bond reaches its date of maturity. In other words, on the call date, the issuer has the right, but not the obligation, to buy back the bonds from the bond holders at a defined call price. Technically speaking, the bonds are not really bought and held by the issuer but are instead cancelled immediately.

Exam Probability: **Low**

24. Answer choices:

(see index for correct answer)

- a. Bond exchange offer
- b. Bid bond
- c. Samurai bond
- d. Amortizing loan

Guidance: level 1

:: Cash flow ::

_____ s are narrowly interconnected with the concepts of value, interest rate and liquidity. A _____ that shall happen on a future day tN can be transformed into a _____ of the same value in t0.

Exam Probability: **High**

25. Answer choices:

(see index for correct answer)

- a. Cash flow hedge
- b. Discounted payback period
- c. Cash flow loan
- d. Cash flow

Guidance: level 1

:: Legal terms ::

_____ s may be governments, corporations or investment trusts. _____ s are legally responsible for the obligations of the issue and for reporting financial conditions, material developments and any other operational activities as required by the regulations of their jurisdictions.

Exam Probability: **High**

26. *Answer choices:*

(see index for correct answer)

- a. Curator bonis
- b. Issuer
- c. Call of duty
- d. Antedated

Guidance: level 1

:: ::

_____ refers to a business or organization attempting to acquire goods or services to accomplish its goals. Although there are several organizations that attempt to set standards in the _____ process, processes can vary greatly between organizations. Typically the word "_____" is not used interchangeably with the word "procurement", since procurement typically includes expediting, supplier quality, and transportation and logistics in addition to _____ .

Exam Probability: **Medium**

27. *Answer choices:*

(see index for correct answer)

- a. open system
- b. hierarchical perspective
- c. co-culture
- d. Purchasing

Guidance: level 1

:: Management accounting ::

In finance, the _____ or net present worth applies to a series of cash flows occurring at different times. The present value of a cash flow depends on the interval of time between now and the cash flow. It also depends on the discount rate. NPV accounts for the time value of money. It provides a method for evaluating and comparing capital projects or financial products with cash flows spread over time, as in loans, investments, payouts from insurance contracts plus many other applications.

Exam Probability: **Medium**

28. *Answer choices:*

(see index for correct answer)

- a. Net present value
- b. Direct material usage variance
- c. Process costing
- d. Operating profit margin

Guidance: level 1

:: Accounting source documents ::

A _____ or account statement is a summary of financial transactions which have occurred over a given period on a bank account held by a person or business with a financial institution.

Exam Probability: **Medium**

29. *Answer choices:*

(see index for correct answer)

- a. Credit memo
- b. Banknote
- c. Bank statement
- d. Purchase order

Guidance: level 1

:: Corporate governance ::

The _____ is the officer of a company that has primary responsibility for managing the company's finances, including financial planning, management of financial risks, record-keeping, and financial reporting. In some sectors, the CFO is also responsible for analysis of data. Some CFOs have the title CFOO for chief financial and operating officer. In the United Kingdom, the typical term for a CFO is finance director . The CFO typically reports to the chief executive officer and the board of directors and may additionally have a seat on the board. The CFO supervises the finance unit and is the chief financial spokesperson for the organization. The CFO directly assists the chief operating officer on all strategic and tactical matters relating to budget management, cost–benefit analysis, forecasting needs, and securing of new funding.

Exam Probability: **Low**

30. *Answer choices:*

(see index for correct answer)

- a. Corner office
- b. Chief financial officer
- c. Directors and officers liability insurance
- d. The Modern Corporation and Private Property

Guidance: level 1

:: Mereology ::

_____ , in the abstract, is what belongs to or with something, whether as an attribute or as a component of said thing. In the context of this article, it is one or more components , whether physical or incorporeal, of a person's estate; or so belonging to, as in being owned by, a person or jointly a group of people or a legal entity like a corporation or even a society. Depending on the nature of the _____ , an owner of _____ has the right to consume, alter, share, redefine, rent, mortgage, pawn, sell, exchange, transfer, give away or destroy it, or to exclude others from doing these things, as well as to perhaps abandon it; whereas regardless of the nature of the _____ , the owner thereof has the right to properly use it , or at the very least exclusively keep it.

Exam Probability: **Medium**

31. *Answer choices:*

(see index for correct answer)

- a. Property
- b. Mereology
- c. Simple
- d. Meronomy

Guidance: level 1

:: Inventory ::

Costs are associated with particular goods using one of the several formulas, including specific identification, first-in first-out, or average cost. Costs include all costs of purchase, costs of conversion and other costs that are incurred in bringing the inventories to their present location and condition. Costs of goods made by the businesses include material, labor, and allocated overhead. The costs of those goods which are not yet sold are deferred as costs of inventory until the inventory is sold or written down in value.

Exam Probability: **Low**

32. *Answer choices:*

(see index for correct answer)

- a. Buffer stock
- b. Cost of goods sold
- c. Stock demands
- d. Stock mix

Guidance: level 1

:: Marketing ::

A _____ is something that is necessary for an organism to live a healthy life. _____ s are distinguished from wants in that, in the case of a _____ , a deficiency causes a clear adverse outcome: a dysfunction or death. In other words, a _____ is something required for a safe, stable and healthy life while a want is a desire, wish or aspiration. When _____ s or wants are backed by purchasing power, they have the potential to become economic demands.

Exam Probability: **Medium**

33. *Answer choices:*

(see index for correct answer)

- a. Private label
- b. Need
- c. Product proliferation
- d. Enterprise marketing management

Guidance: level 1

:: ::

A _____ is the period used by governments for accounting and budget purposes, which varies between countries. It is also used for financial reporting by business and other organizations. Laws in many jurisdictions require company financial reports to be prepared and published on an annual basis, but generally do not require the reporting period to align with the calendar year . Taxation laws generally require accounting records to be maintained and taxes calculated on an annual basis, which usually corresponds to the _____ used for government purposes. The calculation of tax on an annual basis is especially relevant for direct taxation, such as income tax. Many annual government fees—such as Council rates, licence fees, etc.—are also levied on a _____ basis, while others are charged on an anniversary basis.

Exam Probability: **High**

34. Answer choices:

(see index for correct answer)

- a. deep-level diversity
- b. functional perspective
- c. Fiscal year
- d. process perspective

Guidance: level 1

:: Interest rates ::

An _____ is the amount of interest due per period, as a proportion of the amount lent, deposited or borrowed. The total interest on an amount lent or borrowed depends on the principal sum, the _____ , the compounding frequency, and the length of time over which it is lent, deposited or borrowed.

Exam Probability: **Medium**

35. Answer choices:

(see index for correct answer)

- a. Time preference
- b. United States housing bubble
- c. Forex swap
- d. Bank rate

A _____ loan or, simply, _____ is used either by purchasers of real property to raise funds to buy real estate, or alternatively by existing property owners to raise funds for any purpose, while putting a lien on the property being _____ d. The loan is "secured" on the borrower's property through a process known as _____ origination. This means that a legal mechanism is put into place which allows the lender to take possession and sell the secured property to pay off the loan in the event the borrower defaults on the loan or otherwise fails to abide by its terms. The word _____ is derived from a Law French term used in Britain in the Middle Ages meaning "death pledge" and refers to the pledge ending when either the obligation is fulfilled or the property is taken through foreclosure. A _____ can also be described as "a borrower giving consideration in the form of a collateral for a benefit ".

Exam Probability: **High**

36. *Answer choices:*

(see index for correct answer)

- a. deep-level diversity
- b. Mortgage
- c. interpersonal communication
- d. cultural

:: ::

_____s and acquisitions are transactions in which the ownership of companies, other business organizations, or their operating units are transferred or consolidated with other entities. As an aspect of strategic management, M&A can allow enterprises to grow or downsize, and change the nature of their business or competitive position.

Exam Probability: **Low**

37. *Answer choices:*

(see index for correct answer)

- a. hierarchical
- b. imperative
- c. surface-level diversity
- d. Character

Guidance: level 1

:: Management accounting ::

_____s are costs that change as the quantity of the good or service that a business produces changes. _____s are the sum of marginal costs over all units produced. They can also be considered normal costs. Fixed costs and _____s make up the two components of total cost. Direct costs are costs that can easily be associated with a particular cost object. However, not all _____s are direct costs. For example, variable manufacturing overhead costs are _____s that are indirect costs, not direct costs. _____s are sometimes called unit-level costs as they vary with the number of units produced.

Exam Probability: **Medium**

38. *Answer choices:*

(see index for correct answer)

- a. Variable cost
- b. Managerial risk accounting
- c. Responsibility center
- d. Revenue center

Guidance: level 1

:: Currency ::

A _____ , in the most specific sense is money in any form when in use or circulation as a medium of exchange, especially circulating banknotes and coins. A more general definition is that a _____ is a system of money in common use, especially for people in a nation. Under this definition, US dollars , pounds sterling , Australian dollars , European euros , Russian rubles and Indian Rupees are examples of currencies. These various currencies are recognized as stores of value and are traded between nations in foreign exchange markets, which determine the relative values of the different currencies. Currencies in this sense are defined by governments, and each type has limited boundaries of acceptance.

Exam Probability: **Medium**

39. *Answer choices:*

(see index for correct answer)

- a. Swan diagram
- b. Circulation
- c. Unit of account
- d. Remonetisation

Guidance: level 1

:: Stock market ::

A _____ or stock divide increases the number of shares in a company. The price is adjusted such that the before and after market capitalization of the company remains the same and dilution does not occur. Options and warrants are included.

Exam Probability: **Low**

40. *Answer choices:*

(see index for correct answer)

- a. Automated trading system
- b. Issued shares
- c. Mark Twain effect
- d. Stock split

Guidance: level 1

:: Loans ::

In finance, a _____ is the lending of money by one or more individuals, organizations, or other entities to other individuals, organizations etc. The recipient incurs a debt, and is usually liable to pay interest on that debt until it is repaid, and also to repay the principal amount borrowed.

Exam Probability: **Medium**

41. *Answer choices:*

(see index for correct answer)

- a. Forgivable loan
- b. Loan commodities
- c. Mortgage loan

- d. Concessionary loan

Guidance: level 1

:: Marketing ::

_____ or stock is the goods and materials that a business holds for the ultimate goal of resale.

Exam Probability: **Low**

42. *Answer choices:*

(see index for correct answer)

- a. Demand signal repository
- b. Audience segmentation
- c. Multicultural marketing
- d. LIDA

Guidance: level 1

:: ::

From an accounting perspective, _____ is crucial because _____ and _____ taxes considerably affect the net income of most companies and because they are subject to laws and regulations.

Exam Probability: **Medium**

43. *Answer choices:*

(see index for correct answer)

- a. hierarchical perspective
- b. similarity-attraction theory
- c. Character
- d. process perspective

Guidance: level 1

:: ::

_____ is the consumption and saving opportunity gained by an entity within a specified timeframe, which is generally expressed in monetary terms. For households and individuals, " _____ is the sum of all the wages, salaries, profits, interest payments, rents, and other forms of earnings received in a given period of time."

Exam Probability: **Low**

44. *Answer choices:*

(see index for correct answer)

- a. deep-level diversity
- b. Sarbanes-Oxley act of 2002
- c. process perspective
- d. Income

Guidance: level 1

:: ::

In finance, return is a profit on an investment. It comprises any change in value of the investment, and/or cash flows which the investor receives from the investment, such as interest payments or dividends. It may be measured either in absolute terms or as a percentage of the amount invested. The latter is also called the holding period return.

Exam Probability: **Low**

45. *Answer choices:*

(see index for correct answer)

- a. process perspective
- b. empathy
- c. cultural
- d. deep-level diversity

Guidance: level 1

:: Income taxes ::

An _____ is a tax imposed on individuals or entities that varies with respective income or profits . _____ generally is computed as the product of a tax rate times taxable income. Taxation rates may vary by type or characteristics of the taxpayer.

Exam Probability: **Medium**

46. *Answer choices:*

(see index for correct answer)

- a. Income tax in Singapore
- b. State income tax
- c. Income and Corporation Taxes Act 1988
- d. Income tax

Guidance: level 1

:: Bonds (finance) ::

An _____ is a legal contract that reflects or covers a debt or purchase obligation. It specifically refers to two types of practices: in historical usage, an _____ d servant status, and in modern usage, it is an instrument used for commercial debt or real estate transaction.

Exam Probability: **Medium**

47. *Answer choices:*

(see index for correct answer)

- a. Indenture
- b. Land bonds
- c. Auction rate security
- d. Nominal yield

Guidance: level 1

:: Generally Accepted Accounting Principles ::

_____ is a small amount of discretionary funds in the form of cash used for expenditures where it is not sensible to make any disbursement by cheque, because of the inconvenience and costs of writing, signing, and then cashing the cheque.

Exam Probability: **High**

48. *Answer choices:*

(see index for correct answer)

- a. Financial position of the United States
- b. Petty cash
- c. Closing entries
- d. Cost principle

Guidance: level 1

:: ::

_____ , often abbreviated as B/E in finance, is the point of balance making neither a profit nor a loss. The term originates in finance but the concept has been applied in other fields.

Exam Probability: **High**

49. *Answer choices:*
(see index for correct answer)

- a. Break-even
- b. co-culture
- c. imperative
- d. Sarbanes-Oxley act of 2002

Guidance: level 1

:: Financial ratios ::

The _____ shows the percentage of how profitable a company's assets are in generating revenue.

Exam Probability: **High**

50. *Answer choices:*
(see index for correct answer)

- a. Sustainable growth rate
- b. Return of capital
- c. Days in inventory
- d. Return on assets

Guidance: level 1

:: ::

The _____ of a function of a real variable measures the sensitivity to change of the function value with respect to a change in its argument. _____ s are a fundamental tool of calculus. For example, the _____ of the position of a moving object with respect to time is the object's velocity: this measures how quickly the position of the object changes when time advances.

Exam Probability: **High**

51. Answer choices:

(see index for correct answer)

- a. functional perspective
- b. imperative
- c. hierarchical
- d. Derivative

Guidance: level 1

:: Credit cards ::

A _____ is a payment card issued to users to enable the cardholder to pay a merchant for goods and services based on the cardholder's promise to the card issuer to pay them for the amounts plus the other agreed charges. The card issuer creates a revolving account and grants a line of credit to the cardholder, from which the cardholder can borrow money for payment to a merchant or as a cash advance.

Exam Probability: **Low**

52. Answer choices:

(see index for correct answer)

- a. Rail travel card
- b. North American Bancard
- c. Credit card
- d. China UnionPay

Guidance: level 1

:: Management accounting ::

" _____ s are the structural determinants of the cost of an activity, reflecting any linkages or interrelationships that affect it". Therefore we could assume that the _____ s determine the cost behavior within the activities, reflecting the links that these have with other activities and relationships that affect them.

Exam Probability: **Medium**

53. *Answer choices:*
(see index for correct answer)

- a. Variable cost
- b. Financial statement analysis
- c. Semi-variable cost
- d. Contribution margin

Guidance: level 1

:: Stock market ::

_____ is a form of corporate equity ownership, a type of security. The terms voting share and ordinary share are also used frequently in other parts of the world; "_____" being primarily used in the United States. They are known as Equity shares or Ordinary shares in the UK and other Commonwealth realms. This type of share gives the stockholder the right to share in the profits of the company, and to vote on matters of corporate policy and the composition of the members of the board of directors.

Exam Probability: **Medium**

54. *Answer choices:*

(see index for correct answer)

- a. WeSeed
- b. Inet
- c. Chi-X Global
- d. Common stock

Guidance: level 1

:: Consumer theory ::

_____ is the quantity of a good that consumers are willing and able to purchase at various prices during a given period of time.

Exam Probability: **High**

55. Answer choices:

(see index for correct answer)

- a. Snob effect
- b. Cross elasticity of demand
- c. Revealed preference
- d. Demand

Guidance: level 1

:: Generally Accepted Accounting Principles ::

A _____ or reacquired stock is stock which is bought back by the issuing company, reducing the amount of outstanding stock on the open market.

Exam Probability: **Medium**

56. Answer choices:

(see index for correct answer)

- a. Gross profit
- b. Depreciation
- c. deferred revenue
- d. Treasury stock

Guidance: level 1

:: Management ::

_____ is the identification, evaluation, and prioritization of risks followed by coordinated and economical application of resources to minimize, monitor, and control the probability or impact of unfortunate events or to maximize the realization of opportunities.

Exam Probability: **Medium**

57. *Answer choices:*

(see index for correct answer)

- a. Risk management
- b. Failure demand
- c. Wireless informatics
- d. PhD in management

Guidance: level 1

:: Insolvency ::

_____ is a legal process through which people or other entities who cannot repay debts to creditors may seek relief from some or all of their debts. In most jurisdictions, _____ is imposed by a court order, often initiated by the debtor.

Exam Probability: **Low**

58. *Answer choices:*

(see index for correct answer)

- a. Liquidation
- b. Bankruptcy
- c. Insolvency law of Russia
- d. Official Committee of Equity Security Holders

Guidance: level 1

:: Management accounting ::

In economics, _____ s, indirect costs or overheads are business expenses that are not dependent on the level of goods or services produced by the business. They tend to be time-related, such as interest or rents being paid per month, and are often referred to as overhead costs. This is in contrast to variable costs, which are volume-related and unknown at the beginning of the accounting year. For a simple example, such as a bakery, the monthly rent for the baking facilities, and the monthly payments for the security system and basic phone line are _____ s, as they do not change according to how much bread the bakery produces and sells. On the other hand, the wage costs of the bakery are variable, as the bakery will have to hire more workers if the production of bread increases. Economists reckon _____ as a entry barrier for new entrepreneurs.

Exam Probability: **High**

59. *Answer choices:*

(see index for correct answer)

- a. Variable cost
- b. Fixed cost
- c. Overhead
- d. Investment center

Guidance: level 1

Human resource management

Human resource (HR) management is the strategic approach to the effective management of organization workers so that they help the business gain a competitive advantage. It is designed to maximize employee performance in service of an employer's strategic objectives. HR is primarily concerned with the management of people within organizations, focusing on policies and on systems. HR departments are responsible for overseeing employee-benefits design, employee recruitment, training and development, performance appraisal, and rewarding (e.g., managing pay and benefit systems). HR also concerns itself with organizational change and industrial relations, that is, the balancing of organizational practices with requirements arising from collective bargaining and from governmental laws.

:: Human resource management ::

_____ refers to the ability of an organization to retain its employees. _____ can be represented by a simple statistic. However, many consider _____ as relating to the efforts by which employers attempt to retain the employees in their workforce. In this sense, retention becomes the strategies rather than the outcome.

Exam Probability: **Low**

1. *Answer choices:*

(see index for correct answer)

- a. Continuing professional development
- b. Human resource accounting
- c. Employee retention
- d. Chartered Institute of Personnel and Development

Guidance: level 1

:: Packaging ::

In work place, _____ or job _____ means good ranking with the hypothesized conception of requirements of a role. There are two types of job _____ s: contextual and task. Task _____ is related to cognitive ability while contextual _____ is dependent upon personality. Task _____ are behavioral roles that are recognized in job descriptions and by remuneration systems, they are directly related to organizational _____ , whereas, contextual _____ are value based and additional behavioral roles that are not recognized in job descriptions and covered by compensation; they are extra roles that are indirectly related to organizational _____ . Citizenship _____ like contextual _____ means a set of individual activity/contribution that supports the organizational culture.

Exam Probability: **High**

2. *Answer choices:*

(see index for correct answer)

- a. Performance
- b. Waterskin
- c. ISPM 15
- d. Dangerous Substances Directive

Guidance: level 1

:: Business ethics ::

_____ is a pejorative term for a workplace that has very poor, socially unacceptable working conditions. The work may be difficult, dangerous, climatically challenged or underpaid. Workers in _____ s may work long hours with low pay, regardless of laws mandating overtime pay or a minimum wage; child labor laws may also be violated. The Fair Labor Association's "2006 Annual Public Report" inspected factories for FLA compliance in 18 countries including Bangladesh, El Salvador, Colombia, Guatemala, Malaysia, Thailand, Tunisia, Turkey, China, India, Vietnam, Honduras, Indonesia, Brazil, Mexico, and the US. The U.S. Department of Labor's "2015 Findings on the Worst Forms of Child Labor" found that "18 countries did not meet the International Labour Organization's recommendation for an adequate number of inspectors."

Exam Probability: **High**

3. *Answer choices:*

(see index for correct answer)

- a. Business Ethics Quarterly
- b. MBA Oath
- c. Voluntary compliance
- d. Sweatshop

Guidance: level 1

:: ::

_____ is a form of government characterized by strong central power and limited political freedoms. Individual freedoms are subordinate to the state and there is no constitutional accountability and rule of law under an authoritarian regime. Authoritarian regimes can be autocratic with power concentrated in one person or it can be more spread out between multiple officials and government institutions. Juan Linz's influential 1964 description of _____ characterized authoritarian political systems by four qualities.

Exam Probability: **High**

4. *Answer choices:*

(see index for correct answer)

- a. Authoritarianism
- b. functional perspective
- c. corporate values
- d. imperative

Guidance: level 1

:: ::

In business strategy, _____ is establishing a competitive advantage by having the lowest cost of operation in the industry. _____ is often driven by company efficiency, size, scale, scope and cumulative experience. A _____ strategy aims to exploit scale of production, well-defined scope and other economies, producing highly standardized products, using advanced technology. In recent years, more and more companies have chosen a strategic mix to achieve market leadership. These patterns consist of simultaneous _____, superior customer service and product leadership. Walmart has succeeded across the world due to its _____ strategy. The company has cut down on exesses at every point of production and thus are able to provide the consumers with quality products at low prices.

Exam Probability: **Medium**

5. *Answer choices:*

(see index for correct answer)

- a. corporate values
- b. Character
- c. imperative
- d. Cost leadership

Guidance: level 1

:: Sociological terminology ::

In moral and political philosophy, the _____ is a theory or model that originated during the Age of Enlightenment and usually concerns the legitimacy of the authority of the state over the individual. _____ arguments typically posit that individuals have consented, either explicitly or tacitly, to surrender some of their freedoms and submit to the authority in exchange for protection of their remaining rights or maintenance of the social order. The relation between natural and legal rights is often a topic of _____ theory. The term takes its name from The _____ , a 1762 book by Jean-Jacques Rousseau that discussed this concept. Although the antecedents of _____ theory are found in antiquity, in Greek and Stoic philosophy and Roman and Canon Law, the heyday of the _____ was the mid-17th to early 19th centuries, when it emerged as the leading doctrine of political legitimacy.

Exam Probability: **Low**

6. *Answer choices:*

(see index for correct answer)

- a. Social contract
- b. institutional racism
- c. Social engagement
- d. cultural artifact

Guidance: level 1

:: Management ::

In the field of management, _____ involves the formulation and implementation of the major goals and initiatives taken by an organization's top management on behalf of owners, based on consideration of resources and an assessment of the internal and external environments in which the organization operates.

Exam Probability: **Low**

7. *Answer choices:*

(see index for correct answer)

- a. Functional management
- b. Twelve leverage points
- c. Strategic management
- d. IT performance management

Guidance: level 1

:: Management ::

In organizational studies, _____ is the efficient and effective development of an organization's resources when they are needed. Such resources may include financial resources, inventory, human skills, production resources, or information technology and natural resources.

Exam Probability: **Medium**

8. *Answer choices:*

(see index for correct answer)

- a. Event to knowledge
- b. Duality
- c. Concept of the Corporation
- d. Resource management

Guidance: level 1

:: Industrial agreements ::

A _____, in labor relations, is a group of employees with a clear and identifiable community of interests who are represented by a single labor union in collective bargaining and other dealings with management. Examples would be non-management professors, law enforcement professionals, blue-collar workers, clerical and administrative employees, etc. Geographic location as well as the number of facilities included in _____ s can be at issue during representation cases.

Exam Probability: **Low**

9. *Answer choices:*

(see index for correct answer)

- a. Bargaining unit
- b. Court of Arbitration
- c. Federal Labor Relations Act

- d. Compromise agreement

Guidance: level 1

:: ::

_____ is an important topic of Human Resource Management. It helps develop the career of the individual and the prosperous growth of the organization. On the job training is a form of training provided at the workplace. During the training, employees are familiarized with the working environment they will become part of. Employees also get a hands-on experience using machinery, equipment, tools, materials, etc. Part of is to face the challenges that occur during the performance of the job. An experienced employee or a manager are executing the role of the mentor who through written, or verbal instructions and demonstrations are passing on his/her knowledge and company-specific skills to the new employee. Executing the training on at the job location, rather than the classroom, creates a stress-free environment for the employees. _____ is the most popular method of training not only in the United States but in most of the developed countries, such as the United Kingdom, China, Russia, etc. Its effectiveness is based on the use of existing workplace tools, machines, documents and equipment, and the knowledge of specialists who are working in this field. _____ is easy to arrange and manage and it simplifies the process of adapting to the new workplace.OJT is highly used for practical tasks. It is inexpensive, and it doesn't require special equipment that is normally used for a specific job. Upon satisfaction of completion of the training, the employer is expected to retain participants as regular employees.

Exam Probability: **Low**

10. *Answer choices:*

(see index for correct answer)

- a. surface-level diversity
- b. On-the-job training
- c. imperative
- d. hierarchical perspective

Guidance: level 1

:: ::

_____ is an enduring pattern of romantic or sexual attraction to persons of the opposite sex or gender, the same sex or gender, or to both sexes or more than one gender. These attractions are generally subsumed under heterosexuality, homosexuality, and bisexuality, while asexuality is sometimes identified as the fourth category.

Exam Probability: **Low**

11. *Answer choices:*

(see index for correct answer)

- a. personal values
- b. cultural
- c. co-culture
- d. Sexual orientation

Guidance: level 1

:: Job interview ::

An _____ is a survey conducted with an individual who is separating from an organization or relationship. Most commonly, this occurs between an employee and an organization, a student and an educational institution, or a member and an association. An organization can use the information gained from an _____ to assess what should be improved, changed, or remain intact. More so, an organization can use the results from _____ s to reduce employee, student, or member turnover and increase productivity and engagement, thus reducing the high costs associated with turnover. Some examples of the value of conducting _____ s include shortening the recruiting and hiring process, reducing absenteeism, improving innovation, sustaining performance, and reducing possible litigation if issues mentioned in the _____ are addressed. It is important for each organization to customize its own _____ in order to maintain the highest levels of survey validity and reliability.

Exam Probability: **Medium**

12. *Answer choices:*

(see index for correct answer)

- a. Mock interview
- b. Exit interview
- c. Case interview
- d. Programming interview

Guidance: level 1

:: Employment ::

A _____, a concept developed in contemporary research by organizational scholar Denise Rousseau, represents the mutual beliefs, perceptions and informal obligations between an employer and an employee. It sets the dynamics for the relationship and defines the detailed practicality of the work to be done. It is distinguishable from the formal written contract of employment which, for the most part, only identifies mutual duties and responsibilities in a generalized form.

Exam Probability: **High**

13. *Answer choices:*

(see index for correct answer)

- a. Gold-collar worker
- b. Hourly worker
- c. Local hiring
- d. Psychological contract

Guidance: level 1

:: Employment compensation ::

_____s and benefits in kind include various types of non-wage compensation provided to employees in addition to their normal wages or salaries. Instances where an employee exchanges wages for some other form of benefit is generally referred to as a "salary packaging" or "salary exchange" arrangement. In most countries, most kinds of _____ s are taxable to at least some degree. Examples of these benefits include: housing furnished or not, with or without free utilities; group insurance ; disability income protection; retirement benefits; daycare; tuition reimbursement; sick leave; vacation ; social security; profit sharing; employer student loan contributions; conveyancing; domestic help ; and other specialized benefits.

Exam Probability: **Medium**

14. *Answer choices:*

(see index for correct answer)

- a. Basic income
- b. Health Reimbursement Account
- c. Employee benefit
- d. Total Reward

Guidance: level 1

:: Behaviorism ::

In behavioral psychology, _____ is a consequence applied that will strengthen an organism's future behavior whenever that behavior is preceded by a specific antecedent stimulus. This strengthening effect may be measured as a higher frequency of behavior, longer duration, greater magnitude, or shorter latency. There are two types of _____, known as positive _____ and negative _____; positive is where by a reward is offered on expression of the wanted behaviour and negative is taking away an undesirable element in the persons environment whenever the desired behaviour is achieved.

Exam Probability: **Medium**

15. *Answer choices:*

(see index for correct answer)

- a. contingency management
- b. chaining
- c. Systematic desensitization
- d. Reinforcement

Guidance: level 1

:: Labour law ::

A _____ is a legal contract that is meant to limit the liability of an employer whose employees are romantically involved. An employer may choose to require a _____ when a romantic relationship within the company becomes known, in order to indemnify the company in case the employees' romantic relationship fails, primarily so that one party can't bring a sexual harassment lawsuit against the company. To that end, the _____ states that the relationship is consensual, and both parties of the relationship must sign it. The _____ may also stipulate rules for acceptable romantic behavior in the workplace.

Exam Probability: **Low**

16. *Answer choices:*

(see index for correct answer)

- a. Love contract
- b. Work permit
- c. International Association of Labour Law Journals
- d. Works council

Guidance: level 1

:: Labour relations ::

An _____ is a place of employment at which one is not required to join or financially support a union as a condition of hiring or continued employment. _____ is also known as a merit shop.

Exam Probability: **Low**

17. *Answer choices:*

(see index for correct answer)

- a. Disciplinary counseling
- b. Social dialogue
- c. Minnesota Nurses Association
- d. Open shop

Guidance: level 1

:: Free market ::

Piece work is any type of employment in which a worker is paid a fixed _____ for each unit produced or action performed regardless of time.

Exam Probability: **High**

18. *Answer choices:*

(see index for correct answer)

- a. Free market
- b. Piece rate

Guidance: level 1

:: Analysis ::

_____ is the process of breaking a complex topic or substance into smaller parts in order to gain a better understanding of it. The technique has been applied in the study of mathematics and logic since before Aristotle , though _____ as a formal concept is a relatively recent development.

Exam Probability: **Low**

19. *Answer choices:*

(see index for correct answer)

- a. Configurational analysis
- b. Engineering analysis
- c. Analysis
- d. SWOQe

Guidance: level 1

:: Trade union legislation ::

The _____ is the name for several legislative bills on US labor law which have been proposed and sometimes introduced into one or both chambers of the U.S. Congress.

Exam Probability: **Low**

20. *Answer choices:*

(see index for correct answer)

- a. Employee Free Choice Act
- b. Trade Union Reform and Employment Rights Act 1993
- c. Trade Disputes and Trade Unions Act 1927
- d. Trade Disputes and Trade Unions Act 1946

Guidance: level 1

:: ::

In educational development, _____ provides a person, often a student, focus for selecting a career or subject to undertake in the future. Often educational institutions provide career counsellors to assist students with their educational development.

Exam Probability: **Low**

21. *Answer choices:*

(see index for correct answer)

- a. information systems assessment
- b. levels of analysis
- c. Career development

- d. deep-level diversity

Guidance: level 1

:: Persuasion techniques ::

_____ is a psychological technique in which an individual attempts to influence another person by becoming more likeable to their target. This term was coined by social psychologist Edward E. Jones, who further defined _____ as "a class of strategic behaviors illicitly designed to influence a particular other person concerning the attractiveness of one's personal qualities." _____ research has identified some specific tactics of employing _____ .

Exam Probability: **Medium**

22. *Answer choices:*
(see index for correct answer)

- a. Low-ball
- b. Door-in-the-face technique
- c. Crocodile tears
- d. Fairy tale

Guidance: level 1

:: ::

An _____ is a period of work experience offered by an organization for a limited period of time. Once confined to medical graduates, the term is now used for a wide range of placements in businesses, non-profit organizations and government agencies. They are typically undertaken by students and graduates looking to gain relevant skills and experience in a particular field. Employers benefit from these placements because they often recruit employees from their best interns, who have known capabilities, thus saving time and money in the long run. _____ s are usually arranged by third-party organizations which recruit interns on behalf of industry groups. Rules vary from country to country about when interns should be regarded as employees. The system can be open to exploitation by unscrupulous employers.

Exam Probability: **Medium**

23. *Answer choices:*

(see index for correct answer)

- a. personal values
- b. co-culture
- c. cultural
- d. process perspective

Guidance: level 1

:: Unemployment in the United States ::

The _____ is a unit of the United States Department of Labor. It is the principal fact-finding agency for the U.S. government in the broad field of labor economics and statistics and serves as a principal agency of the U.S. Federal Statistical System. The BLS is a governmental statistical agency that collects, processes, analyzes, and disseminates essential statistical data to the American public, the U.S. Congress, other Federal agencies, State and local governments, business, and labor representatives. The BLS also serves as a statistical resource to the United States Department of Labor, and conducts research into how much families need to earn to be able to enjoy a decent standard of living.

Exam Probability: **Low**

24. *Answer choices:*

(see index for correct answer)

- a. Unemployment Compensation Extension Act of 2010
- b. Ticket to Work
- c. Bureau of Labor Statistics
- d. Florida state Unemployment Tax

Guidance: level 1

:: Employment discrimination ::

A _____ is a metaphor used to represent an invisible barrier that keeps a given demographic from rising beyond a certain level in a hierarchy.

Exam Probability: **High**

25. *Answer choices:*

(see index for correct answer)

- a. Glass cliff
- b. Employment Non-Discrimination Act
- c. New South Wales selection bias
- d. Glass ceiling

Guidance: level 1

:: Business law ::

An _____ is a natural person, business, or corporation that provides goods or services to another entity under terms specified in a contract or within a verbal agreement. Unlike an employee, an _____ does not work regularly for an employer but works as and when required, during which time they may be subject to law of agency. _____ s are usually paid on a freelance basis. Contractors often work through a limited company or franchise, which they themselves own, or may work through an umbrella company.

Exam Probability: **Low**

26. *Answer choices:*

(see index for correct answer)

- a. Hundi

- b. Independent contractor
- c. Voting trust
- d. Recharacterisation

Guidance: level 1

:: Human resource management ::

_____ means increasing the scope of a job through extending the range of its job duties and responsibilities generally within the same level and periphery. _____ involves combining various activities at the same level in the organization and adding them to the existing job. It is also called the horizontal expansion of job activities. This contradicts the principles of specialisation and the division of labour whereby work is divided into small units, each of which is performed repetitively by an individual worker and the responsibilities are always clear. Some motivational theories suggest that the boredom and alienation caused by the division of labour can actually cause efficiency to fall. Thus, _____ seeks to motivate workers through reversing the process of specialisation. A typical approach might be to replace assembly lines with modular work; instead of an employee repeating the same step on each product, they perform several tasks on a single item. In order for employees to be provided with _____ they will need to be retrained in new fields to understand how each field works.

Exam Probability: **High**

27. *Answer choices:*

(see index for correct answer)

- a. Workforce planning

- b. Human relations movement
- c. Job enlargement
- d. Employee silence

Guidance: level 1

:: Business terms ::

Centralisation or _____ is the process by which the activities of an organization, particularly those regarding planning and decision-making, framing strategy and policies become concentrated within a particular geographical location group. This moves the important decision-making and planning powers within the center of the organisation.

Exam Probability: **High**

28. *Answer choices:*

(see index for correct answer)

- a. operating cost
- b. front office
- c. organizational capital
- d. noncommercial

Guidance: level 1

:: ::

_____ is overt or covert, often harmful, social interaction with the intention of inflicting damage or other unpleasantness upon another individual. It may occur either reactively or without provocation. In humans, frustration due to blocked goals can cause _____ . Human _____ can be classified into direct and indirect _____ ; whilst the former is characterized by physical or verbal behavior intended to cause harm to someone, the latter is characterized by behavior intended to harm the social relations of an individual or group.

Exam Probability: **Medium**

29. *Answer choices:*

(see index for correct answer)

- a. Aggression
- b. corporate values
- c. imperative
- d. functional perspective

Guidance: level 1

:: Trade union legislation ::

The _____ of 1935 is a foundational statute of United States labor law which guarantees the right of private sector employees to organize into trade unions, engage in collective bargaining, and take collective action such as strikes. The act was written by Senator Robert F. Wagner, passed by the 74th United States Congress, and signed into law by President Franklin D. Roosevelt.

Exam Probability: **High**

30. *Answer choices:*

(see index for correct answer)

- a. Trade Disputes and Trade Unions Act 1927
- b. Trade Disputes Act 1906
- c. National Labor Relations Act
- d. Trade Union Reform and Employment Rights Act 1993

Guidance: level 1

:: Trade unions in the United States ::

The _____ is an American labor union representing over 670,000 employees of the federal government, about 5,000 employees of the District of Columbia, and a few hundred private sector employees, mostly in and around federal facilities. AFGE is the largest union for civilian, non-postal federal employees and the largest union for District of Columbia employees who report directly to the mayor. It is affiliated with the AFL-CIO.

Exam Probability: **High**

31. *Answer choices:*

(see index for correct answer)

- a. National Nurses United
- b. American Federation of Government Employees
- c. Chicago Federation of Labor
- d. Asian Pacific American Labor Alliance

Guidance: level 1

:: Fundamental analysis ::

_____ , also known as letter stock or restricted securities, is stock of a company that is not fully transferable until certain conditions have been met. Upon satisfaction of those conditions, the stock is no longer restricted, and becomes transferable to the person holding the award. _____ is often used as a form of employee compensation, in which case it typically becomes transferrable upon the satisfaction of certain conditions, such as continued employment for a period of time or the achievement of particular product-development milestones, earnings per share goals or other financial targets. _____ is a popular alternative to stock options, particularly for executives, due to favorable accounting rules and income tax treatment.

Exam Probability: **Low**

32. *Answer choices:*

(see index for correct answer)

- a. Market value added

- b. Growth stock
- c. Restricted stock
- d. Public float

Guidance: level 1

:: Business law ::

A pre-entry _____ is a form of union security agreement under which the employer agrees to hire union members only, and employees must remain members of the union at all times in order to remain employed. This is different from a post-entry _____ , which is an agreement requiring all employees to join the union if they are not already members. In a union shop, the union must accept as a member any person hired by the employer.

Exam Probability: **Low**

33. *Answer choices:*
(see index for correct answer)

- a. License
- b. Closed shop
- c. Retroactive overtime
- d. Contract A

Guidance: level 1

:: Business theory ::

_____ or cultural quotient is a term used in business, education, government and academic research. _____ can be understood as the capability to relate and work effectively across cultures. Originally, the term _____ and the abbreviation "CQ" was developed by the research done by Soon Ang and Linn Van Dyne as a researched-based way of measuring and predicting intercultural performance.

Exam Probability: **High**

34. *Answer choices:*

(see index for correct answer)

- a. Brian F. Harris
- b. Cultural intelligence
- c. Robust decision-making
- d. Entrepreneurial leadership

Guidance: level 1

:: Network theory ::

A _____ is a social structure made up of a set of social actors, sets of dyadic ties, and other social interactions between actors. The _____ perspective provides a set of methods for analyzing the structure of whole social entities as well as a variety of theories explaining the patterns observed in these structures. The study of these structures uses _____ analysis to identify local and global patterns, locate influential entities, and examine network dynamics.

Exam Probability: **High**

35. *Answer choices:*

(see index for correct answer)

- a. Complex network
- b. Gephi
- c. Social network
- d. Link analysis

Guidance: level 1

:: Telecommuting ::

_____, also called telework, teleworking, working from home, mobile work, remote work, and flexible workplace, is a work arrangement in which employees do not commute or travel to a central place of work, such as an office building, warehouse, or store. Teleworkers in the 21st century often use mobile telecommunications technology such as Wi-Fi-equipped laptop or tablet computers and smartphones to work from coffee shops; others may use a desktop computer and a landline phone at their home. According to a Reuters poll, approximately "one in five workers around the globe, particularly employees in the Middle East, Latin America and Asia, telecommute frequently and nearly 10 percent work from home every day." In the 2000s, annual leave or vacation in some organizations was seen as absence from the workplace rather than ceasing work, and some office employees used telework to continue to check work e-mails while on vacation.

Exam Probability: **High**

36. *Answer choices:*

(see index for correct answer)

- a. The Conference Group
- b. Telecommuting
- c. ODesk
- d. contracting out

Guidance: level 1

:: ::

_____ is the withdrawal from one's position or occupation or from one's active working life. A person may also semi-retire by reducing work hours.

Exam Probability: **Medium**

37. *Answer choices:*

(see index for correct answer)

- a. functional perspective
- b. corporate values
- c. Character
- d. Retirement

Guidance: level 1

:: Financial statements ::

In financial accounting, a _____ or statement of financial position or statement of financial condition is a summary of the financial balances of an individual or organization, whether it be a sole proprietorship, a business partnership, a corporation, private limited company or other organization such as Government or not-for-profit entity. Assets, liabilities and ownership equity are listed as of a specific date, such as the end of its financial year. A _____ is often described as a "snapshot of a company's financial condition". Of the four basic financial statements, the _____ is the only statement which applies to a single point in time of a business' calendar year.

Exam Probability: **Low**

38. *Answer choices:*

(see index for correct answer)

- a. Statement on Auditing Standards No. 70: Service Organizations
- b. Balance sheet
- c. Consolidated financial statement
- d. Quarterly finance report

Guidance: level 1

:: Labour relations ::

_____ is a form of protest in which people congregate outside a place of work or location where an event is taking place. Often, this is done in an attempt to dissuade others from going in , but it can also be done to draw public attention to a cause. Picketers normally endeavor to be non-violent. It can have a number of aims, but is generally to put pressure on the party targeted to meet particular demands or cease operations. This pressure is achieved by harming the business through loss of customers and negative publicity, or by discouraging or preventing workers or customers from entering the site and thereby preventing the business from operating normally.

Exam Probability: **Low**

39. *Answer choices:*

(see index for correct answer)

- a. Work Order Act
- b. Employee voice
- c. Eurocadres
- d. Picketing

Guidance: level 1

:: Production and manufacturing ::

_____ consists of organization-wide efforts to "install and make permanent climate where employees continuously improve their ability to provide on demand products and services that customers will find of particular value." "Total" emphasizes that departments in addition to production are obligated to improve their operations; "management" emphasizes that executives are obligated to actively manage quality through funding, training, staffing, and goal setting. While there is no widely agreed-upon approach, TQM efforts typically draw heavily on the previously developed tools and techniques of quality control. TQM enjoyed widespread attention during the late 1980s and early 1990s before being overshadowed by ISO 9000, Lean manufacturing, and Six Sigma.

Exam Probability: **High**

40. *Answer choices:*

(see index for correct answer)

- a. Earned value
- b. Resource Breakdown
- c. Simatic S5 PLC
- d. Cycle time variation

Guidance: level 1

:: ::

An _____ is a person temporarily or permanently residing in a country other than their native country. In common usage, the term often refers to professionals, skilled workers, or artists taking positions outside their home country, either independently or sent abroad by their employers, who can be companies, universities, governments, or non-governmental organisations. Effectively migrant workers, they usually earn more than they would at home, and less than local employees. However, the term ` _____ ` is also used for retirees and others who have chosen to live outside their native country. Historically, it has also referred to exiles.

Exam Probability: **Medium**

41. *Answer choices:*

(see index for correct answer)

- a. similarity-attraction theory
- b. process perspective
- c. hierarchical
- d. Expatriate

Guidance: level 1

:: Labour law ::

In law, _____ is to give an immediately secured right of present or future deployment. One has a vested right to an asset that cannot be taken away by any third party, even though one may not yet possess the asset. When the right, interest, or title to the present or future possession of a legal estate can be transferred to any other party, it is termed a vested interest.

Exam Probability: **Medium**

42. *Answer choices:*

(see index for correct answer)

- a. Involvement and Participation Association
- b. Vesting
- c. Principles of Labor Legislation
- d. The Burke Group

Guidance: level 1

:: Employment compensation ::

A _____ is a type of employee benefit plan offered in the United States pursuant to Section 125 of the Internal Revenue Code. Its name comes from the earliest such plans that allowed employees to choose between different types of benefits, similar to the ability of a customer to choose among available items in a cafeteria. Qualified _____ s are excluded from gross income. To qualify, a _____ must allow employees to choose from two or more benefits consisting of cash or qualified benefit plans. The Internal Revenue Code explicitly excludes deferred compensation plans from qualifying as a _____ subject to a gross income exemption. Section 125 also provides two exceptions.

Exam Probability: **High**

43. *Answer choices:*

(see index for correct answer)

- a. Federal Salary Council
- b. Cafeteria plan
- c. Real wage
- d. Wage payment systems

Guidance: level 1

:: Leadership ::

_____ is a theory of leadership where a leader works with teams to identify needed change, creating a vision to guide the change through inspiration, and executing the change in tandem with committed members of a group; it is an integral part of the Full Range Leadership Model. _____ serves to enhance the motivation, morale, and job performance of followers through a variety of mechanisms; these include connecting the follower's sense of identity and self to a project and to the collective identity of the organization; being a role model for followers in order to inspire them and to raise their interest in the project; challenging followers to take greater ownership for their work, and understanding the strengths and weaknesses of followers, allowing the leader to align followers with tasks that enhance their performance.

Exam Probability: **Medium**

44. *Answer choices:*

(see index for correct answer)

- a. European Center for Leadership Development
- b. Situational leadership theory
- c. Outstanding leadership theory
- d. Transformational leadership

Guidance: level 1

:: Industrial relations ::

_____ or employee satisfaction is a measure of workers' contentedness with their job, whether or not they like the job or individual aspects or facets of jobs, such as nature of work or supervision. _____ can be measured in cognitive, affective, and behavioral components. Researchers have also noted that _____ measures vary in the extent to which they measure feelings about the job, or cognitions about the job.

Exam Probability: **High**

45. *Answer choices:*

(see index for correct answer)

- a. Injury prevention
- b. Job satisfaction
- c. European Journal of Industrial Relations
- d. Workforce Investment Board

Guidance: level 1

:: Trade unions ::

A _____ is an association of workers forming a legal unit or legal personhood, usually called a "bargaining unit", which acts as bargaining agent and legal representative for a unit of employees in all matters of law or right arising from or in the administration of a collective agreement. Labour unions typically fund the formal organisation, head office, and legal team functions of the labour union through regular fees or union dues. The delegate staff of the labour union representation in the workforce are made up of workplace volunteers who are appointed by members in democratic elections.

Exam Probability: **High**

46. *Answer choices:*

(see index for correct answer)

- a. Craft unionism
- b. Unfair list
- c. Trade union
- d. General union

Guidance: level 1

:: ::

A _____ is a systematic way of determining the value/worth of a job in relation to other jobs in an organization. It tries to make a systematic comparison between jobs to assess their relative worth for the purpose of establishing a rational pay structure. _____ needs to be differentiated from job analysis. Job analysis is a systematic way of gathering information about a job. Every _____ method requires at least some basic job analysis in order to provide factual information about the jobs concerned. Thus, _____ begins with job analysis and ends at that point where the worth of a job is ascertained for achieving pay equity between jobs and different roles.

Exam Probability: **Medium**

47. *Answer choices:*

(see index for correct answer)

- a. surface-level diversity
- b. functional perspective
- c. hierarchical
- d. Job evaluation

Guidance: level 1

:: ::

_____ is a form of development in which a person called a coach supports a learner or client in achieving a specific personal or professional goal by providing training and guidance. The learner is sometimes called a coachee. Occasionally, _____ may mean an informal relationship between two people, of whom one has more experience and expertise than the other and offers advice and guidance as the latter learns; but _____ differs from mentoring in focusing on specific tasks or objectives, as opposed to more general goals or overall development.

Exam Probability: **High**

48. *Answer choices:*

(see index for correct answer)

- a. co-culture
- b. Coaching
- c. interpersonal communication
- d. hierarchical

Guidance: level 1

:: Employment compensation ::

The formula commonly used by compensation professionals to assess the competitiveness of an employee's pay level involves calculating a "_____". _____ is the short form for Comparative ratio.

Exam Probability: **Medium**

49. *Answer choices:*
(see index for correct answer)

- a. Health Reimbursement Account
- b. Wage regulation
- c. Wages for housework
- d. Compa-ratio

Guidance: level 1

:: Parental leave ::

_____, or family leave, is an employee benefit available in almost all countries. The term "_____" may include maternity, paternity, and adoption leave; or may be used distinctively from "maternity leave" and "paternity leave" to describe separate family leave available to either parent to care for small children. In some countries and jurisdictions, "family leave" also includes leave provided to care for ill family members. Often, the minimum benefits and eligibility requirements are stipulated by law.

Exam Probability: **Medium**

50. *Answer choices:*

(see index for correct answer)

- a. Pregnancy discrimination
- b. Geduldig v. Aiello
- c. Parental leave
- d. Cleveland Board of Education v. LaFleur

Guidance: level 1

:: ::

_____ is the stock of habits, knowledge, social and personality attributes embodied in the ability to perform labor so as to produce economic value.

Exam Probability: **Low**

51. *Answer choices:*

(see index for correct answer)

- a. interpersonal communication
- b. Human capital
- c. surface-level diversity
- d. functional perspective

Guidance: level 1

:: ::

A _____ is a research instrument consisting of a series of questions for the purpose of gathering information from respondents. The _____ was invented by the Statistical Society of London in 1838.

Exam Probability: **High**

52. *Answer choices:*

(see index for correct answer)

- a. Questionnaire
- b. levels of analysis
- c. imperative
- d. hierarchical

Guidance: level 1

:: Minimum wage ::

A _____ is the lowest remuneration that employers can legally pay their workers—the price floor below which workers may not sell their labor. Most countries had introduced _____ legislation by the end of the 20th century.

Exam Probability: **Medium**

53. *Answer choices:*

(see index for correct answer)

- a. Minimum Wage Fairness Act
- b. Minimum wage
- c. Minimum wage in the United States
- d. Guaranteed minimum income

Guidance: level 1

:: Validity (statistics) ::

_____ is "the degree to which a test measures what it claims, or purports, to be measuring." In the classical model of test validity, _____ is one of three main types of validity evidence, alongside content validity and criterion validity. Modern validity theory defines _____ as the overarching concern of validity research, subsuming all other types of validity evidence.

Exam Probability: **High**

54. *Answer choices:*

(see index for correct answer)

- a. Construct validity
- b. Ecological validity
- c. Criterion validity
- d. Concurrent validity

Guidance: level 1

:: Human resource management ::

A _____ is a form of payment from an employer to an employee, which may be specified in an employment contract. It is contrasted with piece wages, where each job, hour or other unit is paid separately, rather than on a periodic basis. From the point of view of running a business, _____ can also be viewed as the cost of acquiring and retaining human resources for running operations, and is then termed personnel expense or _____ expense. In accounting, salaries are recorded in payroll accounts.

Exam Probability: **Low**

55. *Answer choices:*

(see index for correct answer)

- a. Corporate Equality Index
- b. Enterprise architecture
- c. Cross-training
- d. Salary

Guidance: level 1

:: Human resource management ::

This term is often used in an employment or human resources context where rather than terminating employees for first or minor infractions, there is a system of escalating responses intended to correct the negative behavior rather than to punish the employee.

Exam Probability: **High**

56. *Answer choices:*

(see index for correct answer)

- a. Autonomous work group
- b. Progressive discipline
- c. Aspiring Minds

- d. Simultaneous recruiting of new graduates

Guidance: level 1

:: Labor rights ::

The _____ is the concept that people have a human _____ , or engage in productive employment, and may not be prevented from doing so. The _____ is enshrined in the Universal Declaration of Human Rights and recognized in international human rights law through its inclusion in the International Covenant on Economic, Social and Cultural Rights, where the _____ emphasizes economic, social and cultural development.

Exam Probability: **Low**

57. *Answer choices:*
(see index for correct answer)

- a. Labor rights
- b. Kate Mullany House
- c. Right to work
- d. China Labour Bulletin

Guidance: level 1

:: Information systems ::

_____ is the process of creating, sharing, using and managing the knowledge and information of an organisation. It refers to a multidisciplinary approach to achieving organisational objectives by making the best use of knowledge.

Exam Probability: **Low**

58. *Answer choices:*

(see index for correct answer)

- a. Censhare
- b. Hybrid Data Infrastructure
- c. Xcon
- d. Knowledge management

Guidance: level 1

:: Income ::

In business and accounting, net income is an entity's income minus cost of goods sold, expenses and taxes for an accounting period. It is computed as the residual of all revenues and gains over all expenses and losses for the period, and has also been defined as the net increase in shareholders' equity that results from a company's operations. In the context of the presentation of financial statements, the IFRS Foundation defines net income as synonymous with profit and loss. The difference between revenue and the cost of making a product or providing a service, before deducting overheads, payroll, taxation, and interest payments. This is different from operating income .

Exam Probability: **High**

59. *Answer choices:*

(see index for correct answer)

- a. Trinity study
- b. Windfall gain
- c. Bottom line
- d. Net national income

Guidance: level 1

Information systems

Information systems (IS) are formal, sociotechnical, organizational systems designed to collect, process, store, and distribute information. In a sociotechnical perspective Information Systems are composed by four components: technology, process, people and organizational structure.

:: ::

A _____ is a knowledge base website on which users collaboratively modify content and structure directly from the web browser. In a typical _____ , text is written using a simplified markup language and often edited with the help of a rich-text editor.

Exam Probability: **High**

1. *Answer choices:*

(see index for correct answer)

- a. Wiki
- b. co-culture
- c. personal values
- d. cultural

Guidance: level 1

:: ::

A _____ is an abstract model that organizes elements of data and standardizes how they relate to one another and to properties of the real world entities. For instance, a _____ may specify that the data element representing a car be composed of a number of other elements which, in turn, represent the color and size of the car and define its owner.

Exam Probability: **High**

2. *Answer choices:*

(see index for correct answer)

- a. hierarchical
- b. interpersonal communication

- c. cultural
- d. Data model

Guidance: level 1

:: ::

_____ is an American video-sharing website headquartered in San Bruno, California. Three former PayPal employees—Chad Hurley, Steve Chen, and Jawed Karim—created the service in February 2005. Google bought the site in November 2006 for US$1.65 billion; _____ now operates as one of Google's subsidiaries.

Exam Probability: **Medium**

3. *Answer choices:*

(see index for correct answer)

- a. YouTube
- b. surface-level diversity
- c. levels of analysis
- d. Sarbanes-Oxley act of 2002

Guidance: level 1

:: Knowledge engineering ::

The _____ is an extension of the World Wide Web through standards by the World Wide Web Consortium. The standards promote common data formats and exchange protocols on the Web, most fundamentally the Resource Description Framework. According to the W3C, "The _____ provides a common framework that allows data to be shared and reused across application, enterprise, and community boundaries". The _____ is therefore regarded as an integrator across different content, information applications and systems.

Exam Probability: **Medium**

4. *Answer choices:*

(see index for correct answer)

- a. Knowledge Engineering Environment
- b. Semantic Web
- c. D3web
- d. International Journal of Software Engineering and Knowledge Engineering

Guidance: level 1

:: Global Positioning System ::

The _____, originally Navstar GPS, is a satellite-based radionavigation system owned by the United States government and operated by the United States Air Force. It is a global navigation satellite system that provides geolocation and time information to a GPS receiver anywhere on or near the Earth where there is an unobstructed line of sight to four or more GPS satellites. Obstacles such as mountains and buildings block the relatively weak GPS signals.

Exam Probability: **Low**

5. *Answer choices:*
(see index for correct answer)

- a. NMEA 0183
- b. Time to first fix
- c. Interagency GPS Executive Board
- d. Global Positioning System

Guidance: level 1

:: Supply chain management terms ::

In business and finance, _____ is a system of organizations, people, activities, information, and resources involved in moving a product or service from supplier to customer. _____ activities involve the transformation of natural resources, raw materials, and components into a finished product that is delivered to the end customer. In sophisticated _____ systems, used products may re-enter the _____ at any point where residual value is recyclable. _____ s link value chains.

Exam Probability: **Medium**

6. *Answer choices:*

(see index for correct answer)

- a. Most valuable customers
- b. Last mile
- c. Stockout
- d. Supply chain

Guidance: level 1

:: Service-oriented (business computing) ::

_____ is a software licensing and delivery model in which software is licensed on a subscription basis and is centrally hosted. It is sometimes referred to as "on-demand software", and was formerly referred to as "software plus services" by Microsoft. SaaS is typically accessed by users using a thin client, e.g. via a web browser. SaaS has become a common delivery model for many business applications, including office software, messaging software, payroll processing software, DBMS software, management software, CAD software, development software, gamification, virtualization, accounting, collaboration, customer relationship management , Management Information Systems , enterprise resource planning , invoicing, human resource management , talent acquisition, learning management systems, content management , Geographic Information Systems , and service desk management. SaaS has been incorporated into the strategy of nearly all leading enterprise software companies.

Exam Probability: **Medium**

7. Answer choices:

(see index for correct answer)

- a. Software as a service
- b. SEMCI
- c. Digital nervous system
- d. SAP Enterprise Architecture Framework

Guidance: level 1

:: Contract law ::

_____ refers to a situation where a statement's author cannot successfully dispute its authorship or the validity of an associated contract. The term is often seen in a legal setting when the authenticity of a signature is being challenged. In such an instance, the authenticity is being "repudiated".

Exam Probability: **Medium**

8. Answer choices:

(see index for correct answer)

- a. Intention to be legally bound
- b. Peppercorn
- c. Non-repudiation
- d. Invitation to treat

Guidance: level 1

:: Consumer behaviour ::

_____ is the ratio of users who click on a specific link to the number of total users who view a page, email, or advertisement. It is commonly used to measure the success of an online advertising campaign for a particular website as well as the effectiveness of email campaigns.

Exam Probability: **Medium**

9. *Answer choices:*

(see index for correct answer)

- a. Willingness to recommend
- b. Buying decision process
- c. Itamar Simonson
- d. Customer analytics

Guidance: level 1

:: Google services ::

_____ is a time-management and scheduling calendar service developed by Google. It became available in beta release April 13, 2006, and in general release in July 2009, on the web and as mobile apps for the Android and iOS platforms.

Exam Probability: **Low**

10. *Answer choices:*

(see index for correct answer)

- a. Google Moderator
- b. A Google A Day
- c. Google Translator Toolkit
- d. Google Calendar

Guidance: level 1

:: Data management ::

_____ is "data [information] that provides information about other data". Many distinct types of _____ exist, among these descriptive _____, structural _____, administrative _____, reference _____ and statistical _____.

Exam Probability: **Low**

11. *Answer choices:*

(see index for correct answer)

- a. Metadata
- b. Contrast set learning
- c. Nonlinear medium
- d. Holos

Guidance: level 1

:: Management ::

A _____ defines or constrains some aspect of business and always resolves to either true or false. _____ s are intended to assert business structure or to control or influence the behavior of the business. _____ s describe the operations, definitions and constraints that apply to an organization. _____ s can apply to people, processes, corporate behavior and computing systems in an organization, and are put in place to help the organization achieve its goals.

Exam Probability: **Low**

12. *Answer choices:*

(see index for correct answer)

- a. Supplier relationship management
- b. Production flow analysis
- c. Competitive advantage
- d. Business rule

Guidance: level 1

:: Information technology ::

_____ is the use of computers to store, retrieve, transmit, and manipulate data, or information, often in the context of a business or other enterprise. IT is considered to be a subset of information and communications technology . An _____ system is generally an information system, a communications system or, more specifically speaking, a computer system – including all hardware, software and peripheral equipment – operated by a limited group of users.

Exam Probability: **Low**

13. *Answer choices:*

(see index for correct answer)

- a. Omniview technology
- b. Information technology
- c. Henry Bakis
- d. GroupLogic

Guidance: level 1

:: Networking hardware ::

A network interface controller is a computer hardware component that connects a computer to a computer network.

Exam Probability: **Medium**

14. *Answer choices:*

(see index for correct answer)

- a. Console server
- b. Network interface card
- c. Ethernet hub

Guidance: level 1

:: Market research ::

_____ is the action of defining, gathering, analyzing, and distributing intelligence about products, customers, competitors, and any aspect of the environment needed to support executives and managers in strategic decision making for an organization.

Exam Probability: **Low**

15. *Answer choices:*

(see index for correct answer)

- a. CoolBrands
- b. Customer advisory council
- c. Competitive intelligence
- d. IRI

Guidance: level 1

:: Information systems ::

In artificial intelligence, an _____ is a computer system that emulates the decision-making ability of a human expert. _____ s are designed to solve complex problems by reasoning through bodies of knowledge, represented mainly as if–then rules rather than through conventional procedural code. The first _____ s were created in the 1970s and then proliferated in the 1980s. _____ s were among the first truly successful forms of artificial intelligence software. However, some experts point out that _____ s were not part of true artificial intelligence since they lack the ability to learn autonomously from external data. An _____ is divided into two subsystems: the inference engine and the knowledge base. The knowledge base represents facts and rules. The inference engine applies the rules to the known facts to deduce new facts. Inference engines can also include explanation and debugging abilities.

Exam Probability: **Low**

16. *Answer choices:*

(see index for correct answer)

- a. Social Study of Information Systems
- b. Expert system

- c. 3D city models
- d. European Research Center for Information Systems

Guidance: level 1

:: Information technology management ::

_____ s or pop-ups are forms of online advertising on the World Wide Web. A pop-up is a graphical user interface display area, usually a small window, that suddenly appears in the foreground of the visual interface. The pop-up window containing an advertisement is usually generated by JavaScript that uses cross-site scripting , sometimes with a secondary payload that uses Adobe Flash. They can also be generated by other vulnerabilities/security holes in browser security.

Exam Probability: **High**

17. *Answer choices:*

(see index for correct answer)

- a. Global delivery model
- b. Pop-up ad
- c. Many-to-many
- d. Microsoft Customer Care Framework

Guidance: level 1

:: Policy ::

A _____ is a statement or a legal document that discloses some or all of the ways a party gathers, uses, discloses, and manages a customer or client's data. It fulfills a legal requirement to protect a customer or client's privacy. Personal information can be anything that can be used to identify an individual, not limited to the person's name, address, date of birth, marital status, contact information, ID issue, and expiry date, financial records, credit information, medical history, where one travels, and intentions to acquire goods and services. In the case of a business it is often a statement that declares a party's policy on how it collects, stores, and releases personal information it collects. It informs the client what specific information is collected, and whether it is kept confidential, shared with partners, or sold to other firms or enterprises. Privacy policies typically represent a broader, more generalized treatment, as opposed to data use statements, which tend to be more detailed and specific.

Exam Probability: **Low**

18. *Answer choices:*

(see index for correct answer)

- a. Overton window
- b. Policy transfer
- c. Privacy policy
- d. Nosokinetics

Guidance: level 1

:: Information technology management ::

In information technology to _____ means to move from one place to another, information to detailed data by focusing in on something. In a GUI-environment, "drilling-down" may involve clicking on some representation in order to reveal more detail.

Exam Probability: **Medium**

19. *Answer choices:*

(see index for correct answer)

- a. Drill down
- b. Speech analytics
- c. Professional Petroleum Data Management Association
- d. IT portfolio management

Guidance: level 1

:: Information technology organisations ::

The Internet Corporation for Assigned Names and Numbers is a nonprofit organization responsible for coordinating the maintenance and procedures of several databases related to the namespaces and numerical spaces of the Internet, ensuring the network's stable and secure operation. _____ performs the actual technical maintenance work of the Central Internet Address pools and DNS root zone registries pursuant to the Internet Assigned Numbers Authority function contract. The contract regarding the IANA stewardship functions between _____ and the National Telecommunications and Information Administration of the United States Department of Commerce ended on October 1, 2016, formally transitioning the functions to the global multistakeholder community.

Exam Probability: **High**

20. *Answer choices:*

(see index for correct answer)

- a. GreenNet
- b. WOUGNET
- c. C2Net
- d. ICANN

Guidance: level 1

:: Automatic identification and data capture ::

_____ is human–computer interaction in which a computer is expected to be transported during normal usage, which allows for transmission of data, voice and video. _____ involves mobile communication, mobile hardware, and mobile software. Communication issues include ad hoc networks and infrastructure networks as well as communication properties, protocols, data formats and concrete technologies. Hardware includes mobile devices or device components. Mobile software deals with the characteristics and requirements of mobile applications.

Exam Probability: **Medium**

21. *Answer choices:*

(see index for correct answer)

- a. Mobile computing
- b. Digital Automated Identification SYstem
- c. Transmitter hunting
- d. Magnetic ink character recognition

Guidance: level 1

:: ::

Collaborative software or _____ is application software designed to help people involved in a common task to achieve their goals. One of the earliest definitions of collaborative software is "intentional group processes plus software to support them".

Exam Probability: **High**

22. *Answer choices:*

(see index for correct answer)

- a. hierarchical
- b. functional perspective
- c. Groupware
- d. information systems assessment

Guidance: level 1

:: Business models ::

_____ , or The Computer Utility, is a service provisioning model in which a service provider makes computing resources and infrastructure management available to the customer as needed, and charges them for specific usage rather than a flat rate. Like other types of on-demand computing , the utility model seeks to maximize the efficient use of resources and/or minimize associated costs. Utility is the packaging of system resources, such as computation, storage and services, as a metered service. This model has the advantage of a low or no initial cost to acquire computer resources; instead, resources are essentially rented.

Exam Probability: **High**

23. *Answer choices:*

(see index for correct answer)

- a. Utility computing
- b. Blended value
- c. InnovationXchange
- d. Independent business

Guidance: level 1

:: ::

A _____ is a research instrument consisting of a series of questions for the purpose of gathering information from respondents. The _____ was invented by the Statistical Society of London in 1838.

Exam Probability: **Low**

24. *Answer choices:*

(see index for correct answer)

- a. interpersonal communication
- b. Questionnaire
- c. hierarchical
- d. cultural

Guidance: level 1

:: Computing input devices ::

In computing, an _____ is a piece of computer hardware equipment used to provide data and control signals to an information processing system such as a computer or information appliance. Examples of _____ s include keyboards, mouse, scanners, digital cameras and joysticks. Audio _____ s may be used for purposes including speech recognition. Many companies are utilizing speech recognition to help assist users to use their device.

Exam Probability: **Medium**

25. *Answer choices:*

(see index for correct answer)

- a. Input device
- b. Planetary scanner
- c. Image scanner
- d. Ergonomic keyboard

Guidance: level 1

:: Management ::

In organizational studies, _____ is the efficient and effective development of an organization's resources when they are needed. Such resources may include financial resources, inventory, human skills, production resources, or information technology and natural resources.

Exam Probability: **Low**

26. *Answer choices:*

(see index for correct answer)

- a. Power structure
- b. Relevance paradox
- c. Resource management
- d. Process capability

Guidance: level 1

:: Market research ::

_____ s are many different distantly related animals that typically have a long cylindrical tube-like body and no limbs. _____ s vary in size from microscopic to over 1 metre in length for marine polychaete _____ s , 6.7 metres for the African giant earth _____ , Microchaetus rappi, and 58 metres for the marine nemertean _____ , Lineus longissimus. Various types of _____ occupy a small variety of parasitic niches, living inside the bodies of other animals. Free-living _____ species do not live on land, but instead, live in marine or freshwater environments, or underground by burrowing. In biology, " _____ " refers to an obsolete taxon, vermes, used by Carolus Linnaeus and Jean-Baptiste Lamarck for all non-arthropod invertebrate animals, now seen to be paraphyletic. The name stems from the Old English word wyrm. Most animals called " _____ s" are invertebrates, but the term is also used for the amphibian caecilians and the slow _____ Anguis, a legless burrowing lizard. Invertebrate animals commonly called " _____ s" include annelids , nematodes , platyhelminthes , marine nemertean _____ s , marine Chaetognatha , priapulid _____ s, and insect larvae such as grubs and maggots.

Exam Probability: **High**

27. *Answer choices:*

(see index for correct answer)

- a. Mode effect
- b. Competitive intelligence
- c. Cogent Research
- d. Worm

Guidance: level 1

:: Domain name system ::

The _____ is a hierarchical and decentralized naming system for computers, services, or other resources connected to the Internet or a private network. It associates various information with domain names assigned to each of the participating entities. Most prominently, it translates more readily memorized domain names to the numerical IP addresses needed for locating and identifying computer services and devices with the underlying network protocols. By providing a worldwide, distributed directory service, the _____ has been an essential component of the functionality of the Internet since 1985.

Exam Probability: **Low**

28. *Answer choices:*

(see index for correct answer)

- a. Domain Name System
- b. RACE encoding

- c. Global Name Registry
- d. Domain Name System Security Extensions

Guidance: level 1

:: ::

_____ LLC is an American multinational technology company that specializes in Internet-related services and products, which include online advertising technologies, search engine, cloud computing, software, and hardware. It is considered one of the Big Four technology companies, alongside Amazon, Apple and Facebook.

Exam Probability: **High**

29. *Answer choices:*

(see index for correct answer)

- a. hierarchical
- b. Google
- c. information systems assessment
- d. co-culture

Guidance: level 1

:: E-commerce ::

_____ is a method of e-commerce where shoppers' friends become involved in the shopping experience. _____ attempts to use technology to mimic the social interactions found in physical malls and stores. With the rise of mobile devices, _____ is now extending beyond the online world and into the offline world of shopping.

Exam Probability: **High**

30. *Answer choices:*

(see index for correct answer)

- a. UsedSoft
- b. EatOye
- c. Extended Validation Certificate
- d. Tor

Guidance: level 1

:: E-commerce ::

_____ is a type of fraud that occurs on the Internet in pay-per-click online advertising. In this type of advertising, the owners of websites that post the ads are paid an amount of money determined by how many visitors to the sites click on the ads. Fraud occurs when a person, automated script or computer program imitates a legitimate user of a web browser, clicking on such an ad without having an actual interest in the target of the ad's link. _____ is the subject of some controversy and increasing litigation due to the advertising networks being a key beneficiary of the fraud.

Exam Probability: **Low**

31. *Answer choices:*

(see index for correct answer)

- a. Click fraud
- b. Feefighters
- c. PagSeguro
- d. Shipping portal

Guidance: level 1

:: Credit cards ::

A _____ is a payment card issued to users to enable the cardholder to pay a merchant for goods and services based on the cardholder's promise to the card issuer to pay them for the amounts plus the other agreed charges. The card issuer creates a revolving account and grants a line of credit to the cardholder, from which the cardholder can borrow money for payment to a merchant or as a cash advance.

Exam Probability: **Low**

32. *Answer choices:*

(see index for correct answer)

- a. EnRoute
- b. Cashplus

- c. Visa Inc.
- d. Credit card

Guidance: level 1

:: ::

The _____ , commonly known as the Web, is an information system where documents and other web resources are identified by Uniform Resource Locators , which may be interlinked by hypertext, and are accessible over the Internet.
The resources of the WWW may be accessed by users by a software application called a web browser.

Exam Probability: **Medium**

33. *Answer choices:*

(see index for correct answer)

- a. Sarbanes-Oxley act of 2002
- b. World Wide Web
- c. levels of analysis
- d. surface-level diversity

Guidance: level 1

:: Information systems ::

_____ , Chief Digital Information Officer or Information Technology Director, is a job title commonly given to the most senior executive in an enterprise who works for the traditional information technology and computer systems that support enterprise goals.

Exam Probability: **Low**

34. *Answer choices:*

(see index for correct answer)

- a. Chief information officer
- b. Mi-Case
- c. Dataspaces
- d. Physical Internet

Guidance: level 1

:: Industrial design ::

Across the many fields concerned with _____ , including information science, computer science, human-computer interaction, communication, and industrial design, there is little agreement over the meaning of the term "_____", although all are related to interaction with computers and other machines with a user interface.

Exam Probability: **Low**

35. *Answer choices:*

(see index for correct answer)

- a. Electronic packaging
- b. Dimension
- c. Community design
- d. Interactivity

Guidance: level 1

:: ::

_____ is a kind of action that occur as two or more objects have an effect upon one another. The idea of a two-way effect is essential in the concept of _____ , as opposed to a one-way causal effect. A closely related term is interconnectivity, which deals with the _____ s of _____ s within systems: combinations of many simple _____ s can lead to surprising emergent phenomena. _____ has different tailored meanings in various sciences. Changes can also involve _____ .

Exam Probability: **Low**

36. *Answer choices:*

(see index for correct answer)

- a. process perspective
- b. information systems assessment
- c. Interaction

- d. Sarbanes-Oxley act of 2002

Guidance: level 1

:: Data management ::

_____ , or OLAP , is an approach to answer multi-dimensional analytical queries swiftly in computing. OLAP is part of the broader category of business intelligence, which also encompasses relational databases, report writing and data mining. Typical applications of OLAP include business reporting for sales, marketing, management reporting, business process management , budgeting and forecasting, financial reporting and similar areas, with new applications emerging, such as agriculture. The term OLAP was created as a slight modification of the traditional database term online transaction processing .

Exam Probability: **Low**

37. *Answer choices:*

(see index for correct answer)

- a. Automated tiered storage
- b. Online analytical processing
- c. Data extraction
- d. Match report

Guidance: level 1

:: Information systems ::

An _____, or a group of such silos, is an insular management system in which one information system or subsystem is incapable of reciprocal operation with others that are, or should be, related. Thus information is not adequately shared but rather remains sequestered within each system or subsystem, figuratively trapped within a container like grain is trapped within a silo: there may be a lot of it, and it may be stacked quite high and freely available within those limits, but it has no effect outside those limits. Such data silos are proving to be an obstacle for businesses wishing to use data mining to make productive use of their data.

Exam Probability: **Low**

38. *Answer choices:*

(see index for correct answer)

- a. Manufacturing execution system
- b. Self-service software vendors
- c. Information silo
- d. CGA

Guidance: level 1

:: Data analysis ::

_____, also referred to as text data mining, roughly equivalent to text analytics, is the process of deriving high-quality information from text. High-quality information is typically derived through the devising of patterns and trends through means such as statistical pattern learning. _____ usually involves the process of structuring the input text, deriving patterns within the structured data, and finally evaluation and interpretation of the output. 'High quality' in _____ usually refers to some combination of relevance, novelty, and interest. Typical _____ tasks include text categorization, text clustering, concept/entity extraction, production of granular taxonomies, sentiment analysis, document summarization, and entity relation modeling.

Exam Probability: **Low**

39. *Answer choices:*

(see index for correct answer)

- a. Text mining
- b. Contingency table
- c. Visual comparison
- d. Proxy

Guidance: level 1

:: ::

A _____ is a published declaration of the intentions, motives, or views of the issuer, be it an individual, group, political party or government. A _____ usually accepts a previously published opinion or public consensus or promotes a new idea with prescriptive notions for carrying out changes the author believes should be made. It often is political or artistic in nature, but may present an individual's life stance. _____ s relating to religious belief are generally referred to as creeds.

Exam Probability: **Low**

40. *Answer choices:*

(see index for correct answer)

- a. surface-level diversity
- b. Sarbanes-Oxley act of 2002
- c. Manifesto
- d. hierarchical perspective

Guidance: level 1

:: Production economics ::

_____ is a way of producing goods and services that relies on self-organizing communities of individuals. In such communities, the labor of a large number of people is coordinated towards a shared outcome.

Exam Probability: **Medium**

41. Answer choices:

(see index for correct answer)

- a. Peer production
- b. Industrial production index
- c. Productivity Alpha
- d. Economies of scale

Guidance: level 1

:: ::

A _____ is server software, or hardware dedicated to running said software, that can satisfy World Wide Web client requests. A _____ can, in general, contain one or more websites. A _____ processes incoming network requests over HTTP and several other related protocols.

Exam Probability: **Low**

42. Answer choices:

(see index for correct answer)

- a. hierarchical perspective
- b. Web server
- c. process perspective
- d. surface-level diversity

Guidance: level 1

:: Help desk ::

Data center management is the collection of tasks performed by those responsible for managing ongoing operation of a data center This includes Business service management and planning for the future.

Exam Probability: **Medium**

43. *Answer choices:*

(see index for correct answer)

- a. Help desk
- b. KnowledgeBase Manager Pro
- c. Technical support
- d. SysAid Technologies

Guidance: level 1

:: Data management ::

In computing, a _____ , also known as an enterprise _____ , is a system used for reporting and data analysis, and is considered a core component of business intelligence. DWs are central repositories of integrated data from one or more disparate sources. They store current and historical data in one single place that are used for creating analytical reports for workers throughout the enterprise.

Exam Probability: **High**

44. *Answer choices:*

(see index for correct answer)

- a. Retention period
- b. Data warehouse
- c. Meta-data management
- d. Enterprise Objects Framework

Guidance: level 1

:: Data management ::

_____ is a data management concept concerning the capability that enables an organization to ensure that high data quality exists throughout the complete lifecycle of the data. The key focus areas of _____ include availability, usability, consistency, data integrity and data security and includes establishing processes to ensure effective data management throughout the enterprise such as accountability for the adverse effects of poor data quality and ensuring that the data which an enterprise has can be used by the entire organization.

Exam Probability: **Medium**

45. *Answer choices:*

(see index for correct answer)

- a. Data auditing
- b. Single source publishing
- c. Data governance
- d. Storage area network

Guidance: level 1

:: Information technology management ::

_____ is a good-practice framework created by international professional association ISACA for information technology management and IT governance. _____ provides an implementable "set of controls over information technology and organizes them around a logical framework of IT-related processes and enablers."

Exam Probability: **Medium**

46. *Answer choices:*

(see index for correct answer)

- a. Capability Maturity Model
- b. One-to-one

- c. Mobile business development
- d. Infoblox

Guidance: level 1

:: Network theory ::

A _____ is a social structure made up of a set of social actors, sets of dyadic ties, and other social interactions between actors. The _____ perspective provides a set of methods for analyzing the structure of whole social entities as well as a variety of theories explaining the patterns observed in these structures. The study of these structures uses _____ analysis to identify local and global patterns, locate influential entities, and examine network dynamics.

Exam Probability: **High**

47. *Answer choices:*

(see index for correct answer)

- a. Assortative mixing
- b. Network controllability
- c. Social network
- d. Centrality

Guidance: level 1

:: Remote administration software ::

_____ is a protocol used on the Internet or local area network to provide a bidirectional interactive text-oriented communication facility using a virtual terminal connection. User data is interspersed in-band with _____ control information in an 8-bit byte oriented data connection over the Transmission Control Protocol.

Exam Probability: **Medium**

48. *Answer choices:*

(see index for correct answer)

- a. Apple Remote Desktop
- b. RealVNC
- c. TightVNC
- d. VIA3

Guidance: level 1

:: Costs ::

In economics, _____ is the total economic cost of production and is made up of variable cost, which varies according to the quantity of a good produced and includes inputs such as labour and raw materials, plus fixed cost, which is independent of the quantity of a good produced and includes inputs that cannot be varied in the short term: fixed costs such as buildings and machinery, including sunk costs if any. Since cost is measured per unit of time, it is a flow variable.

Exam Probability: **Medium**

49. *Answer choices:*

(see index for correct answer)

- a. Manufacturing cost
- b. Total cost
- c. Customer Cost
- d. Psychic cost

Guidance: level 1

:: ::

_____ are electronic transfer of money from one bank account to another, either within a single financial institution or across multiple institutions, via computer-based systems, without the direct intervention of bank staff.

Exam Probability: **Low**

50. Answer choices:

(see index for correct answer)

- a. co-culture
- b. functional perspective
- c. surface-level diversity
- d. Electronic funds transfer

Guidance: level 1

:: ::

_____ consists of tailoring a service or a product to accommodate specific individuals, sometimes tied to groups or segments of individuals. A wide variety of organizations use _____ to improve customer satisfaction, digital sales conversion, marketing results, branding, and improved website metrics as well as for advertising. _____ is a key element in social media and recommender systems.

Exam Probability: **Low**

51. Answer choices:

(see index for correct answer)

- a. Personalization
- b. imperative
- c. personal values
- d. cultural

Guidance: level 1

:: Management systems ::

An _____ , also known as an <u>Executive support system </u>, is a type of management support system that facilitates and supports senior executive information and decision-making needs. It provides easy access to internal and external information relevant to organizational goals. It is commonly considered a specialized form of decision support system .

Exam Probability: **Medium**

52. *Answer choices:*
(see index for correct answer)

- a. Service network
- b. Policy Governance
- c. Executive information system
- d. Holacracy

Guidance: level 1

:: Information technology management ::

_____ within quality management systems and information technology systems is a process—either formal or informal—used to ensure that changes to a product or system are introduced in a controlled and coordinated manner. It reduces the possibility that unnecessary changes will be introduced to a system without forethought, introducing faults into the system or undoing changes made by other users of software. The goals of a _____ procedure usually include minimal disruption to services, reduction in back-out activities, and cost-effective utilization of resources involved in implementing change.

Exam Probability: **Low**

53. *Answer choices:*

(see index for correct answer)

- a. Definitive Media Library
- b. Early-arriving fact
- c. ESCM
- d. Change control

Guidance: level 1

:: Computer access control ::

_____ is the act of confirming the truth of an attribute of a single piece of data claimed true by an entity. In contrast with identification, which refers to the act of stating or otherwise indicating a claim purportedly attesting to a person or thing's identity, _____ is the process of actually confirming that identity. It might involve confirming the identity of a person by validating their identity documents, verifying the authenticity of a website with a digital certificate, determining the age of an artifact by carbon dating, or ensuring that a product is what its packaging and labeling claim to be. In other words, _____ often involves verifying the validity of at least one form of identification.

Exam Probability: **Low**

54. *Answer choices:*

(see index for correct answer)

- a. MultiOTP
- b. Authentication
- c. two-factor
- d. Internet Authentication Service

Guidance: level 1

:: Fraud ::

In law, _____ is intentional deception to secure unfair or unlawful gain, or to deprive a victim of a legal right. _____ can violate civil law, a criminal law, or it may cause no loss of money, property or legal right but still be an element of another civil or criminal wrong. The purpose of _____ may be monetary gain or other benefits, for example by obtaining a passport, travel document, or driver's license, or mortgage _____, where the perpetrator may attempt to qualify for a mortgage by way of false statements.

Exam Probability: **Medium**

55. *Answer choices:*

(see index for correct answer)

- a. Romance scam
- b. Customer not present
- c. Fraud
- d. Lebanese loop

Guidance: level 1

:: Information technology management ::

_____ is the use of software to control machine tools and related ones in the manufacturing of workpieces. This is not the only definition for CAM, but it is the most common; CAM may also refer to the use of a computer to assist in all operations of a manufacturing plant, including planning, management, transportation and storage. Its primary purpose is to create a faster production process and components and tooling with more precise dimensions and material consistency, which in some cases, uses only the required amount of raw material, while simultaneously reducing energy consumption. CAM is now a system used in schools and lower educational purposes. CAM is a subsequent computer-aided process after computer-aided design and sometimes computer-aided engineering, as the model generated in CAD and verified in CAE can be input into CAM software, which then controls the machine tool. CAM is used in many schools alongside Computer-Aided Design to create objects.

Exam Probability: **Low**

56. *Answer choices:*

(see index for correct answer)

- a. 25U signal support systems specialist
- b. Computer-aided manufacturing
- c. Operations architecture
- d. Computer-aided facility management

Guidance: level 1

:: Information systems ::

_____ is a process used in the life cycle area of the dynamic systems development method to collect business requirements while developing new information systems for a company. "The JAD process also includes approaches for enhancing user participation, expediting development, and improving the quality of specifications." It consists of a workshop where "knowledge workers and IT specialists meet, sometimes for several days, to define and review the business requirements for the system." The attendees include high level management officials who will ensure the product provides the needed reports and information at the end. This acts as "a management process which allows Corporate Information Services departments to work more effectively with users in a shorter time frame".

Exam Probability: **Low**

57. *Answer choices:*

(see index for correct answer)

- a. Geographical Operations System
- b. Expert system
- c. Joint application design
- d. DIKW Pyramid

Guidance: level 1

:: Information technology management ::

_____ concerns a cycle of organizational activity: the acquisition of information from one or more sources, the custodianship and the distribution of that information to those who need it, and its ultimate disposition through archiving or deletion.

Exam Probability: **Low**

58. *Answer choices:*

(see index for correct answer)

- a. Web commerce
- b. Accelops
- c. Information repository
- d. Ekatva

Guidance: level 1

:: Data transmission ::

In telecommunications and computing, _____ is the number of bits that are conveyed or processed per unit of time.

Exam Probability: **Low**

59. *Answer choices:*

(see index for correct answer)

- a. Distributed source coding
- b. Character interval
- c. Distributed antenna system
- d. Digital Media Access Protocol

Guidance: level 1

Marketing

Marketing is the study and management of exchange relationships. Marketing is the business process of creating relationships with and satisfying customers. With its focus on the customer, marketing is one of the premier components of business management.

Marketing is defined by the American Marketing Association as "the activity, set of institutions, and processes for creating, communicating, delivering, and exchanging offerings that have value for customers, clients, partners, and society at large."

In international relations, _____ is – from the perspective of governments – a voluntary transfer of resources from one country to another.

Exam Probability: **High**

1. *Answer choices:*

(see index for correct answer)

- a. hierarchical
- b. personal values
- c. Aid
- d. information systems assessment

Guidance: level 1

:: Investment ::

In finance, the benefit from an _____ is called a return. The return may consist of a gain realised from the sale of property or an _____, unrealised capital appreciation, or _____ income such as dividends, interest, rental income etc., or a combination of capital gain and income. The return may also include currency gains or losses due to changes in foreign currency exchange rates.

Exam Probability: **High**

2. *Answer choices:*

(see index for correct answer)

- a. Tangible investment
- b. Market exposure
- c. Investment style
- d. Investment

Guidance: level 1

:: Communication design ::

An _____ is a series of advertisement messages that share a single idea and theme which make up an integrated marketing communication. An IMC is a platform in which a group of people can group their ideas, beliefs, and concepts into one large media base. _____ s utilize diverse media channels over a particular time frame and target identified audiences.

Exam Probability: **High**

3. *Answer choices:*

(see index for correct answer)

- a. Advertising campaign
- b. Lithography
- c. Grapus
- d. Central Saint Martins

Guidance: level 1

:: ::

_____ Company, commonly referred to as _____ , is an American multinational corporation headquartered in Detroit that designs, manufactures, markets, and distributes vehicles and vehicle parts, and sells financial services, with global headquarters in Detroit's Renaissance Center. It was originally founded by William C. Durant on September 16, 1908 as a holding company. The company is the largest American automobile manufacturer, and one of the world's largest. As of 2018, _____ is ranked #10 on the Fortune 500 rankings of the largest United States corporations by total revenue.

Exam Probability: **High**

4. *Answer choices:*

(see index for correct answer)

- a. hierarchical perspective
- b. General Motors
- c. similarity-attraction theory
- d. open system

Guidance: level 1

:: ::

A _____ is a person who trades in commodities produced by other people. Historically, a _____ is anyone who is involved in business or trade. _____ s have operated for as long as industry, commerce, and trade have existed. During the 16th-century, in Europe, two different terms for _____ s emerged: One term, meerseniers, described local traders such as bakers, grocers, etc.; while a new term, koopman (Dutch: koopman, described _____ s who operated on a global stage, importing and exporting goods over vast distances, and offering added-value services such as credit and finance.

Exam Probability: **Medium**

5. *Answer choices:*

(see index for correct answer)

- a. co-culture
- b. deep-level diversity
- c. functional perspective
- d. process perspective

Guidance: level 1

:: Market research ::

An _____ or lighthouse customer is an early customer of a given company, product, or technology. The term originates from Everett M. Rogers' Diffusion of Innovations .

Exam Probability: **High**

6. *Answer choices:*

(see index for correct answer)

- a. High Mark Credit Information Services
- b. AQH Share
- c. Early adopter
- d. Customer satisfaction research

Guidance: level 1

:: Marketing ::

_____ s are structured marketing strategies designed by merchants to encourage customers to continue to shop at or use the services of businesses associated with each program. These programs exist covering most types of commerce, each one having varying features and rewards-schemes.

Exam Probability: **High**

7. *Answer choices:*

(see index for correct answer)

- a. Marketspace
- b. Patronage concentration
- c. Jonathan Grado
- d. Inventory

Guidance: level 1

:: ::

In the broadest sense, _____ is any practice which contributes to the sale of products to a retail consumer. At a retail in-store level, _____ refers to the variety of products available for sale and the display of those products in such a way that it stimulates interest and entices customers to make a purchase.

Exam Probability: **Medium**

8. *Answer choices:*

(see index for correct answer)

- a. similarity-attraction theory
- b. surface-level diversity
- c. Sarbanes-Oxley act of 2002
- d. Merchandising

Guidance: level 1

:: Direct selling ::

_____ consists of two main business models: single-level marketing, in which a direct seller makes money by buying products from a parent organization and selling them directly to customers, and multi-level marketing, in which the direct seller may earn money from both direct sales to customers and by sponsoring new direct sellers and potentially earning a commission from their efforts.

Exam Probability: **High**

9. *Answer choices:*

(see index for correct answer)

- a. CVSL
- b. Direct Selling News
- c. Direct Selling Association
- d. Direct selling

Guidance: level 1

:: ::

A _____ consists of one people who live in the same dwelling and share meals. It may also consist of a single family or another group of people. A dwelling is considered to contain multiple _____ s if meals or living spaces are not shared. The _____ is the basic unit of analysis in many social, microeconomic and government models, and is important to economics and inheritance.

Exam Probability: **High**

10. *Answer choices:*

(see index for correct answer)

- a. co-culture
- b. corporate values
- c. functional perspective
- d. Household

Guidance: level 1

:: Advertising techniques ::

In promotion and of advertising, a _____ or show consists of a person's written or spoken statement extolling the virtue of a product. The term "_____" most commonly applies to the sales-pitches attributed to ordinary citizens, whereas the word "endorsement" usually applies to pitches by celebrities. _____ s can be part of communal marketing. Sometimes, the cartoon character can be a _____ in a commercial.

Exam Probability: **High**

11. *Answer choices:*

(see index for correct answer)

- a. Testimonial
- b. Hard sell

- c. Display window
- d. FAST marketing

Guidance: level 1

:: Business planning ::

_____ is an organization's process of defining its strategy, or direction, and making decisions on allocating its resources to pursue this strategy. It may also extend to control mechanisms for guiding the implementation of the strategy. _____ became prominent in corporations during the 1960s and remains an important aspect of strategic management. It is executed by strategic planners or strategists, who involve many parties and research sources in their analysis of the organization and its relationship to the environment in which it competes.

Exam Probability: **High**

12. *Answer choices:*
(see index for correct answer)

- a. Strategic planning
- b. Stakeholder management
- c. Open Options Corporation
- d. Joint decision trap

Guidance: level 1

:: Business terms ::

A _____ is a short statement of why an organization exists, what its overall goal is, identifying the goal of its operations: what kind of product or service it provides, its primary customers or market, and its geographical region of operation. It may include a short statement of such fundamental matters as the organization's values or philosophies, a business's main competitive advantages, or a desired future state—the "vision".

Exam Probability: **Low**

13. *Answer choices:*

(see index for correct answer)

- a. Strategic partner
- b. centralization
- c. churn rate
- d. Mission statement

Guidance: level 1

:: Types of marketing ::

_____ is "marketing on a worldwide scale reconciling or taking commercial advantage of global operational differences, similarities and opportunities in order to meet global objectives".

Exam Probability: **Low**

14. *Answer choices:*

(see index for correct answer)

- a. Global marketing
- b. Diversity marketing
- c. Ambush marketing
- d. Community marketing

Guidance: level 1

:: Marketing by medium ::

_____ or viral advertising is a business strategy that uses existing social networks to promote a product. Its name refers to how consumers spread information about a product with other people in their social networks, much in the same way that a virus spreads from one person to another. It can be delivered by word of mouth or enhanced by the network effects of the Internet and mobile networks.

Exam Probability: **Low**

15. *Answer choices:*

(see index for correct answer)

- a. Digital marketing
- b. Social intelligence architect

- c. Social marketing intelligence
- d. Viral marketing

Guidance: level 1

:: International trade ::

_____ or globalisation is the process of interaction and integration among people, companies, and governments worldwide. As a complex and multifaceted phenomenon, _____ is considered by some as a form of capitalist expansion which entails the integration of local and national economies into a global, unregulated market economy. _____ has grown due to advances in transportation and communication technology. With the increased global interactions comes the growth of international trade, ideas, and culture. _____ is primarily an economic process of interaction and integration that's associated with social and cultural aspects. However, conflicts and diplomacy are also large parts of the history of _____, and modern _____.

Exam Probability: **High**

16. *Answer choices:*
(see index for correct answer)

- a. Orderly marketing arrangement
- b. Free trade agreement
- c. European Union Customs Union
- d. Globalization

Guidance: level 1

:: Brand management ::

_____ is defined as positive feelings towards a brand and dedication to purchase the same product or service repeatedly now and in the future from the same brand, regardless of a competitor's actions or changes in the environment. It can also be demonstrated with other behaviors such as positive word-of-mouth advocacy. _____ is where an individual buys products from the same manufacturer repeatedly rather than from other suppliers. Businesses whose financial and ethical values, for example ESG responsibilities, rest in large part on their _____ are said to use the loyalty business model.

Exam Probability: **Medium**

17. *Answer choices:*

(see index for correct answer)

- a. Merck Consumer Health
- b. Sanrio
- c. Brand loyalty
- d. Giant Step

Guidance: level 1

:: Consumer behaviour ::

_____ refers to the ability of a company or product to retain its customers over some specified period. High _____ means customers of the product or business tend to return to, continue to buy or in some other way not defect to another product or business, or to non-use entirely. Selling organizations generally attempt to reduce customer defections. _____ starts with the first contact an organization has with a customer and continues throughout the entire lifetime of a relationship and successful retention efforts take this entire lifecycle into account. A company's ability to attract and retain new customers is related not only to its product or services, but also to the way it services its existing customers, the value the customers actually generate as a result of utilizing the solutions, and the reputation it creates within and across the marketplace.

Exam Probability: **Medium**

18. *Answer choices:*

(see index for correct answer)

- a. Internality
- b. Daniel Starch
- c. Hoarding
- d. Household production function

Guidance: level 1

:: Marketing ::

The _____ is a foundation model for businesses. The _____ has been defined as the "set of marketing tools that the firm uses to pursue its marketing objectives in the target market". Thus the _____ refers to four broad levels of marketing decision, namely: product, price, place, and promotion. Marketing practice has been occurring for millennia, but marketing theory emerged in the early twentieth century. The contemporary _____, or the 4 Ps, which has become the dominant framework for marketing management decisions, was first published in 1960. In services marketing, an extended _____ is used, typically comprising 7 Ps, made up of the original 4 Ps extended by process, people, and physical evidence. Occasionally service marketers will refer to 8 Ps, comprising these 7 Ps plus performance.

Exam Probability: **High**

19. *Answer choices:*

(see index for correct answer)

- a. Gift suite
- b. Breakthrough Moments
- c. Jobbing house
- d. Marketing in schools

Guidance: level 1

:: Cultural appropriation ::

_____ is a social and economic order that encourages the acquisition of goods and services in ever-increasing amounts. With the industrial revolution, but particularly in the 20th century, mass production led to an economic crisis: there was overproduction—the supply of goods would grow beyond consumer demand, and so manufacturers turned to planned obsolescence and advertising to manipulate consumer spending. In 1899, a book on _____ published by Thorstein Veblen, called The Theory of the Leisure Class, examined the widespread values and economic institutions emerging along with the widespread "leisure time" in the beginning of the 20th century. In it Veblen "views the activities and spending habits of this leisure class in terms of conspicuous and vicarious consumption and waste. Both are related to the display of status and not to functionality or usefulness."

Exam Probability: **Medium**

20. *Answer choices:*

(see index for correct answer)

- a. Yoga piracy
- b. Plastic Paddy
- c. Cool
- d. Consumerism

Guidance: level 1

:: Problem solving ::

In other words, _____ is a situation where a group of people meet to generate new ideas and solutions around a specific domain of interest by removing inhibitions. People are able to think more freely and they suggest as many spontaneous new ideas as possible. All the ideas are noted down and those ideas are not criticized and after _____ session the ideas are evaluated. The term was popularized by Alex Faickney Osborn in the 1953 book Applied Imagination.

Exam Probability: **Low**

21. *Answer choices:*

(see index for correct answer)

- a. Brainstorming
- b. Cognitive acceleration
- c. Computational thinking
- d. Candle problem

Guidance: level 1

:: Materials ::

A _____ , also known as a feedstock, unprocessed material, or primary commodity, is a basic material that is used to produce goods, finished products, energy, or intermediate materials which are feedstock for future finished products. As feedstock, the term connotes these materials are bottleneck assets and are highly important with regard to producing other products. An example of this is crude oil, which is a _____ and a feedstock used in the production of industrial chemicals, fuels, plastics, and pharmaceutical goods; lumber is a _____ used to produce a variety of products including all types of furniture. The term "_____" denotes materials in minimally processed or unprocessed in states; e.g., raw latex, crude oil, cotton, coal, raw biomass, iron ore, air, logs, or water i.e. "...any product of agriculture, forestry, fishing and any other mineral that is in its natural form or which has undergone the transformation required to prepare it for internationally marketing in substantial volumes."

Exam Probability: **High**

22. *Answer choices:*

(see index for correct answer)

- a. Carbon grid
- b. Layered double hydroxides
- c. Raw material
- d. Auxetics

Guidance: level 1

:: Business economics ::

In economics, _____ is demand for a factor of production or intermediate good that occurs as a result of the demand for another intermediate or final good. In essence, the demand for, say, a factor of production by a firm is dependent on the demand by consumers for the product produced by the firm. The term was first introduced by Alfred Marshall in his Principles of Economics in 1890.

Exam Probability: **High**

23. *Answer choices:*

(see index for correct answer)

- a. Staple financing
- b. Derived demand
- c. Financial risk modeling
- d. Function cost analysis

Guidance: level 1

:: ::

_____ are interactive computer-mediated technologies that facilitate the creation and sharing of information, ideas, career interests and other forms of expression via virtual communities and networks. The variety of stand-alone and built-in _____ services currently available introduces challenges of definition; however, there are some common features.

Exam Probability: **Medium**

24. Answer choices:

(see index for correct answer)

- a. corporate values
- b. imperative
- c. similarity-attraction theory
- d. Character

Guidance: level 1

:: Management ::

_____ is the process of thinking about the activities required to achieve a desired goal. It is the first and foremost activity to achieve desired results. It involves the creation and maintenance of a plan, such as psychological aspects that require conceptual skills. There are even a couple of tests to measure someone's capability of _____ well. As such, _____ is a fundamental property of intelligent behavior. An important further meaning, often just called " _____ " is the legal context of permitted building developments.

Exam Probability: **High**

25. Answer choices:

(see index for correct answer)

- a. Planning
- b. Six phases of a big project

- c. Systems analysis
- d. Customer Benefit Package

Guidance: level 1

:: Market research ::

_____ is "the process or set of processes that links the producers, customers, and end users to the marketer through information used to identify and define marketing opportunities and problems; generate, refine, and evaluate marketing actions; monitor marketing performance; and improve understanding of marketing as a process. _____ specifies the information required to address these issues, designs the method for collecting information, manages and implements the data collection process, analyzes the results, and communicates the findings and their implications."

Exam Probability: **Medium**

26. *Answer choices:*

(see index for correct answer)

- a. IModerate
- b. Marketing research
- c. Nielsen VideoScan
- d. AQH Share

Guidance: level 1

:: Consumer theory ::

A _____ is a technical term in psychology, economics and philosophy usually used in relation to choosing between alternatives. For example, someone prefers A over B if they would rather choose A than B.

Exam Probability: **High**

27. *Answer choices:*
(see index for correct answer)

- a. Permanent income hypothesis
- b. Time-based pricing
- c. Preference
- d. Demand

Guidance: level 1

:: ::

Bloomberg Businessweek is an American weekly business magazine published since 2009 by Bloomberg L.P. Businessweek, founded in 1929, aimed to provide information and interpretation about events in the business world. The magazine is headquartered in New York City. Megan Murphy served as editor from November 2016; she stepped down from the role in January 2018 and Joel Weber was appointed in her place. The magazine is published 47 times a year.

Exam Probability: **High**

28. *Answer choices:*

(see index for correct answer)

- a. levels of analysis
- b. Business Week
- c. surface-level diversity
- d. Sarbanes-Oxley act of 2002

Guidance: level 1

:: Project management ::

Contemporary business and science treat as a _____ any undertaking, carried out individually or collaboratively and possibly involving research or design, that is carefully planned to achieve a particular aim.

Exam Probability: **Medium**

29. *Answer choices:*

(see index for correct answer)

- a. Aggregate planning
- b. Case competition
- c. Bid manager
- d. Project

Guidance: level 1

:: Consumer theory ::

_____ is the quantity of a good that consumers are willing and able to purchase at various prices during a given period of time.

Exam Probability: **High**

30. *Answer choices:*
(see index for correct answer)

- a. Demand
- b. Lexicographic preferences
- c. Elasticity of substitution
- d. Consumer service

Guidance: level 1

:: ::

A _____ is a research instrument consisting of a series of questions for the purpose of gathering information from respondents. The _____ was invented by the Statistical Society of London in 1838.

Exam Probability: **Medium**

31. *Answer choices:*

(see index for correct answer)

- a. co-culture
- b. similarity-attraction theory
- c. interpersonal communication
- d. Questionnaire

Guidance: level 1

:: Income ::

_____ is a ratio between the net profit and cost of investment resulting from an investment of some resources. A high ROI means the investment's gains favorably to its cost. As a performance measure, ROI is used to evaluate the efficiency of an investment or to compare the efficiencies of several different investments. In purely economic terms, it is one way of relating profits to capital invested. _____ is a performance measure used by businesses to identify the efficiency of an investment or number of different investments.

Exam Probability: **High**

32. *Answer choices:*

(see index for correct answer)

- a. Return on investment
- b. National average salary
- c. Salary inversion
- d. Aggregate income

Guidance: level 1

:: Advertising ::

_____ is the behavioral and cognitive process of selectively concentrating on a discrete aspect of information, whether deemed subjective or objective, while ignoring other perceivable information. It is a state of arousal. It is the taking possession by the mind in clear and vivid form of one out of what seem several simultaneous objects or trains of thought. Focalization, the concentration of consciousness, is of its essence. _____ has also been described as the allocation of limited cognitive processing resources.

Exam Probability: **Medium**

33. *Answer choices:*
(see index for correct answer)

- a. Under the Anheuser Bush
- b. International Tourism Advertising
- c. Thetextpage
- d. Recruitment tool

Guidance: level 1

:: Pricing ::

_____ is a pricing strategy in which the selling price is determined by adding a specific amount markup to a product's unit cost. An alternative pricing method is value-based pricing.

Exam Probability: **High**

34. *Answer choices:*

(see index for correct answer)

- a. Cost-plus pricing
- b. Guaranteed Maximum Price
- c. Invoice price
- d. Best Rate Guaranteed

Guidance: level 1

:: Data management ::

In computing, a _____ , also known as an enterprise _____ , is a system used for reporting and data analysis, and is considered a core component of business intelligence. DWs are central repositories of integrated data from one or more disparate sources. They store current and historical data in one single place that are used for creating analytical reports for workers throughout the enterprise.

Exam Probability: **High**

35. *Answer choices:*

(see index for correct answer)

- a. Data steward
- b. Data warehouse
- c. BBC Archives
- d. Consumer relationship system

Guidance: level 1

:: Market research ::

_____ refers to a collection of methods that managers use to analyze an organization's internal and external environment to understand the organization's capabilities, customers, and business environment. The _____ consists of several methods of analysis: The 5Cs Analysis, SWOT analysis and Porter five forces analysis. A Marketing Plan is created to guide businesses on how to communicate the benefits of their products to the needs of potential customer. The _____ is the second step in the marketing plan and is a critical step in establishing a long term relationship with customers.

Exam Probability: **High**

36. *Answer choices:*

(see index for correct answer)

- a. PreTesting Company
- b. Automated Measurement of Lineups
- c. Customer experience analytics
- d. Situation analysis

Guidance: level 1

:: Project management ::

_____ is the right to exercise power, which can be formalized by a state and exercised by way of judges, appointed executives of government, or the ecclesiastical or priestly appointed representatives of a God or other deities.

Exam Probability: **Low**

37. *Answer choices:*

(see index for correct answer)

- a. Structured data analysis
- b. Project risk management
- c. Authority

- d. Stages of project finance

Guidance: level 1

:: ::

In communications and information processing, _____ is a system of rules to convert information—such as a letter, word, sound, image, or gesture—into another form or representation, sometimes shortened or secret, for communication through a communication channel or storage in a storage medium. An early example is the invention of language, which enabled a person, through speech, to communicate what they saw, heard, felt, or thought to others. But speech limits the range of communication to the distance a voice can carry, and limits the audience to those present when the speech is uttered. The invention of writing, which converted spoken language into visual symbols, extended the range of communication across space and time.

Exam Probability: **High**

38. *Answer choices:*
(see index for correct answer)

- a. interpersonal communication
- b. hierarchical perspective
- c. information systems assessment
- d. Code

Guidance: level 1

:: Promotion and marketing communications ::

Advertising mail, also known as _____ , junk mail , mailshot or admail, is the delivery of advertising material to recipients of postal mail. The delivery of advertising mail forms a large and growing service for many postal services, and direct-mail marketing forms a significant portion of the direct marketing industry. Some organizations attempt to help people opt out of receiving advertising mail, in many cases motivated by a concern over its negative environmental impact.

Exam Probability: **Low**

39. *Answer choices:*
(see index for correct answer)

- a. Propaganda
- b. Direct mail
- c. Social network advertising
- d. Popworld Promotes

Guidance: level 1

:: ::

A _____ is an organization, usually a group of people or a company, authorized to act as a single entity and recognized as such in law. Early incorporated entities were established by charter . Most jurisdictions now allow the creation of new _____ s through registration.

Exam Probability: **Medium**

40. *Answer choices:*

(see index for correct answer)

- a. Corporation
- b. open system
- c. co-culture
- d. information systems assessment

Guidance: level 1

:: ::

_____ Corporation is an American multinational technology company with headquarters in Redmond, Washington. It develops, manufactures, licenses, supports and sells computer software, consumer electronics, personal computers, and related services. Its best known software products are the _____ Windows line of operating systems, the _____ Office suite, and the Internet Explorer and Edge Web browsers. Its flagship hardware products are the Xbox video game consoles and the _____ Surface lineup of touchscreen personal computers. As of 2016, it is the world's largest software maker by revenue, and one of the world's most valuable companies. The word "_____" is a portmanteau of "microcomputer" and "software". _____ is ranked No. 30 in the 2018 Fortune 500 rankings of the largest United States corporations by total revenue.

Exam Probability: **High**

41. *Answer choices:*

(see index for correct answer)

- a. Microsoft
- b. Character
- c. open system
- d. levels of analysis

Guidance: level 1

:: Management ::

A _____ describes the rationale of how an organization creates, delivers, and captures value, in economic, social, cultural or other contexts. The process of _____ construction and modification is also called _____ innovation and forms a part of business strategy.

Exam Probability: **Medium**

42. *Answer choices:*

(see index for correct answer)

- a. Design leadership
- b. Double linking
- c. Business model
- d. Six phases of a big project

Guidance: level 1

:: Organizational structure ::

An _____ defines how activities such as task allocation, coordination, and supervision are directed toward the achievement of organizational aims.

Exam Probability: **High**

43. *Answer choices:*

(see index for correct answer)

- a. Organizational structure
- b. Followership
- c. Automated Bureaucracy
- d. Blessed Unrest

Guidance: level 1

:: Health promotion ::

_____, as defined by the World _____ Organization, is "a state of complete physical, mental and social well-being and not merely the absence of disease or infirmity." This definition has been subject to controversy, as it may have limited value for implementation. _____ may be defined as the ability to adapt and manage physical, mental and social challenges throughout life.

Exam Probability: **Low**

44. Answer choices:

(see index for correct answer)

- a. Peer education
- b. NHS Health Scotland
- c. Carers rights movement
- d. Health

Guidance: level 1

:: Business ::

The seller, or the provider of the goods or services, completes a sale in response to an acquisition, appropriation, requisition or a direct interaction with the buyer at the point of sale. There is a passing of title of the item, and the settlement of a price, in which agreement is reached on a price for which transfer of ownership of the item will occur. The seller, not the purchaser typically executes the sale and it may be completed prior to the obligation of payment. In the case of indirect interaction, a person who sells goods or service on behalf of the owner is known as a _____ man or _____ woman or _____ person, but this often refers to someone selling goods in a store/shop, in which case other terms are also common, including _____ clerk, shop assistant, and retail clerk.

Exam Probability: **Low**

45. *Answer choices:*

(see index for correct answer)

- a. Business statistics
- b. Customer experience
- c. Student@Home
- d. Sales

Guidance: level 1

:: Decision theory ::

Within economics the concept of _____ is used to model worth or value, but its usage has evolved significantly over time. The term was introduced initially as a measure of pleasure or satisfaction within the theory of utilitarianism by moral philosophers such as Jeremy Bentham and John Stuart Mill. But the term has been adapted and reapplied within neoclassical economics, which dominates modern economic theory, as a _____ function that represents a consumer's preference ordering over a choice set. As such, it is devoid of its original interpretation as a measurement of the pleasure or satisfaction obtained by the consumer from that choice.

Exam Probability: **High**

46. *Answer choices:*

(see index for correct answer)

- a. Psychological pricing
- b. Clarity test
- c. Utility
- d. Secretary problem

Guidance: level 1

:: ::

A _____ service is an online platform which people use to build social networks or social relationship with other people who share similar personal or career interests, activities, backgrounds or real-life connections.

Exam Probability: **Medium**

47. *Answer choices:*

(see index for correct answer)

- a. information systems assessment
- b. hierarchical
- c. open system
- d. Social networking

Guidance: level 1

:: Data interchange standards ::

_____ is the concept of businesses electronically communicating information that was traditionally communicated on paper, such as purchase orders and invoices. Technical standards for EDI exist to facilitate parties transacting such instruments without having to make special arrangements.

Exam Probability: **Medium**

48. *Answer choices:*

(see index for correct answer)

- a. ASC X12
- b. Electronic data interchange
- c. Domain Application Protocol

- d. Data Interchange Standards Association

Guidance: level 1

:: Product development ::

In business and engineering, _____ covers the complete process of bringing a new product to market. A central aspect of NPD is product design, along with various business considerations. _____ is described broadly as the transformation of a market opportunity into a product available for sale. The product can be tangible or intangible, though sometimes services and other processes are distinguished from "products." NPD requires an understanding of customer needs and wants, the competitive environment, and the nature of the market. Cost, time and quality are the main variables that drive customer needs. Aiming at these three variables, innovative companies develop continuous practices and strategies to better satisfy customer requirements and to increase their own market share by a regular development of new products. There are many uncertainties and challenges which companies must face throughout the process. The use of best practices and the elimination of barriers to communication are the main concerns for the management of the NPD.

Exam Probability: **Medium**

49. *Answer choices:*

(see index for correct answer)

- a. New product development
- b. Virtual prototyping
- c. Product line extension
- d. Brief

Guidance: level 1

:: ::

_____ LLC is an American multinational technology company that specializes in Internet-related services and products, which include online advertising technologies, search engine, cloud computing, software, and hardware. It is considered one of the Big Four technology companies, alongside Amazon, Apple and Facebook.

Exam Probability: **Low**

50. *Answer choices:*

(see index for correct answer)

- a. deep-level diversity
- b. surface-level diversity
- c. Google
- d. interpersonal communication

Guidance: level 1

:: Industrial design ::

In physics and mathematics, the _____ of a mathematical space is informally defined as the minimum number of coordinates needed to specify any point within it. Thus a line has a _____ of one because only one coordinate is needed to specify a point on it for example, the point at 5 on a number line. A surface such as a plane or the surface of a cylinder or sphere has a _____ of two because two coordinates are needed to specify a point on it for example, both a latitude and longitude are required to locate a point on the surface of a sphere. The inside of a cube, a cylinder or a sphere is three-_____al because three coordinates are needed to locate a point within these spaces.

Exam Probability: **High**

51. *Answer choices:*

(see index for correct answer)

- a. WikID
- b. Dimension
- c. Fab Lab Barcelona
- d. International Archive of Women in Architecture

Guidance: level 1

:: Evaluation methods ::

In natural and social sciences, and sometimes in other fields, _____ is the systematic empirical investigation of observable phenomena via statistical, mathematical, or computational techniques. The objective of _____ is to develop and employ mathematical models, theories, and hypotheses pertaining to phenomena. The process of measurement is central to _____ because it provides the fundamental connection between empirical observation and mathematical expression of quantitative relationships.

Exam Probability: **Low**

52. *Answer choices:*

(see index for correct answer)

- a. Poll average
- b. Transformative assessment
- c. Business excellence
- d. Economic impact analysis

Guidance: level 1

:: ::

An _____ is the production of goods or related services within an economy. The major source of revenue of a group or company is the indicator of its relevant _____. When a large group has multiple sources of revenue generation, it is considered to be working in different industries. Manufacturing _____ became a key sector of production and labour in European and North American countries during the Industrial Revolution, upsetting previous mercantile and feudal economies. This came through many successive rapid advances in technology, such as the production of steel and coal.

Exam Probability: **High**

53. *Answer choices:*

(see index for correct answer)

- a. Character
- b. corporate values
- c. Industry
- d. deep-level diversity

Guidance: level 1

:: Marketing ::

_____ is the process of using surveys to evaluate consumer acceptance of a new product idea prior to the introduction of a product to the market. It is important not to confuse _____ with advertising testing, brand testing and packaging testing; as is sometimes done. _____ focuses on the basic product idea, without the embellishments and puffery inherent in advertising.

Exam Probability: **Low**

54. Answer choices:

(see index for correct answer)

- a. Market orientation
- b. Customer value proposition
- c. Paddock girl
- d. Icon brand

Guidance: level 1

:: Marketing ::

_____ , sometimes called trigger-based or event-driven marketing, is a marketing strategy that uses two-way communication channels to allow consumers to connect with a company directly. Although this exchange can take place in person, in the last decade it has increasingly taken place almost exclusively online through email, social media, and blogs.

Exam Probability: **Low**

55. Answer choices:

(see index for correct answer)

- a. Customer interaction tracker
- b. Interactive marketing

- c. Primary research
- d. Affective design

Guidance: level 1

:: ::

_____ is the collection of techniques, skills, methods, and processes used in the production of goods or services or in the accomplishment of objectives, such as scientific investigation. _____ can be the knowledge of techniques, processes, and the like, or it can be embedded in machines to allow for operation without detailed knowledge of their workings. Systems applying _____ by taking an input, changing it according to the system's use, and then producing an outcome are referred to as _____ systems or technological systems.

Exam Probability: **High**

56. *Answer choices:*

(see index for correct answer)

- a. imperative
- b. information systems assessment
- c. co-culture
- d. Technology

Guidance: level 1

:: ::

Management is the administration of an organization, whether it is a business, a not-for-profit organization, or government body. Management includes the activities of setting the strategy of an organization and coordinating the efforts of its employees to accomplish its objectives through the application of available resources, such as financial, natural, technological, and human resources. The term "management" may also refer to those people who manage an organization.

Exam Probability: **Low**

57. *Answer choices:*

(see index for correct answer)

- a. interpersonal communication
- b. surface-level diversity
- c. hierarchical perspective
- d. Manager

Guidance: level 1

:: Data ::

Data has two ways of being created or generated. The first is what is called 'captured data', and is found through purposeful investigation or analysis. The second is called 'exhaust data', and is gathered usually by machines or terminals as a secondary function. For example, cash registers, smartphones, and speedometers serve a main function but may collect data as a secondary task. Exhaustive data is usually too large or of little use to process and becomes 'transient' or thrown away.

Exam Probability: **Medium**

58. *Answer choices:*

(see index for correct answer)

- a. Primary data
- b. Humanities Indicators
- c. Empress Embedded Database
- d. Data visualization

Guidance: level 1

:: Basic financial concepts ::

_____ is a sustained increase in the general price level of goods and services in an economy over a period of time. When the general price level rises, each unit of currency buys fewer goods and services; consequently, _____ reflects a reduction in the purchasing power per unit of money a loss of real value in the medium of exchange and unit of account within the economy. The measure of _____ is the _____ rate, the annualized percentage change in a general price index, usually the consumer price index, over time. The opposite of _____ is deflation.

Exam Probability: **High**

59. *Answer choices:*

(see index for correct answer)

- a. Future-oriented
- b. Present value of benefits
- c. Forward guidance
- d. Inflation

Guidance: level 1

Manufacturing

Manufacturing is the production of merchandise for use or sale using labor and machines, tools, chemical and biological processing, or formulation. The term may refer to a range of human activity, from handicraft to high tech, but is most commonly applied to industrial design, in which raw materials are transformed into finished goods on a large scale. Such finished goods may be sold to other manufacturers for the production of other, more complex products, such as aircraft, household appliances, furniture, sports equipment or automobiles, or sold to wholesalers, who in turn sell them to retailers, who then sell them to end users and consumers.

:: Quality management ::

_____ is a not-for-profit membership foundation in Brussels, established in 1989 to increase the competitiveness of the European economy. The initial impetus for forming _____ was a response to the work of W. Edwards Deming and the development of the concepts of Total Quality Management.

Exam Probability: **High**

1. *Answer choices:*

(see index for correct answer)

- a. EFQM
- b. PQASSO
- c. Dana Ulery
- d. China Quality Course

Guidance: level 1

:: Inventory ::

The _____ is the level of inventory which triggers an action to replenish that particular inventory stock. It is a minimum amount of an item which a firm holds in stock, such that, when stock falls to this amount, the item must be reordered. It is normally calculated as the forecast usage during the replenishment lead time plus safety stock. In the EOQ model, it was assumed that there is no time lag between ordering and procuring of materials. Therefore the _____ for replenishing the stocks occurs at that level when the inventory level drops to zero and because instant delivery by suppliers, the stock level bounce back.

Exam Probability: **Medium**

2. *Answer choices:*

(see index for correct answer)

- a. Inventory optimization
- b. Stock control
- c. Cost of goods available for sale
- d. Safety stock

Guidance: level 1

:: Costs ::

The _____ is computed by dividing the total cost of goods available for sale by the total units available for sale. This gives a weighted-average unit cost that is applied to the units in the ending inventory.

Exam Probability: **Medium**

3. *Answer choices:*

(see index for correct answer)

- a. Direct materials cost
- b. Cost per paper
- c. Average cost
- d. Total cost of acquisition

Guidance: level 1

:: Industrial processes ::

_____ is a technique involving the condensation of vapors and the return of this condensate to the system from which it originated. It is used in industrial and laboratory distillations. It is also used in chemistry to supply energy to reactions over a long period of time.

Exam Probability: **High**

4. *Answer choices:*

(see index for correct answer)

- a. Isoelectric focusing
- b. Alberger process
- c. Reflux
- d. Rendering

Guidance: level 1

:: Production economics ::

_____ is the joint use of a resource or space. It is also the process of dividing and distributing. In its narrow sense, it refers to joint or alternating use of inherently finite goods, such as a common pasture or a shared residence. Still more loosely, "_____" can actually mean giving something as an outright gift: for example, to "share" one's food really means to give some of it as a gift. _____ is a basic component of human interaction, and is responsible for strengthening social ties and ensuring a person's well-being.

Exam Probability: **Low**

5. *Answer choices:*

(see index for correct answer)

- a. short run
- b. Product pipeline
- c. Sectoral output
- d. Transaction cost

Guidance: level 1

:: Production and manufacturing ::

A BOM can define products as they are designed, as they are ordered, as they are built, or as they are maintained. The different types of BOMs depend on the business need and use for which they are intended. In process industries, the BOM is also known as the formula, recipe, or ingredients list. The phrase "bill of material" is frequently used by engineers as an adjective to refer not to the literal bill, but to the current production configuration of a product, to distinguish it from modified or improved versions under study or in test.

Exam Probability: **High**

6. *Answer choices:*

(see index for correct answer)

- a. Production part approval process
- b. Experience curve
- c. ERPNEXT
- d. Job shop

Guidance: level 1

:: Commerce ::

A _____ is an employee within a company, business or other organization who is responsible at some level for buying or approving the acquisition of goods and services needed by the company. Responsible for buying the best quality products, goods and services for their company at the most competitive prices, _____ s work in a wide range of sectors for many different organizations. The position responsibilities may be the same as that of a buyer or purchasing agent, or may include wider supervisory or managerial responsibilities. A _____ may oversee the acquisition of materials needed for production, general supplies for offices and facilities, equipment, or construction contracts. A _____ often supervises purchasing agents and buyers, but in small companies the _____ may also be the purchasing agent or buyer. The _____ position may also carry the title "Procurement Manager" or in the public sector, "Procurement Officer". He or she can come from both an Engineering or Economics background.

Exam Probability: **High**

7. *Answer choices:*

(see index for correct answer)

- a. Purchasing manager
- b. Quickbrowse
- c. Reseller
- d. Linestanding

Guidance: level 1

:: Monopoly (economics) ::

_____ are "efficiencies formed by variety, not volume". For example, a gas station that sells gasoline can sell soda, milk, baked goods, etc through their customer service representatives and thus achieve gasoline companies _____ .

Exam Probability: **Medium**

8. *Answer choices:*

(see index for correct answer)

- a. Economies of scope
- b. Coercive monopoly
- c. Regulatory economics
- d. Complementary monopoly

Guidance: level 1

:: Distribution, retailing, and wholesaling ::

The _____ is a distribution channel phenomenon in which forecasts yield supply chain inefficiencies. It refers to increasing swings in inventory in response to shifts in customer demand as one moves further up the supply chain. The concept first appeared in Jay Forrester's Industrial Dynamics and thus it is also known as the Forrester effect. The _____ was named for the way the amplitude of a whip increases down its length. The further from the originating signal, the greater the distortion of the wave pattern. In a similar manner, forecast accuracy decreases as one moves upstream along the supply chain. For example, many consumer goods have fairly consistent consumption at retail but this signal becomes more chaotic and unpredictable as the focus moves away from consumer purchasing behavior.

Exam Probability: **High**

9. *Answer choices:*

(see index for correct answer)

- a. Bullwhip effect
- b. Direct market
- c. 350 West Mart Center
- d. Pallet rack mover

Guidance: level 1

:: Management ::

A process is a unique combination of tools, materials, methods, and people engaged in producing a measurable output; for example a manufacturing line for machine parts. All processes have inherent statistical variability which can be evaluated by statistical methods.

Exam Probability: **Medium**

10. *Answer choices:*

(see index for correct answer)

- a. Porter five forces analysis
- b. Supply management
- c. Process capability
- d. Middle management

Guidance: level 1

:: Business process ::

A _____ or business method is a collection of related, structured activities or tasks by people or equipment which in a specific sequence produce a service or product for a particular customer or customers. _____ es occur at all organizational levels and may or may not be visible to the customers. A _____ may often be visualized as a flowchart of a sequence of activities with interleaving decision points or as a process matrix of a sequence of activities with relevance rules based on data in the process. The benefits of using _____ es include improved customer satisfaction and improved agility for reacting to rapid market change. Process-oriented organizations break down the barriers of structural departments and try to avoid functional silos.

Exam Probability: **High**

11. *Answer choices:*

(see index for correct answer)

- a. Tenant screening
- b. Business process
- c. Software Ideas Modeler
- d. International business development

Guidance: level 1

:: Project management ::

_____ is a work methodology emphasizing the parallelisation of tasks, which is sometimes called simultaneous engineering or integrated product development using an integrated product team approach. It refers to an approach used in product development in which functions of design engineering, manufacturing engineering, and other functions are integrated to reduce the time required to bring a new product to market.

Exam Probability: **Medium**

12. *Answer choices:*

(see index for correct answer)

- a. Project engineering
- b. Concurrent engineering
- c. Project cancellation
- d. Theory Z of Ouchi

Guidance: level 1

:: Semiconductor companies ::

_____ Corporation is a Japanese multinational conglomerate corporation headquartered in Konan, Minato, Tokyo. Its diversified business includes consumer and professional electronics, gaming, entertainment and financial services. The company owns the largest music entertainment business in the world, the largest video game console business and one of the largest video game publishing businesses, and is one of the leading manufacturers of electronic products for the consumer and professional markets, and a leading player in the film and television entertainment industry. _____ was ranked 97th on the 2018 Fortune Global 500 list.

Exam Probability: **Medium**

13. *Answer choices:*

(see index for correct answer)

- a. Sony
- b. IXYS Corporation
- c. Hana Micron
- d. Qulsar

Guidance: level 1

:: Industrial organization ::

In economics, specifically general equilibrium theory, a perfect market is defined by several idealizing conditions, collectively called _____ . In theoretical models where conditions of _____ hold, it has been theoretically demonstrated that a market will reach an equilibrium in which the quantity supplied for every product or service, including labor, equals the quantity demanded at the current price. This equilibrium would be a Pareto optimum.

Exam Probability: **Medium**

14. *Answer choices:*

(see index for correct answer)

- a. Minimum efficient scale
- b. Organizational studies
- c. Worldwide Responsible Accredited Production
- d. Hold-up problem

Guidance: level 1

:: Distribution, retailing, and wholesaling ::

_____ measures the performance of a system. Certain goals are defined and the _____ gives the percentage to which those goals should be achieved. Fill rate is different from _____ .

Exam Probability: **High**

15. Answer choices:

(see index for correct answer)

- a. National
- b. Filling station
- c. Sales variance
- d. Curtis Circulation

Guidance: level 1

:: Management accounting ::

_____ are costs that are not directly accountable to a cost object. _____ may be either fixed or variable. _____ include administration, personnel and security costs. These are those costs which are not directly related to production. Some _____ may be overhead. But some overhead costs can be directly attributed to a project and are direct costs.

Exam Probability: **Medium**

16. Answer choices:

(see index for correct answer)

- a. Standard cost
- b. Process costing
- c. Factory overhead
- d. Indirect costs

Guidance: level 1

:: Industrial equipment ::

_____ s are heat exchangers typically used to provide heat to the bottom of industrial distillation columns. They boil the liquid from the bottom of a distillation column to generate vapors which are returned to the column to drive the distillation separation. The heat supplied to the column by the _____ at the bottom of the column is removed by the condenser at the top of the column.

Exam Probability: **Low**

17. *Answer choices:*

(see index for correct answer)

- a. Material-handling equipment
- b. Reboiler
- c. Choke manifold
- d. Gravimetric blender

Guidance: level 1

:: Mereology ::

_____, in the abstract, is what belongs to or with something, whether as an attribute or as a component of said thing. In the context of this article, it is one or more components, whether physical or incorporeal, of a person's estate; or so belonging to, as in being owned by, a person or jointly a group of people or a legal entity like a corporation or even a society. Depending on the nature of the _____, an owner of _____ has the right to consume, alter, share, redefine, rent, mortgage, pawn, sell, exchange, transfer, give away or destroy it, or to exclude others from doing these things, as well as to perhaps abandon it; whereas regardless of the nature of the _____, the owner thereof has the right to properly use it, or at the very least exclusively keep it.

Exam Probability: **High**

18. *Answer choices:*

(see index for correct answer)

- a. Mereology
- b. Simple
- c. Meronomy
- d. Mereological essentialism

Guidance: level 1

:: Metalworking ::

A _____ is a round object with various uses. It is used in _____ games, where the play of the game follows the state of the _____ as it is hit, kicked or thrown by players. _____ s can also be used for simpler activities, such as catch or juggling. _____ s made from hard-wearing materials are used in engineering applications to provide very low friction bearings, known as _____ bearings. Black-powder weapons use stone and metal _____ s as projectiles.

Exam Probability: **High**

19. *Answer choices:*

(see index for correct answer)

- a. Ball
- b. Industrial finishing
- c. Metal injection molding
- d. Laser peening

Guidance: level 1

:: Production and manufacturing ::

_____ is a systematic method to improve the "value" of goods or products and services by using an examination of function. Value, as defined, is the ratio of function to cost. Value can therefore be manipulated by either improving the function or reducing the cost. It is a primary tenet of _____ that basic functions be preserved and not be reduced as a consequence of pursuing value improvements.

Exam Probability: **High**

20. *Answer choices:*

(see index for correct answer)

- a. Bill of materials
- b. Value engineering
- c. Multi-Point Interface
- d. Advanced product quality planning

Guidance: level 1

:: Information technology management ::

The term _____ is used to refer to periods when a system is unavailable. _____ or outage duration refers to a period of time that a system fails to provide or perform its primary function. Reliability, availability, recovery, and unavailability are related concepts. The unavailability is the proportion of a time-span that a system is unavailable or offline. This is usually a result of the system failing to function because of an unplanned event, or because of routine maintenance .

Exam Probability: **Low**

21. *Answer choices:*

(see index for correct answer)

- a. Business transaction performance

- b. EFx Factory
- c. Contract management
- d. ITIL security management

Guidance: level 1

:: Promotion and marketing communications ::

The _____ of American Manufacturers, now ThomasNet, is an online platform for supplier discovery and product sourcing in the US and Canada. It was once known as the "big green books" and "Thomas Registry", and was a multi-volume directory of industrial product information covering 650,000 distributors, manufacturers and service companies within 67,000-plus industrial categories that is now published on ThomasNet.

Exam Probability: **High**

22. *Answer choices:*

(see index for correct answer)

- a. The Best Job In The World
- b. Helter Skelter
- c. Valpak
- d. Promotional representative

Guidance: level 1

:: Project management ::

A _____ is one of a series of numbered markers placed along a road or boundary at intervals of one mile or occasionally, parts of a mile. They are typically located at the side of the road or in a median or central reservation. They are alternatively known as mile markers, mileposts or mile posts . Mileage is the distance along the road from a fixed commencement point. Commonly the term " _____ " may also refer to markers placed at other distances, such as every kilometre.

Exam Probability: **Low**

23. *Answer choices:*

(see index for correct answer)

- a. Transport Initiatives Edinburgh
- b. Milestone
- c. Duration
- d. Fast-track construction

Guidance: level 1

:: Management ::

_____ , also known as natural process limits, are horizontal lines drawn on a statistical process control chart, usually at a distance of ±3 standard deviations of the plotted statistic from the statistic's mean.

Exam Probability: **Low**

24. *Answer choices:*

(see index for correct answer)

- a. Leadership Series
- b. Management fad
- c. Control limits
- d. Association management company

Guidance: level 1

:: Business planning ::

_____ is a critical component to the successful delivery of any project, programme or activity. A stakeholder is any individual, group or organization that can affect, be affected by, or perceive itself to be affected by a programme.

Exam Probability: **High**

25. *Answer choices:*

(see index for correct answer)

- a. Gap analysis
- b. Stakeholder management
- c. operational planning

- d. Open Options Corporation

Guidance: level 1

:: Consortia ::

A _____ is an association of two or more individuals, companies, organizations or governments with the objective of participating in a common activity or pooling their resources for achieving a common goal.

Exam Probability: **High**

26. *Answer choices:*

(see index for correct answer)

- a. IPSO Alliance
- b. Service Availability Forum
- c. International Internet Preservation Consortium
- d. Consortium

Guidance: level 1

:: Industrial engineering ::

_____ , in its contemporary conceptualisation, is a comparison of perceived expectations of a service with perceived performance, giving rise to the equation SQ=P-E. This conceptualistion of _____ has its origins in the expectancy-disconfirmation paradigm.

Exam Probability: **High**

27. *Answer choices:*

(see index for correct answer)

- a. Service quality
- b. Work Measurement
- c. Response surface methodology
- d. Operations and technology management

Guidance: level 1

:: Industrial processes ::

A _____ is a device used for high-temperature heating. The name derives from Latin word fornax, which means oven. The heat energy to fuel a _____ may be supplied directly by fuel combustion, by electricity such as the electric arc _____ , or through induction heating in induction _____ s.

Exam Probability: **Low**

28. *Answer choices:*

(see index for correct answer)

- a. Scrubber
- b. Leaching
- c. Metallizing
- d. Furnace

Guidance: level 1

:: Production and manufacturing ::

_____ was a management-led program to eliminate defects in industrial production that enjoyed brief popularity in American industry from 1964 to the early 1970s. Quality expert Philip Crosby later incorporated it into his "Absolutes of Quality Management" and it enjoyed a renaissance in the American automobile industry—as a performance goal more than as a program—in the 1990s. Although applicable to any type of enterprise, it has been primarily adopted within supply chains wherever large volumes of components are being purchased .

Exam Probability: **Medium**

29. *Answer choices:*

(see index for correct answer)

- a. Fab lab
- b. Profibus
- c. Detailed division of labor

- d. MAPICS

Guidance: level 1

:: Management ::

A _____ is an idea of the future or desired result that a person or a group of people envisions, plans and commits to achieve. People endeavor to reach _____ s within a finite time by setting deadlines.

Exam Probability: **Medium**

30. *Answer choices:*

(see index for correct answer)

- a. Tacit knowledge
- b. Instruction creep
- c. Certified management consultant
- d. Goal

Guidance: level 1

:: ::

An _____ is a company that produces parts and equipment that may be marketed by another manufacturer. For example, Foxconn, a Taiwanese electronics contract manufacturing company, which produces a variety of parts and equipment for companies such as Apple Inc., Dell, Google, Huawei, Nintendo, etc., is the largest OEM company in the world by both scale and revenue.

Exam Probability: **Low**

31. *Answer choices:*

(see index for correct answer)

- a. corporate values
- b. co-culture
- c. cultural
- d. Original equipment manufacturer

Guidance: level 1

:: Process management ::

A _____ is a diagram commonly used in chemical and process engineering to indicate the general flow of plant processes and equipment. The PFD displays the relationship between major equipment of a plant facility and does not show minor details such as piping details and designations. Another commonly used term for a PFD is a flowsheet.

Exam Probability: **Low**

32. *Answer choices:*

(see index for correct answer)

- a. Process flow diagram
- b. Ideal tasks
- c. business process re-engineering
- d. Business process discovery

Guidance: level 1

:: Management ::

_____ is a category of business activity made possible by software tools that aim to provide customers with both independence from vendors and better means for engaging with vendors. These same tools can also apply to individuals' relations with other institutions and organizations.

Exam Probability: **Medium**

33. *Answer choices:*

(see index for correct answer)

- a. Infrastructure asset management
- b. Porter five forces analysis
- c. Strategic management
- d. Vendor relationship management

Guidance: level 1

:: Project management ::

Contemporary business and science treat as a _____ any undertaking, carried out individually or collaboratively and possibly involving research or design, that is carefully planned to achieve a particular aim.

Exam Probability: **Medium**

34. *Answer choices:*

(see index for correct answer)

- a. Disciplined Agile Delivery
- b. Project
- c. Level of Effort
- d. Theory Z

Guidance: level 1

:: Information systems ::

_____ is the process of creating, sharing, using and managing the knowledge and information of an organisation. It refers to a multidisciplinary approach to achieving organisational objectives by making the best use of knowledge.

Exam Probability: **Medium**

35. *Answer choices:*

(see index for correct answer)

- a. Knowledge management
- b. CountrySTAT
- c. Personal knowledge management
- d. Cold start

Guidance: level 1

:: Management ::

_____ is a term used in business and Information Technology to describe the in-depth process of capturing customer's expectations, preferences and aversions. Specifically, the _____ is a market research technique that produces a detailed set of customer wants and needs, organized into a hierarchical structure, and then prioritized in terms of relative importance and satisfaction with current alternatives. _____ studies typically consist of both qualitative and quantitative research steps. They are generally conducted at the start of any new product, process, or service design initiative in order to better understand the customer's wants and needs, and as the key input for new product definition, Quality Function Deployment, and the setting of detailed design specifications.

Exam Probability: **Low**

36. *Answer choices:*

(see index for correct answer)

- a. Logistics support analysis
- b. Executive development
- c. Behavioral risk management
- d. Event management

Guidance: level 1

:: Project management ::

In economics and business decision-making, a sunk cost is a cost that has already been incurred and cannot be recovered.

Exam Probability: **High**

37. *Answer choices:*

(see index for correct answer)

- a. Kickoff meeting
- b. Sunk costs
- c. Extreme project management
- d. Burn down chart

Guidance: level 1

:: Process management ::

_____ is a statistics package developed at the Pennsylvania State University by researchers Barbara F. Ryan, Thomas A. Ryan, Jr., and Brian L. Joiner in 1972. It began as a light version of OMNITAB 80, a statistical analysis program by NIST. Statistical analysis software such as _____ automates calculations and the creation of graphs, allowing the user to focus more on the analysis of data and the interpretation of results. It is compatible with other _____ , Inc. software.

Exam Probability: **High**

38. *Answer choices:*

(see index for correct answer)

- a. Throughput

- b. Value grid
- c. Modular process skid
- d. White Space

Guidance: level 1

:: Costs ::

In economics, _____ is the total economic cost of production and is made up of variable cost, which varies according to the quantity of a good produced and includes inputs such as labour and raw materials, plus fixed cost, which is independent of the quantity of a good produced and includes inputs that cannot be varied in the short term: fixed costs such as buildings and machinery, including sunk costs if any. Since cost is measured per unit of time, it is a flow variable.

Exam Probability: **High**

39. *Answer choices:*
(see index for correct answer)

- a. labor cost
- b. Total cost
- c. Direct materials cost
- d. Cost competitiveness of fuel sources

Guidance: level 1

:: Business planning ::

_____ is an organization's process of defining its strategy, or direction, and making decisions on allocating its resources to pursue this strategy. It may also extend to control mechanisms for guiding the implementation of the strategy. _____ became prominent in corporations during the 1960s and remains an important aspect of strategic management. It is executed by strategic planners or strategists, who involve many parties and research sources in their analysis of the organization and its relationship to the environment in which it competes.

Exam Probability: **High**

40. *Answer choices:*

(see index for correct answer)

- a. operational planning
- b. Joint decision trap
- c. Exit planning
- d. Community Futures

Guidance: level 1

:: Product management ::

_____ s, also known as Shewhart charts or process-behavior charts, are a statistical process control tool used to determine if a manufacturing or business process is in a state of control.

Exam Probability: **Low**

41. *Answer choices:*

(see index for correct answer)

- a. Swing tag
- b. Control chart
- c. Brand alliances
- d. Service product management

Guidance: level 1

:: Production and manufacturing ::

In industry, _____ is a system of maintaining and improving the integrity of production and quality systems through the machines, equipment, processes, and employees that add business value to an organization.

Exam Probability: **Low**

42. *Answer choices:*

(see index for correct answer)

- a. Feeder line
- b. Low rate initial production
- c. Enterprise control
- d. Total productive maintenance

Guidance: level 1

:: ::

_____ is the process of making predictions of the future based on past and present data and most commonly by analysis of trends. A commonplace example might be estimation of some variable of interest at some specified future date. Prediction is a similar, but more general term. Both might refer to formal statistical methods employing time series, cross-sectional or longitudinal data, or alternatively to less formal judgmental methods. Usage can differ between areas of application: for example, in hydrology the terms "forecast" and "_____" are sometimes reserved for estimates of values at certain specific future times, while the term "prediction" is used for more general estimates, such as the number of times floods will occur over a long period.

Exam Probability: **Low**

43. *Answer choices:*
(see index for correct answer)

- a. Forecasting
- b. hierarchical perspective
- c. empathy
- d. open system

Guidance: level 1

:: E-commerce ::

_____ is the business-to-business or business-to-consumer or business-to-government purchase and sale of supplies, work, and services through the Internet as well as other information and networking systems, such as electronic data interchange and enterprise resource planning.

Exam Probability: **High**

44. *Answer choices:*

(see index for correct answer)

- a. Triton
- b. Discovery shopping
- c. DVD-by-mail
- d. E-procurement

Guidance: level 1

:: ::

In production, research, retail, and accounting, a _____ is the value of money that has been used up to produce something or deliver a service, and hence is not available for use anymore. In business, the _____ may be one of acquisition, in which case the amount of money expended to acquire it is counted as _____ . In this case, money is the input that is gone in order to acquire the thing. This acquisition _____ may be the sum of the _____ of production as incurred by the original producer, and further _____ s of transaction as incurred by the acquirer over and above the price paid to the producer. Usually, the price also includes a mark-up for profit over the _____ of production.

Exam Probability: **Low**

45. *Answer choices:*

(see index for correct answer)

- a. Cost
- b. process perspective
- c. Sarbanes-Oxley act of 2002
- d. surface-level diversity

Guidance: level 1

:: Casting (manufacturing) ::

A _____ is a regularity in the world, man-made design, or abstract ideas. As such, the elements of a _____ repeat in a predictable manner. A geometric _____ is a kind of _____ formed of geometric shapes and typically repeated like a wallpaper design.

Exam Probability: **Medium**

46. *Answer choices:*

(see index for correct answer)

- a. Steel casting
- b. Castability
- c. Pattern

- d. Cope and drag

Guidance: level 1

:: ::

_____ is the process of finding an estimate, or approximation, which is a value that is usable for some purpose even if input data may be incomplete, uncertain, or unstable. The value is nonetheless usable because it is derived from the best information available. Typically, _____ involves "using the value of a statistic derived from a sample to estimate the value of a corresponding population parameter". The sample provides information that can be projected, through various formal or informal processes, to determine a range most likely to describe the missing information. An estimate that turns out to be incorrect will be an overestimate if the estimate exceeded the actual result, and an underestimate if the estimate fell short of the actual result.

Exam Probability: **Low**

47. *Answer choices:*
(see index for correct answer)

- a. open system
- b. co-culture
- c. interpersonal communication
- d. Estimation

Guidance: level 1

:: Project management ::

A _____ is a type of bar chart that illustrates a project schedule, named after its inventor, Henry Gantt , who designed such a chart around the years 1910–1915. Modern _____ s also show the dependency relationships between activities and current schedule status.

Exam Probability: **High**

48. *Answer choices:*

(see index for correct answer)

- a. A Guide to the Project Management Body of Knowledge
- b. Virtual design and construction
- c. Gantt chart
- d. Project cancellation

Guidance: level 1

:: Metals ::

A _____ is a material that, when freshly prepared, polished, or fractured, shows a lustrous appearance, and conducts electricity and heat relatively well. _____ s are typically malleable or ductile . A _____ may be a chemical element such as iron, or an alloy such as stainless steel.

Exam Probability: **High**

49. *Answer choices:*

(see index for correct answer)

- a. Light metal
- b. Forging temperature
- c. Thulium
- d. Metal

Guidance: level 1

:: Production and manufacturing ::

_____ is the process of determining the production capacity needed by an organization to meet changing demands for its products. In the context of _____ , design capacity is the maximum amount of work that an organization is capable of completing in a given period. Effective capacity is the maximum amount of work that an organization is capable of completing in a given period due to constraints such as quality problems, delays, material handling, etc.

Exam Probability: **Medium**

50. *Answer choices:*

(see index for correct answer)

- a. Workmanship
- b. Job production

- c. Hydrosila
- d. Cycle time variation

Guidance: level 1

:: Project management ::

In general usage, a _____ is a comprehensive evaluation of an individual's current pay and future financial state by using current known variables to predict future income, asset values and withdrawal plans. This often includes a budget which organizes an individual's finances and sometimes includes a series of steps or specific goals for spending and saving in the future. This plan allocates future income to various types of expenses, such as rent or utilities, and also reserves some income for short-term and long-term savings. A _____ is sometimes referred to as an investment plan, but in personal finance a _____ can focus on other specific areas such as risk management, estates, college, or retirement.

Exam Probability: **Low**

51. *Answer choices:*
(see index for correct answer)

- a. Work package
- b. Financial plan
- c. Basis of estimate
- d. Theory X

Guidance: level 1

:: ::

_____ is the production of products for use or sale using labour and machines, tools, chemical and biological processing, or formulation. The term may refer to a range of human activity, from handicraft to high tech, but is most commonly applied to industrial design, in which raw materials are transformed into finished goods on a large scale. Such finished goods may be sold to other manufacturers for the production of other, more complex products, such as aircraft, household appliances, furniture, sports equipment or automobiles, or sold to wholesalers, who in turn sell them to retailers, who then sell them to end users and consumers.

Exam Probability: **Medium**

52. *Answer choices:*

(see index for correct answer)

- a. hierarchical perspective
- b. Manufacturing
- c. open system
- d. levels of analysis

Guidance: level 1

:: Infographics ::

The _____ is a form used to collect data in real time at the location where the data is generated. The data it captures can be quantitative or qualitative. When the information is quantitative, the _____ is sometimes called a tally sheet.

Exam Probability: **High**

53. *Answer choices:*

(see index for correct answer)

- a. Check sheet
- b. Engineering drawing
- c. Vis5D
- d. Baby on board

Guidance: level 1

:: Production and manufacturing ::

_____ is the production under license of technology developed elsewhere. It is an especially prominent commercial practice in developing nations, which often approach _____ as a starting point for indigenous industrial development.

Exam Probability: **Low**

54. *Answer choices:*

(see index for correct answer)

- a. Craft production
- b. Licensed production
- c. Predetermined motion time system
- d. product lifecycle

Guidance: level 1

:: Project management ::

A _____ is the approximation of the cost of a program, project, or operation. The _____ is the product of the cost estimating process. The _____ has a single total value and may have identifiable component values. A problem with a cost overrun can be avoided with a credible, reliable, and accurate _____ . A cost estimator is the professional who prepares _____ s. There are different types of cost estimators, whose title may be preceded by a modifier, such as building estimator, or electrical estimator, or chief estimator. Other professionals such as quantity surveyors and cost engineers may also prepare _____ s or contribute to _____ s. In the US, according to the Bureau of Labor Statistics, there were 185,400 cost estimators in 2010. There are around 75,000 professional quantity surveyors working in the UK.

Exam Probability: **Medium**

55. *Answer choices:*

(see index for correct answer)

- a. Cash flow diagram

- b. Project manufacturing
- c. Cost estimate
- d. Work package

Guidance: level 1

:: Production and manufacturing ::

Automatic _____ in continuous production processes is a combination of control engineering and chemical engineering disciplines that uses industrial control systems to achieve a production level of consistency, economy and safety which could not be achieved purely by human manual control. It is implemented widely in industries such as oil refining, pulp and paper manufacturing, chemical processing and power generating plants.

Exam Probability: **Low**

56. *Answer choices:*

(see index for correct answer)

- a. Process control
- b. Variable rate feeder
- c. Computer-aided process planning
- d. Piece work

Guidance: level 1

:: Non-parametric statistics ::

A _____ is an accurate representation of the distribution of numerical data. It is an estimate of the probability distribution of a continuous variable and was first introduced by Karl Pearson. It differs from a bar graph, in the sense that a bar graph relates two variables, but a _____ relates only one. To construct a _____, the first step is to "bin" the range of values—that is, divide the entire range of values into a series of intervals—and then count how many values fall into each interval. The bins are usually specified as consecutive, non-overlapping intervals of a variable. The bins must be adjacent, and are often of equal size.

Exam Probability: **Medium**

57. *Answer choices:*
(see index for correct answer)

- a. Histogram
- b. Nonparametric regression
- c. Nemenyi test
- d. Order statistic

Guidance: level 1

:: Quality assurance ::

The _____ is a United States-based nonprofit tax-exempt 501 organization that accredits more than 21,000 US health care organizations and programs. The international branch accredits medical services from around the world. A majority of US state governments recognize _____ accreditation as a condition of licensure for the receipt of Medicaid and Medicare reimbursements.

Exam Probability: **High**

58. *Answer choices:*

(see index for correct answer)

- a. Trent Accreditation Scheme
- b. Software assurance
- c. The Compliance Team
- d. Community Health Accreditation Program

Guidance: level 1

:: Information technology management ::

_____ is a collective term for all approaches to prepare, support and help individuals, teams, and organizations in making organizational change. The most common change drivers include: technological evolution, process reviews, crisis, and consumer habit changes; pressure from new business entrants, acquisitions, mergers, and organizational restructuring. It includes methods that redirect or redefine the use of resources, business process, budget allocations, or other modes of operation that significantly change a company or organization. Organizational _____ considers the full organization and what needs to change, while _____ may be used solely to refer to how people and teams are affected by such organizational transition. It deals with many different disciplines, from behavioral and social sciences to information technology and business solutions.

Exam Probability: **High**

59. *Answer choices:*
(see index for correct answer)

- a. Business transformation
- b. Grey problem
- c. IT risk
- d. Mung

Guidance: level 1

Commerce

Commerce relates to "the exchange of goods and services, especially on a large scale." It includes legal, economic, political, social, cultural and technological systems that operate in any country or internationally.

:: Business ethics ::

_____ is a type of harassment technique that relates to a sexual nature and the unwelcome or inappropriate promise of rewards in exchange for sexual favors. _____ includes a range of actions from mild transgressions to sexual abuse or assault. Harassment can occur in many different social settings such as the workplace, the home, school, churches, etc. Harassers or victims may be of any gender.

Exam Probability: **Low**

1. *Answer choices:*

(see index for correct answer)

- a. Bribery Act 2010
- b. Philosophy of business
- c. Contingent work
- d. Moral hazard

Guidance: level 1

:: ::

A _____ is any person who contracts to acquire an asset in return for some form of consideration.

Exam Probability: **Medium**

2. *Answer choices:*

(see index for correct answer)

- a. Buyer
- b. information systems assessment
- c. process perspective
- d. hierarchical perspective

Guidance: level 1

:: Industry ::

_____ , also known as flow production or continuous production, is the production of large amounts of standardized products, including and especially on assembly lines. Together with job production and batch production, it is one of the three main production methods.

Exam Probability: **High**

3. *Answer choices:*

(see index for correct answer)

- a. The Year in Industry
- b. Mass production
- c. Fordism
- d. Eco-industrial development

Guidance: level 1

:: Consortia ::

A _____ is an association of two or more individuals, companies, organizations or governments with the objective of participating in a common activity or pooling their resources for achieving a common goal.

Exam Probability: **Low**

4. *Answer choices:*

(see index for correct answer)

- a. Asian American and Pacific Islander Policy Research Consortium
- b. Consortium
- c. World Information Technology and Services Alliance
- d. Open Data Center Alliance

Guidance: level 1

:: ::

In logic and philosophy, an _____ is a series of statements, called the premises or premisses, intended to determine the degree of truth of another statement, the conclusion. The logical form of an _____ in a natural language can be represented in a symbolic formal language, and independently of natural language formally defined "_____ s" can be made in math and computer science.

Exam Probability: **Low**

5. *Answer choices:*

(see index for correct answer)

- a. Character
- b. Argument
- c. surface-level diversity
- d. Sarbanes-Oxley act of 2002

Guidance: level 1

:: Management ::

In business, a _____ is the attribute that allows an organization to outperform its competitors. A _____ may include access to natural resources, such as high-grade ores or a low-cost power source, highly skilled labor, geographic location, high entry barriers, and access to new technology.

Exam Probability: **High**

6. *Answer choices:*

(see index for correct answer)

- a. Competitive advantage
- b. Value migration
- c. Best current practice
- d. Dominant design

Guidance: level 1

:: ::

_____ is the principled guide to action taken by the administrative executive branches of the state with regard to a class of issues, in a manner consistent with law and institutional customs.

Exam Probability: **Medium**

7. *Answer choices:*

(see index for correct answer)

- a. Sarbanes-Oxley act of 2002
- b. Public policy
- c. open system
- d. functional perspective

Guidance: level 1

:: ::

_____ is a marketing communication that employs an openly sponsored, non-personal message to promote or sell a product, service or idea. Sponsors of _____ are typically businesses wishing to promote their products or services. _____ is differentiated from public relations in that an advertiser pays for and has control over the message. It differs from personal selling in that the message is non-personal, i.e., not directed to a particular individual. _____ is communicated through various mass media, including traditional media such as newspapers, magazines, television, radio, outdoor _____ or direct mail; and new media such as search results, blogs, social media, websites or text messages. The actual presentation of the message in a medium is referred to as an advertisement, or "ad" or advert for short.

Exam Probability: **High**

8. *Answer choices:*

(see index for correct answer)

- a. personal values
- b. surface-level diversity
- c. process perspective
- d. Advertising

Guidance: level 1

:: ::

Regulatory economics is the economics of regulation. It is the application of law by government or independent administrative agencies for various purposes, including remedying market failure, protecting the environment, centrally-planning an economy, enriching well-connected firms, or benefiting politicians.

Exam Probability: **Medium**

9. *Answer choices:*

(see index for correct answer)

- a. similarity-attraction theory
- b. process perspective
- c. interpersonal communication
- d. functional perspective

Guidance: level 1

:: ::

The _____ of 1990 is a civil rights law that prohibits discrimination based on disability. It affords similar protections against discrimination to Americans with disabilities as the Civil Rights Act of 1964, which made discrimination based on race, religion, sex, national origin, and other characteristics illegal. In addition, unlike the Civil Rights Act, the ADA also requires covered employers to provide reasonable accommodations to employees with disabilities, and imposes accessibility requirements on public accommodations.

Exam Probability: **Low**

10. *Answer choices:*

(see index for correct answer)

- a. imperative
- b. similarity-attraction theory
- c. surface-level diversity
- d. process perspective

Guidance: level 1

:: Economics terminology ::

_____ is the total receipts a seller can obtain from selling goods or services to buyers. It can be written as P × Q, which is the price of the goods multiplied by the quantity of the sold goods.

Exam Probability: **High**

11. *Answer choices:*

(see index for correct answer)

- a. Price variance
- b. Profit motive
- c. Normal profit
- d. Bond issue

Guidance: level 1

:: Information retrieval ::

_____ is a technique used by recommender systems. _____ has two senses, a narrow one and a more general one.

Exam Probability: **Medium**

12. *Answer choices:*

(see index for correct answer)

- a. Cosine similarity
- b. 30 Digits
- c. European Summer School in Information Retrieval
- d. Collaborative filtering

Guidance: level 1

:: E-commerce ::

_____ is the business-to-business or business-to-consumer or business-to-government purchase and sale of supplies, work, and services through the Internet as well as other information and networking systems, such as electronic data interchange and enterprise resource planning.

Exam Probability: **Low**

13. *Answer choices:*

(see index for correct answer)

- a. PapiNet
- b. DigiCash
- c. Inventory Information Approval System
- d. Online shopping

Guidance: level 1

:: Banking ::

A _____ is a financial institution that accepts deposits from the public and creates credit. Lending activities can be performed either directly or indirectly through capital markets. Due to their importance in the financial stability of a country, _____ s are highly regulated in most countries. Most nations have institutionalized a system known as fractional reserve _____ ing under which _____ s hold liquid assets equal to only a portion of their current liabilities. In addition to other regulations intended to ensure liquidity, _____ s are generally subject to minimum capital requirements based on an international set of capital standards, known as the Basel Accords.

Exam Probability: **High**

14. *Answer choices:*

(see index for correct answer)

- a. Banq
- b. Intermediation
- c. Arranger
- d. Bank

Guidance: level 1

:: Trading posts of the Hanseatic League ::

_____ is a city and unitary authority area in North _____ shire, England, with a population of 208,200 as of 2017. Located at the confluence of the Rivers Ouse and Foss, it is the county town of the historic county of _____ shire and was the home of the House of _____ throughout its existence. The city is known for its famous historical landmarks such as _____ Minster and the city walls, as well as a variety of cultural and sporting activities, which makes it a popular tourist destination in England. The local authority is the City of _____ Council, a single tier governing body responsible for providing all local services and facilities throughout the city. The City of _____ local government district includes rural areas beyond the old city boundaries.

Exam Probability: **High**

15. *Answer choices:*

(see index for correct answer)

- a. York
- b. Falsterbo
- c. Polotsk

- d. Antwerp

Guidance: level 1

:: Information technology management ::

_____ s or pop-ups are forms of online advertising on the World Wide Web. A pop-up is a graphical user interface display area, usually a small window, that suddenly appears in the foreground of the visual interface. The pop-up window containing an advertisement is usually generated by JavaScript that uses cross-site scripting, sometimes with a secondary payload that uses Adobe Flash. They can also be generated by other vulnerabilities/security holes in browser security.

Exam Probability: **High**

16. *Answer choices:*

(see index for correct answer)

- a. Pop-up ad
- b. Cumulus
- c. Building lifecycle management
- d. Enterprise content management

Guidance: level 1

:: ::

A _____ is a sworn body of people convened to render an impartial verdict officially submitted to them by a court, or to set a penalty or judgment. Modern juries tend to be found in courts to ascertain the guilt or lack thereof in a crime. In Anglophone jurisdictions, the verdict may be guilty or not guilty. The old institution of grand juries still exists in some places, particularly the United States, to investigate whether enough evidence of a crime exists to bring someone to trial.

Exam Probability: **Low**

17. *Answer choices:*

(see index for correct answer)

- a. Jury
- b. process perspective
- c. functional perspective
- d. cultural

Guidance: level 1

:: ::

_____ is the provision of service to customers before, during and after a purchase. The perception of success of such interactions is dependent on employees "who can adjust themselves to the personality of the guest". _____ concerns the priority an organization assigns to _____ relative to components such as product innovation and pricing. In this sense, an organization that values good _____ may spend more money in training employees than the average organization or may proactively interview customers for feedback.

Exam Probability: **Low**

18. *Answer choices:*

(see index for correct answer)

- a. Customer service
- b. process perspective
- c. deep-level diversity
- d. information systems assessment

Guidance: level 1

:: ::

A federation is a political entity characterized by a union of partially self-governing provinces, states, or other regions under a central _____. In a federation, the self-governing status of the component states, as well as the division of power between them and the central government, is typically constitutionally entrenched and may not be altered by a unilateral decision of either party, the states or the federal political body. Alternatively, federation is a form of government in which sovereign power is formally divided between a central authority and a number of constituent regions so that each region retains some degree of control over its internal affairs. It is often argued that federal states where the central government has the constitutional authority to suspend a constituent state's government by invoking gross mismanagement or civil unrest, or to adopt national legislation that overrides or infringe on the constituent states' powers by invoking the central government's constitutional authority to ensure "peace and good government" or to implement obligations contracted under an international treaty, are not truly federal states.

Exam Probability: **Medium**

19. *Answer choices:*

(see index for correct answer)

- a. personal values
- b. cultural
- c. levels of analysis
- d. Federal government

Guidance: level 1

:: Strategic alliances ::

A _____ is an agreement between two or more parties to pursue a set of agreed upon objectives needed while remaining independent organizations. A _____ will usually fall short of a legal partnership entity, agency, or corporate affiliate relationship. Typically, two companies form a _____ when each possesses one or more business assets or have expertise that will help the other by enhancing their businesses. _____s can develop in outsourcing relationships where the parties desire to achieve long-term win-win benefits and innovation based on mutually desired outcomes.

Exam Probability: **Medium**

20. *Answer choices:*

(see index for correct answer)

- a. Bridge Alliance
- b. Strategic alliance
- c. Defensive termination
- d. International joint venture

Guidance: level 1

:: Marketing analytics ::

_____ is a long-term, forward-looking approach to planning with the fundamental goal of achieving a sustainable competitive advantage. Strategic planning involves an analysis of the company's strategic initial situation prior to the formulation, evaluation and selection of market-oriented competitive position that contributes to the company's goals and marketing objectives.

Exam Probability: **Low**

21. *Answer choices:*

(see index for correct answer)

- a. Marketing performance measurement and management
- b. Marketing strategy
- c. Gross rating point
- d. Advertising adstock

Guidance: level 1

:: ::

In legal terminology, a _____ is any formal legal document that sets out the facts and legal reasons that the filing party or parties believes are sufficient to support a claim against the party or parties against whom the claim is brought that entitles the plaintiff to a remedy. For example, the Federal Rules of Civil Procedure that govern civil litigation in United States courts provide that a civil action is commenced with the filing or service of a pleading called a _____ . Civil court rules in states that have incorporated the Federal Rules of Civil Procedure use the same term for the same pleading.

Exam Probability: **Medium**

22. *Answer choices:*

(see index for correct answer)

- a. co-culture
- b. information systems assessment
- c. corporate values
- d. Complaint

Guidance: level 1

:: Globalization-related theories ::

_____ is the process in which a nation is being improved in the sector of the economic, political, and social well-being of its people. The term has been used frequently by economists, politicians, and others in the 20th and 21st centuries. The concept, however, has been in existence in the West for centuries. "Modernization, "westernization", and especially "industrialization" are other terms often used while discussing _____ . _____ has a direct relationship with the environment and environmental issues. _____ is very often confused with industrial development, even in some academic sources.

Exam Probability: **High**

23. *Answer choices:*
(see index for correct answer)

- a. postmodernism
- b. Economic development
- c. post-industrial

Guidance: level 1

:: Logistics ::

_____ is generally the detailed organization and implementation of a complex operation. In a general business sense, _____ is the management of the flow of things between the point of origin and the point of consumption in order to meet requirements of customers or corporations. The resources managed in _____ may include tangible goods such as materials, equipment, and supplies, as well as food and other consumable items. The _____ of physical items usually involves the integration of information flow, materials handling, production, packaging, inventory, transportation, warehousing, and often security.

Exam Probability: **Medium**

24. *Answer choices:*

(see index for correct answer)

- a. Savi Technology
- b. ISO/IEC 18000-3
- c. Hubs and Nodes
- d. Loading dock

Guidance: level 1

:: ::

In mathematics, computer science and operations research, mathematical optimization or mathematical programming is the selection of a best element from some set of available alternatives.

Exam Probability: **Low**

25. *Answer choices:*

(see index for correct answer)

- a. Optimum
- b. hierarchical perspective
- c. imperative
- d. personal values

Guidance: level 1

:: ::

_____ refers to the overall process of attracting, shortlisting, selecting and appointing suitable candidates for jobs within an organization. _____ can also refer to processes involved in choosing individuals for unpaid roles. Managers, human resource generalists and _____ specialists may be tasked with carrying out _____, but in some cases public-sector employment agencies, commercial _____ agencies, or specialist search consultancies are used to undertake parts of the process. Internet-based technologies which support all aspects of _____ have become widespread.

Exam Probability: **Low**

26. *Answer choices:*

(see index for correct answer)

- a. functional perspective
- b. imperative
- c. Recruitment
- d. hierarchical perspective

Guidance: level 1

:: E-commerce ::

IBM _____ also known as WCS is a software platform framework for e-commerce, including marketing, sales, customer and order processing functionality in a tailorable, integrated package. It is a single, unified platform which offers the ability to do business directly with consumers, with businesses, indirectly through channel partners, or all of these simultaneously. _____ is a customizable, scalable and high availability solution built on the Java - Java EE platform using open standards, such as XML, and Web services.

Exam Probability: **Medium**

27. *Answer choices:*

(see index for correct answer)

- a. Segundamano
- b. ROPO

- c. WebSphere Commerce
- d. Point of sale

Guidance: level 1

:: Production economics ::

In economics and related disciplines, a _____ is a cost in making any economic trade when participating in a market.

Exam Probability: **High**

28. *Answer choices:*
(see index for correct answer)

- a. Transaction cost
- b. Foundations of Economic Analysis
- c. HMI quality
- d. Constant elasticity of transformation

Guidance: level 1

:: Costs ::

In economics, _____ is the total economic cost of production and is made up of variable cost, which varies according to the quantity of a good produced and includes inputs such as labour and raw materials, plus fixed cost, which is independent of the quantity of a good produced and includes inputs that cannot be varied in the short term: fixed costs such as buildings and machinery, including sunk costs if any. Since cost is measured per unit of time, it is a flow variable.

Exam Probability: **Low**

29. *Answer choices:*

(see index for correct answer)

- a. Search cost
- b. Customer Cost
- c. Opportunity cost of capital
- d. Incremental cost-effectiveness ratio

Guidance: level 1

:: Regulators ::

A _____ is a public authority or government agency responsible for exercising autonomous authority over some area of human activity in a regulatory or supervisory capacity. An independent _____ is a _____ that is independent from other branches or arms of the government.

Exam Probability: **High**

30. Answer choices:

(see index for correct answer)

- a. Crofters Commission
- b. Energy and Utilities Board
- c. Regulatory agency
- d. Croatian Regulatory Authority for Network Industries

Guidance: level 1

:: Supply chain management ::

_____ is the removal of intermediaries in economics from a supply chain, or cutting out the middlemen in connection with a transaction or a series of transactions. Instead of going through traditional distribution channels, which had some type of intermediary, companies may now deal with customers directly, for example via the Internet. Hence, the use of factory direct and direct from the factory to mean the same thing.

Exam Probability: **Medium**

31. Answer choices:

(see index for correct answer)

- a. Demand sensing
- b. Disintermediation
- c. Global supply-chain finance
- d. Institute for Supply Management

Guidance: level 1

:: Public relations ::

_____ is the public visibility or awareness for any product, service or company. It may also refer to the movement of information from its source to the general public, often but not always via the media. The subjects of _____ include people, goods and services, organizations, and works of art or entertainment.

Exam Probability: **Low**

32. *Answer choices:*

(see index for correct answer)

- a. LaunchSquad
- b. Upstate California
- c. Publicity
- d. Public diplomacy

Guidance: level 1

:: Marketing ::

The _____ is a foundation model for businesses. The _____ has been defined as the "set of marketing tools that the firm uses to pursue its marketing objectives in the target market". Thus the _____ refers to four broad levels of marketing decision, namely: product, price, place, and promotion. Marketing practice has been occurring for millennia, but marketing theory emerged in the early twentieth century. The contemporary _____ , or the 4 Ps, which has become the dominant framework for marketing management decisions, was first published in 1960. In services marketing, an extended _____ is used, typically comprising 7 Ps, made up of the original 4 Ps extended by process, people, and physical evidence. Occasionally service marketers will refer to 8 Ps, comprising these 7 Ps plus performance.

Exam Probability: **Medium**

33. *Answer choices:*
(see index for correct answer)

- a. Price point
- b. Aftermarket
- c. Marketing mix
- d. Marketing operations

Guidance: level 1

:: ::

In marketing jargon, product lining is offering several related products for sale individually. Unlike product bundling, where several products are combined into one group, which is then offered for sale as a units, product lining involves offering the products for sale separately. A line can comprise related products of various sizes, types, colors, qualities, or prices. Line depth refers to the number of subcategories a category has. Line consistency refers to how closely related the products that make up the line are. Line vulnerability refers to the percentage of sales or profits that are derived from only a few products in the line.

Exam Probability: **Medium**

34. *Answer choices:*

(see index for correct answer)

- a. imperative
- b. deep-level diversity
- c. information systems assessment
- d. Sarbanes-Oxley act of 2002

Guidance: level 1

:: Income ::

In business and accounting, net income is an entity's income minus cost of goods sold, expenses and taxes for an accounting period. It is computed as the residual of all revenues and gains over all expenses and losses for the period, and has also been defined as the net increase in shareholders' equity that results from a company's operations. In the context of the presentation of financial statements, the IFRS Foundation defines net income as synonymous with profit and loss. The difference between revenue and the cost of making a product or providing a service, before deducting overheads, payroll, taxation, and interest payments. This is different from operating income.

Exam Probability: **Low**

35. *Answer choices:*

(see index for correct answer)

- a. Bottom line
- b. Signing bonus
- c. Salary inversion
- d. Creative real estate investing

Guidance: level 1

:: ::

_____ is the amount of time someone works beyond normal working hours. The term is also used for the pay received for this time. Normal hours may be determined in several ways.

Exam Probability: **High**

36. *Answer choices:*

(see index for correct answer)

- a. cultural
- b. interpersonal communication
- c. imperative
- d. personal values

Guidance: level 1

:: Industrial automation ::

_____ is the technology by which a process or procedure is performed with minimal human assistance. _____ or automatic control is the use of various control systems for operating equipment such as machinery, processes in factories, boilers and heat treating ovens, switching on telephone networks, steering and stabilization of ships, aircraft and other applications and vehicles with minimal or reduced human intervention.

Exam Probability: **High**

37. *Answer choices:*

(see index for correct answer)

- a. EtherCAT
- b. IODD

- c. Automation surprise
- d. PLCopen

Guidance: level 1

:: ::

An _____ is the production of goods or related services within an economy. The major source of revenue of a group or company is the indicator of its relevant _____ . When a large group has multiple sources of revenue generation, it is considered to be working in different industries. Manufacturing _____ became a key sector of production and labour in European and North American countries during the Industrial Revolution, upsetting previous mercantile and feudal economies. This came through many successive rapid advances in technology, such as the production of steel and coal.

Exam Probability: **High**

38. *Answer choices:*

(see index for correct answer)

- a. hierarchical perspective
- b. surface-level diversity
- c. information systems assessment
- d. Industry

Guidance: level 1

:: Minimum wage ::

A _____ is the lowest remuneration that employers can legally pay their workers—the price floor below which workers may not sell their labor. Most countries had introduced _____ legislation by the end of the 20th century.

Exam Probability: **Low**

39. *Answer choices:*

(see index for correct answer)

- a. National Anti-Sweating League
- b. Minimum Wage Fairness Act
- c. Minimum wage in the United States
- d. Minimum wage

Guidance: level 1

:: Information technology management ::

B2B is often contrasted with business-to-consumer. In B2B commerce, it is often the case that the parties to the relationship have comparable negotiating power, and even when they do not, each party typically involves professional staff and legal counsel in the negotiation of terms, whereas B2C is shaped to a far greater degree by economic implications of information asymmetry. However, within a B2B context, large companies may have many commercial, resource and information advantages over smaller businesses. The United Kingdom government, for example, created the post of Small Business Commissioner under the Enterprise Act 2016 to "enable small businesses to resolve disputes" and "consider complaints by small business suppliers about payment issues with larger businesses that they supply."

Exam Probability: **High**

40. *Answer choices:*

(see index for correct answer)

- a. E-Booking
- b. The International Records Management Trust
- c. High Availability Application Architecture
- d. Business-to-business

Guidance: level 1

_____ is a qualitative measure used to relate the quality of motor vehicle traffic service. LOS is used to analyze roadways and intersections by categorizing traffic flow and assigning quality levels of traffic based on performance measure like vehicle speed, density, congestion, etc.

Exam Probability: **Low**

41. *Answer choices:*

(see index for correct answer)

- a. personal values
- b. Level of service
- c. empathy
- d. co-culture

Guidance: level 1

:: ::

_____ are electronic transfer of money from one bank account to another, either within a single financial institution or across multiple institutions, via computer-based systems, without the direct intervention of bank staff.

Exam Probability: **High**

42. *Answer choices:*

(see index for correct answer)

- a. corporate values
- b. hierarchical perspective
- c. deep-level diversity
- d. Electronic funds transfer

Guidance: level 1

:: ::

_____ is the social science that studies the production, distribution, and consumption of goods and services.

Exam Probability: **High**

43. *Answer choices:*

(see index for correct answer)

- a. Sarbanes-Oxley act of 2002
- b. interpersonal communication
- c. Economics
- d. corporate values

Guidance: level 1

:: Insolvency ::

_____ is a legal process through which people or other entities who cannot repay debts to creditors may seek relief from some or all of their debts. In most jurisdictions, _____ is imposed by a court order, often initiated by the debtor.

Exam Probability: **High**

44. *Answer choices:*

(see index for correct answer)

- a. Insolvency law of Russia
- b. Bankruptcy
- c. Preferential creditor
- d. Conservatorship

Guidance: level 1

:: ::

A trade fair is an exhibition organized so that companies in a specific industry can showcase and demonstrate their latest products and services, meet with industry partners and customers, study activities of rivals, and examine recent market trends and opportunities. In contrast to consumer fairs, only some trade fairs are open to the public, while others can only be attended by company representatives and members of the press, therefore _____ s are classified as either "public" or "trade only". A few fairs are hybrids of the two; one example is the Frankfurt Book Fair, which is trade only for its first three days and open to the general public on its final two days. They are held on a continuing basis in virtually all markets and normally attract companies from around the globe. For example, in the U.S., there are currently over 10,000 _____ s held every year, and several online directories have been established to help organizers, attendees, and marketers identify appropriate events.

Exam Probability: **Low**

45. *Answer choices:*

(see index for correct answer)

- a. corporate values
- b. hierarchical
- c. Trade show
- d. levels of analysis

Guidance: level 1

:: Confidence tricks ::

_____ is the fraudulent attempt to obtain sensitive information such as usernames, passwords and credit card details by disguising oneself as a trustworthy entity in an electronic communication. Typically carried out by email spoofing or instant messaging, it often directs users to enter personal information at a fake website which matches the look and feel of the legitimate site.

Exam Probability: **Medium**

46. *Answer choices:*

(see index for correct answer)

- a. Phishing
- b. Black money scam
- c. First International Bank of Grenada
- d. Hot reading

Guidance: level 1

:: Management accounting ::

In economics, _____ s, indirect costs or overheads are business expenses that are not dependent on the level of goods or services produced by the business. They tend to be time-related, such as interest or rents being paid per month, and are often referred to as overhead costs. This is in contrast to variable costs, which are volume-related and unknown at the beginning of the accounting year. For a simple example, such as a bakery, the monthly rent for the baking facilities, and the monthly payments for the security system and basic phone line are _____ s, as they do not change according to how much bread the bakery produces and sells. On the other hand, the wage costs of the bakery are variable, as the bakery will have to hire more workers if the production of bread increases. Economists reckon _____ as a entry barrier for new entrepreneurs.

Exam Probability: **Medium**

47. *Answer choices:*

(see index for correct answer)

- a. Overhead
- b. Average per-bit delivery cost
- c. Fixed cost
- d. Extended cost

Guidance: level 1

:: ::

The _____ or just chief executive, is the most senior corporate, executive, or administrative officer in charge of managing an organization especially an independent legal entity such as a company or nonprofit institution. CEOs lead a range of organizations, including public and private corporations, non-profit organizations and even some government organizations. The CEO of a corporation or company typically reports to the board of directors and is charged with maximizing the value of the entity, which may include maximizing the share price, market share, revenues or another element. In the non-profit and government sector, CEOs typically aim at achieving outcomes related to the organization's mission, such as reducing poverty, increasing literacy, etc.

Exam Probability: **Low**

48. *Answer choices:*

(see index for correct answer)

- a. Chief executive officer
- b. personal values
- c. hierarchical perspective
- d. interpersonal communication

Guidance: level 1

:: Business law ::

A _____ is a contractual arrangement calling for the lessee to pay the lessor for use of an asset. Property, buildings and vehicles are common assets that are _____ d. Industrial or business equipment is also _____ d.

Exam Probability: **High**

49. *Answer choices:*

(see index for correct answer)

- a. Holder
- b. Lease
- c. Administration
- d. Partnership

Guidance: level 1

:: Commerce ::

_____ relates to "the exchange of goods and services, especially on a large scale". It includes legal, economic, political, social, cultural and technological systems that operate in a country or in international trade.

Exam Probability: **Low**

50. *Answer choices:*

(see index for correct answer)

- a. Staple right
- b. Reseller
- c. International Marketmakers Combination
- d. Factory

Guidance: level 1

:: ::

> Employment is a relationship between two parties, usually based on a contract where work is paid for, where one party, which may be a corporation, for profit, not-for-profit organization, co-operative or other entity is the employer and the other is the employee. Employees work in return for payment, which may be in the form of an hourly wage, by piecework or an annual salary, depending on the type of work an employee does or which sector she or he is working in. Employees in some fields or sectors may receive gratuities, bonus payment or stock options. In some types of employment, employees may receive benefits in addition to payment. Benefits can include health insurance, housing, disability insurance or use of a gym. Employment is typically governed by employment laws, regulations or legal contracts.

Exam Probability: **High**

51. *Answer choices:*

(see index for correct answer)

- a. Sarbanes-Oxley act of 2002
- b. surface-level diversity
- c. interpersonal communication
- d. Personnel

Guidance: level 1

:: ::

A _____ is monetary compensation paid by an employer to an employee in exchange for work done. Payment may be calculated as a fixed amount for each task completed, or at an hourly or daily rate, or based on an easily measured quantity of work done.

Exam Probability: **Low**

52. *Answer choices:*

(see index for correct answer)

- a. hierarchical
- b. surface-level diversity
- c. hierarchical perspective
- d. functional perspective

Guidance: level 1

:: ::

_____ Holdings, Inc. is an American company operating a worldwide online payments system that supports online money transfers and serves as an electronic alternative to traditional paper methods like checks and money orders. The company operates as a payment processor for online vendors, auction sites, and many other commercial users, for which it charges a fee in exchange for benefits such as one-click transactions and password memory. _____'s payment system, also called _____, is considered a type of payment rail.

Exam Probability: **High**

53. *Answer choices:*

(see index for correct answer)

- a. empathy
- b. cultural
- c. PayPal
- d. Sarbanes-Oxley act of 2002

Guidance: level 1

:: Manufacturing ::

A _____ is a building for storing goods. _____ s are used by manufacturers, importers, exporters, wholesalers, transport businesses, customs, etc. They are usually large plain buildings in industrial parks on the outskirts of cities, towns or villages.

Exam Probability: **Low**

54. *Answer choices:*

(see index for correct answer)

- a. Air bearing
- b. Kit-of-parts
- c. Discrete manufacturing

- d. Sewing

Guidance: level 1

:: ::

_____ is the extraction of valuable minerals or other geological materials from the earth, usually from an ore body, lode, vein, seam, reef or placer deposit. These deposits form a mineralized package that is of economic interest to the miner.

Exam Probability: **Low**

55. *Answer choices:*

(see index for correct answer)

- a. Mining
- b. personal values
- c. cultural
- d. process perspective

Guidance: level 1

:: Auctioneering ::

Unlike sealed-bid auctions, an _____ is "open" or fully transparent, as the identity of all bidders is disclosed to each other during the auction. More generally, an auction mechanism is considered "English" if it involves an iterative process of adjusting the price in a direction that is unfavorable to the bidders. In contrast, a Dutch auction would adjust the price in a direction that favored the bidders.

Exam Probability: **Medium**

56. *Answer choices:*

(see index for correct answer)

- a. Name Your Own Price
- b. Estate sale
- c. World Livestock Auctioneer Championship
- d. English auction

Guidance: level 1

:: ::

A _____ or GM is an executive who has overall responsibility for managing both the revenue and cost elements of a company's income statement, known as profit & loss responsibility. A _____ usually oversees most or all of the firm's marketing and sales functions as well as the day-to-day operations of the business. Frequently, the _____ is responsible for effective planning, delegating, coordinating, staffing, organizing, and decision making to attain desirable profit making results for an organization.

Exam Probability: **Medium**

57. *Answer choices:*

(see index for correct answer)

- a. process perspective
- b. deep-level diversity
- c. empathy
- d. imperative

Guidance: level 1

:: Market research ::

_____ is an organized effort to gather information about target markets or customers. It is a very important component of business strategy. The term is commonly interchanged with marketing research; however, expert practitioners may wish to draw a distinction, in that marketing research is concerned specifically about marketing processes, while _____ is concerned specifically with markets.

Exam Probability: **Low**

58. *Answer choices:*

(see index for correct answer)

- a. AttentionTracking
- b. Ad Tracking

- c. CoolBrands
- d. Market research

Guidance: level 1

:: ::

_____ is a concept of English common law and is a necessity for simple contracts but not for special contracts. The concept has been adopted by other common law jurisdictions, including the US.

Exam Probability: **Medium**

59. *Answer choices:*
(see index for correct answer)

- a. hierarchical perspective
- b. surface-level diversity
- c. process perspective
- d. Consideration

Guidance: level 1

Business ethics

Business ethics (also known as corporate ethics) is a form of applied ethics or professional ethics, that examines ethical principles and moral or ethical problems that can arise in a business environment. It applies to all aspects of business conduct and is relevant to the conduct of individuals and entire organizations. These ethics originate from individuals, organizational statements or from the legal system. These norms, values, ethical, and unethical practices are what is used to guide business. They help those businesses maintain a better connection with their stakeholders.

Revenge is a form of justice enacted in the absence or defiance of the norms of formal law and jurisprudence. Often, revenge is defined as being a harmful action against a person or group in response to a grievance, be it real or perceived. It is used to punish a wrong by going outside the law. Francis Bacon described revenge as a kind of "wild justice" that "does... offend the law [and] putteth the law out of office." Primitive justice or retributive justice is often differentiated from more formal and refined forms of justice such as distributive justice and divine judgment.

Exam Probability: **High**

1. *Answer choices:*

(see index for correct answer)

- a. co-culture
- b. cultural
- c. information systems assessment
- d. empathy

Guidance: level 1

:: False advertising law ::

The Lanham Act is the primary federal trademark statute of law in the United States. The Act prohibits a number of activities, including trademark infringement, trademark dilution, and false advertising.

Exam Probability: **Medium**

2. *Answer choices:*

(see index for correct answer)

- a. Rebecca Tushnet
- b. Lanham Act

Guidance: level 1

:: Cognitive biases ::

In personality psychology, _____ is the degree to which people believe that they have control over the outcome of events in their lives, as opposed to external forces beyond their control. Understanding of the concept was developed by Julian B. Rotter in 1954, and has since become an aspect of personality studies. A person's "locus" is conceptualized as internal or external.

Exam Probability: **Medium**

3. *Answer choices:*

(see index for correct answer)

- a. Picture superiority effect
- b. Telescoping effect
- c. Neglect of probability
- d. Familiarity heuristic

Guidance: level 1

:: ::

Cannabis, also known as _____ among other names, is a psychoactive drug from the Cannabis plant used for medical or recreational purposes. The main psychoactive part of cannabis is tetrahydrocannabinol, one of 483 known compounds in the plant, including at least 65 other cannabinoids. Cannabis can be used by smoking, vaporizing, within food, or as an extract.

Exam Probability: **Low**

4. *Answer choices:*

(see index for correct answer)

- a. cultural
- b. Marijuana
- c. information systems assessment
- d. levels of analysis

Guidance: level 1

:: White-collar criminals ::

_____ refers to financially motivated, nonviolent crime committed by businesses and government professionals. It was first defined by the sociologist Edwin Sutherland in 1939 as "a crime committed by a person of respectability and high social status in the course of their occupation". Typical _____ s could include wage theft, fraud, bribery, Ponzi schemes, insider trading, labor racketeering, embezzlement, cybercrime, copyright infringement, money laundering, identity theft, and forgery. Lawyers can specialize in _____ .

Exam Probability: **Medium**

5. *Answer choices:*

(see index for correct answer)

- a. White-collar crime
- b. Tongsun Park

Guidance: level 1

:: Private equity ::

In finance, a high-yield bond is a bond that is rated below investment grade. These bonds have a higher risk of default or other adverse credit events, but typically pay higher yields than better quality bonds in order to make them attractive to investors.

Exam Probability: **Low**

6. *Answer choices:*

(see index for correct answer)

- a. Junk bond
- b. Robin Hood Ventures
- c. Carried interest
- d. Earnout

Guidance: level 1

:: Carbon finance ::

The _____ is an international treaty which extends the 1992 United Nations Framework Convention on Climate Change that commits state parties to reduce greenhouse gas emissions, based on the scientific consensus that global warming is occurring and it is extremely likely that human-made CO_2 emissions have predominantly caused it. The _____ was adopted in Kyoto, Japan on 11 December 1997 and entered into force on 16 February 2005. There are currently 192 parties to the Protocol.

Exam Probability: **High**

7. *Answer choices:*

(see index for correct answer)

- a. Kyoto Protocol
- b. Marginal abatement cost
- c. Plant A Tree Today Foundation

- d. EcoAid

Guidance: level 1

:: Agricultural labor ::

The _____ of America, or more commonly just _____ , is a labor union for farmworkers in the United States. It originated from the merger of two workers' rights organizations, the Agricultural Workers Organizing Committee led by organizer Larry Itliong, and the National Farm Workers Association led by César Chávez and Dolores Huerta. They became allied and transformed from workers' rights organizations into a union as a result of a series of strikes in 1965, when the mostly Filipino farmworkers of the AWOC in Delano, California initiated a grape strike, and the NFWA went on strike in support. As a result of the commonality in goals and methods, the NFWA and the AWOC formed the _____ Organizing Committee on August 22, 1966. This organization was accepted into the AFL-CIO in 1972 and changed its name to the _____ Union.

Exam Probability: **Low**

8. *Answer choices:*
(see index for correct answer)

- a. H-2A Visa
- b. State Agricultural Farm
- c. Rural tenancy
- d. Subsistence agriculture

Guidance: level 1

:: ::

_____ is a region of India consisting of the Indian states of Bihar, Jharkhand, West Bengal, Odisha and also the union territory Andaman and Nicobar Islands. West Bengal's capital Kolkata is the largest city of this region. The Kolkata Metropolitan Area is the country's third largest.

Exam Probability: **Low**

9. *Answer choices:*

(see index for correct answer)

- a. levels of analysis
- b. functional perspective
- c. East India
- d. similarity-attraction theory

Guidance: level 1

:: Business ethics ::

The _____ are the names of two corporate codes of conduct, developed by the African-American preacher Rev. Leon Sullivan, promoting corporate social responsibility.

Exam Probability: **Medium**

10. *Answer choices:*

(see index for correct answer)

- a. Corporate Knights
- b. Anti-consumerism
- c. University of Illinois clout scandal
- d. Equator Principles

Guidance: level 1

:: ::

_____ in the United States is a federal and state program that helps with medical costs for some people with limited income and resources. _____ also offers benefits not normally covered by Medicare, including nursing home care and personal care services. The Health Insurance Association of America describes _____ as "a government insurance program for persons of all ages whose income and resources are insufficient to pay for health care." _____ is the largest source of funding for medical and health-related services for people with low income in the United States, providing free health insurance to 74 million low-income and disabled people as of 2017. It is a means-tested program that is jointly funded by the state and federal governments and managed by the states, with each state currently having broad leeway to determine who is eligible for its implementation of the program. States are not required to participate in the program, although all have since 1982. _____ recipients must be U.S. citizens or qualified non-citizens, and may include low-income adults, their children, and people with certain disabilities. Poverty alone does not necessarily qualify someone for _____ .

Exam Probability: **High**

11. *Answer choices:*

(see index for correct answer)

- a. Sarbanes-Oxley act of 2002
- b. open system
- c. Medicaid
- d. co-culture

Guidance: level 1

:: ::

The _____ is an 1848 political pamphlet by the German philosophers Karl Marx and Friedrich Engels. Commissioned by the Communist League and originally published in London just as the Revolutions of 1848 began to erupt, the Manifesto was later recognised as one of the world's most influential political documents. It presents an analytical approach to the class struggle and the conflicts of capitalism and the capitalist mode of production, rather than a prediction of communism's potential future forms.

Exam Probability: **Medium**

12. *Answer choices:*

(see index for correct answer)

- a. open system

- b. Communist Manifesto
- c. process perspective
- d. hierarchical perspective

Guidance: level 1

:: Management ::

The term _____ refers to measures designed to increase the degree of autonomy and self-determination in people and in communities in order to enable them to represent their interests in a responsible and self-determined way, acting on their own authority. It is the process of becoming stronger and more confident, especially in controlling one's life and claiming one's rights. _____ as action refers both to the process of self-_____ and to professional support of people, which enables them to overcome their sense of powerlessness and lack of influence, and to recognize and use their resources. To do work with power.

Exam Probability: **Medium**

13. *Answer choices:*

(see index for correct answer)

- a. Radical transparency
- b. Best current practice
- c. Court of Assistants
- d. Cross ownership

Guidance: level 1

:: Globalization-related theories ::

_____ is an economic system based on the private ownership of the means of production and their operation for profit. Characteristics central to _____ include private property, capital accumulation, wage labor, voluntary exchange, a price system, and competitive markets. In a capitalist market economy, decision-making and investment are determined by every owner of wealth, property or production ability in financial and capital markets, whereas prices and the distribution of goods and services are mainly determined by competition in goods and services markets.

Exam Probability: **Low**

14. *Answer choices:*

(see index for correct answer)

- a. postmodernism
- b. Economic Development
- c. Capitalism

Guidance: level 1

:: Utilitarianism ::

_____ is a school of thought that argues that the pursuit of pleasure and intrinsic goods are the primary or most important goals of human life. A hedonist strives to maximize net pleasure. However upon finally gaining said pleasure, happiness may remain stationary.

Exam Probability: **Low**

15. *Answer choices:*

(see index for correct answer)

- a. Informed judge
- b. Global Happiness Organization
- c. Utilitarianism
- d. The Collected Works of Jeremy Bentham

Guidance: level 1

:: ::

_____ is a private Dominican liberal arts college in Madison, Wisconsin. The college occupies a 55 acres campus overlooking the shores of Lake Wingra.

Exam Probability: **High**

16. *Answer choices:*

(see index for correct answer)

- a. Edgewood College
- b. personal values
- c. open system
- d. levels of analysis

Guidance: level 1

:: Fraud ::

In law, _____ is intentional deception to secure unfair or unlawful gain, or to deprive a victim of a legal right. _____ can violate civil law, a criminal law, or it may cause no loss of money, property or legal right but still be an element of another civil or criminal wrong. The purpose of _____ may be monetary gain or other benefits, for example by obtaining a passport, travel document, or driver's license, or mortgage _____, where the perpetrator may attempt to qualify for a mortgage by way of false statements.

Exam Probability: **High**

17. *Answer choices:*
(see index for correct answer)

- a. Missing trader fraud
- b. Unconscious fraud
- c. Corporate scandal
- d. Fraud

Guidance: level 1

:: ::

_____ is the practice of deliberately managing the spread of information between an individual or an organization and the public. _____ may include an organization or individual gaining exposure to their audiences using topics of public interest and news items that do not require direct payment. This differentiates it from advertising as a form of marketing communications. _____ is the idea of creating coverage for clients for free, rather than marketing or advertising. But now, advertising is also a part of greater PR Activities. An example of good _____ would be generating an article featuring a client, rather than paying for the client to be advertised next to the article. The aim of _____ is to inform the public, prospective customers, investors, partners, employees, and other stakeholders and ultimately persuade them to maintain a positive or favorable view about the organization, its leadership, products, or political decisions. _____ professionals typically work for PR and marketing firms, businesses and companies, government, and public officials as PIOs and nongovernmental organizations, and nonprofit organizations. Jobs central to _____ include account coordinator, account executive, account supervisor, and media relations manager.

Exam Probability: **Medium**

18. *Answer choices:*

(see index for correct answer)

- a. information systems assessment
- b. Public relations
- c. Character

- d. surface-level diversity

Guidance: level 1

:: ::

The _____ of 1906 was the first of a series of significant consumer protection laws which was enacted by Congress in the 20th century and led to the creation of the Food and Drug Administration. Its main purpose was to ban foreign and interstate traffic in adulterated or mislabeled food and drug products, and it directed the U.S. Bureau of Chemistry to inspect products and refer offenders to prosecutors. It required that active ingredients be placed on the label of a drug's packaging and that drugs could not fall below purity levels established by the United States Pharmacopeia or the National Formulary. The Jungle by Upton Sinclair with its graphic and revolting descriptions of unsanitary conditions and unscrupulous practices rampant in the meatpacking industry, was an inspirational piece that kept the public's attention on the important issue of unhygienic meat processing plants that later led to food inspection legislation. Sinclair quipped, "I aimed at the public's heart and by accident I hit it in the stomach," as outraged readers demanded and got the pure food law.

Exam Probability: **Low**

19. *Answer choices:*

(see index for correct answer)

- a. open system
- b. personal values
- c. similarity-attraction theory

- d. cultural

Guidance: level 1

:: ::

_____ Corporation was an American energy, commodities, and services company based in Houston, Texas. It was founded in 1985 as a merger between Houston Natural Gas and InterNorth, both relatively small regional companies. Before its bankruptcy on December 3, 2001, _____ employed approximately 29,000 staff and was a major electricity, natural gas, communications and pulp and paper company, with claimed revenues of nearly $101 billion during 2000. Fortune named _____ "America's Most Innovative Company" for six consecutive years.

Exam Probability: **Medium**

20. *Answer choices:*

(see index for correct answer)

- a. information systems assessment
- b. Enron
- c. process perspective
- d. imperative

Guidance: level 1

:: United States federal labor legislation ::

The _____ of 1988 is a United States federal law that generally prevents employers from using polygraph tests, either for pre-employment screening or during the course of employment, with certain exemptions.

Exam Probability: **Low**

21. *Answer choices:*
(see index for correct answer)

- a. Employment Act of 1946
- b. Erdman Act
- c. Title 29 of the United States Code
- d. Alien Contract Labor Law

Guidance: level 1

:: Business ethics ::

A _____ is a person who exposes any kind of information or activity that is deemed illegal, unethical, or not correct within an organization that is either private or public. The information of alleged wrongdoing can be classified in many ways: violation of company policy/rules, law, regulation, or threat to public interest/national security, as well as fraud, and corruption. Those who become _____ s can choose to bring information or allegations to surface either internally or externally. Internally, a _____ can bring his/her accusations to the attention of other people within the accused organization such as an immediate supervisor. Externally, a _____ can bring allegations to light by contacting a third party outside of an accused organization such as the media, government, law enforcement, or those who are concerned. _____ s, however, take the risk of facing stiff reprisal and retaliation from those who are accused or alleged of wrongdoing.

Exam Probability: **Low**

22. *Answer choices:*

(see index for correct answer)

- a. Society of Corporate Compliance and Ethics
- b. Business and Professional Ethics Journal
- c. Accounting ethics
- d. Whistleblower

Guidance: level 1

:: ::

In ecology, a _____ is the type of natural environment in which a particular species of organism lives. It is characterized by both physical and biological features. A species' _____ is those places where it can find food, shelter, protection and mates for reproduction.

Exam Probability: **High**

23. *Answer choices:*

(see index for correct answer)

- a. Sarbanes-Oxley act of 2002
- b. hierarchical
- c. Habitat
- d. process perspective

Guidance: level 1

:: ::

The _____ Group is a global financial investment management and insurance company headquartered in Des Moines, Iowa.

Exam Probability: **Low**

24. *Answer choices:*

(see index for correct answer)

- a. levels of analysis
- b. hierarchical perspective
- c. Character
- d. Sarbanes-Oxley act of 2002

Guidance: level 1

:: Confidence tricks ::

A _____ is a business model that recruits members via a promise of payments or services for enrolling others into the scheme, rather than supplying investments or sale of products. As recruiting multiplies, recruiting becomes quickly impossible, and most members are unable to profit; as such, _____ s are unsustainable and often illegal.

Exam Probability: **High**

25. *Answer choices:*

(see index for correct answer)

- a. Blessing scam
- b. Patent safe
- c. Fortune telling fraud
- d. Pyramid scheme

Guidance: level 1

Bernard Lawrence _____ is an American former market maker, investment advisor, financier, fraudster, and convicted felon, who is currently serving a federal prison sentence for offenses related to a massive Ponzi scheme. He is the former non-executive chairman of the NASDAQ stock market, the confessed operator of the largest Ponzi scheme in world history, and the largest financial fraud in U.S. history. Prosecutors estimated the fraud to be worth $64.8 billion based on the amounts in the accounts of _____ 's 4,800 clients as of November 30, 2008.

Exam Probability: **High**

26. *Answer choices:*

(see index for correct answer)

- a. Character
- b. deep-level diversity
- c. Madoff
- d. interpersonal communication

Guidance: level 1

An _____ is the release of a liquid petroleum hydrocarbon into the environment, especially the marine ecosystem, due to human activity, and is a form of pollution. The term is usually given to marine _____ s, where oil is released into the ocean or coastal waters, but spills may also occur on land. _____ s may be due to releases of crude oil from tankers, offshore platforms, drilling rigs and wells, as well as spills of refined petroleum products and their by-products, heavier fuels used by large ships such as bunker fuel, or the spill of any oily refuse or waste oil.

Exam Probability: **Low**

27. *Answer choices:*

(see index for correct answer)

- a. imperative
- b. cultural
- c. Character
- d. interpersonal communication

Guidance: level 1

:: Leadership ::

_____ is a theory of leadership where a leader works with teams to identify needed change, creating a vision to guide the change through inspiration, and executing the change in tandem with committed members of a group; it is an integral part of the Full Range Leadership Model. _____ serves to enhance the motivation, morale, and job performance of followers through a variety of mechanisms; these include connecting the follower's sense of identity and self to a project and to the collective identity of the organization; being a role model for followers in order to inspire them and to raise their interest in the project; challenging followers to take greater ownership for their work, and understanding the strengths and weaknesses of followers, allowing the leader to align followers with tasks that enhance their performance.

Exam Probability: **Medium**

28. *Answer choices:*

(see index for correct answer)

- a. Love leadership
- b. Transactional leadership
- c. Agentic leadership
- d. Transformational leadership

Guidance: level 1

:: Separation of investment and commercial banking ::

The _____ refers to § 619 of the Dodd–Frank Wall Street Reform and Consumer Protection Act. The rule was originally proposed by American economist and former United States Federal Reserve Chairman Paul Volcker to restrict United States banks from making certain kinds of speculative investments that do not benefit their customers. Volcker argued that such speculative activity played a key role in the financial crisis of 2007–2008. The rule is often referred to as a ban on proprietary trading by commercial banks, whereby deposits are used to trade on the bank's own accounts, although a number of exceptions to this ban were included in the Dodd-Frank law.

Exam Probability: **Medium**

29. *Answer choices:*

(see index for correct answer)

- a. investment bank
- b. Bank Holding Company Act
- c. Volcker Rule
- d. Independent Commission on Banking

Guidance: level 1

:: Business ethics ::

_____ is a type of international private business self-regulation. While once it was possible to describe CSR as an internal organisational policy or a corporate ethic strategy, that time has passed as various international laws have been developed and various organisations have used their authority to push it beyond individual or even industry-wide initiatives. While it has been considered a form of corporate self-regulation for some time, over the last decade or so it has moved considerably from voluntary decisions at the level of individual organisations, to mandatory schemes at regional, national and even transnational levels.

Exam Probability: **Medium**

30. *Answer choices:*

(see index for correct answer)

- a. Corporate social responsibility
- b. Product stewardship
- c. Interfaith Center on Corporate Responsibility
- d. Symantec

Guidance: level 1

:: Renewable energy ::

_____ is the conversion of energy from sunlight into electricity, either directly using photovoltaics , indirectly using concentrated _____ , or a combination. Concentrated _____ systems use lenses or mirrors and tracking systems to focus a large area of sunlight into a small beam. Photovoltaic cells convert light into an electric current using the photovoltaic effect.

Exam Probability: **High**

31. *Answer choices:*

(see index for correct answer)

- a. Solar power
- b. Yield co
- c. Wildpoldsried
- d. National Solar Conference and World Renewable Energy Forum 2012

Guidance: level 1

:: ::

The _____ is an agency of the United States Department of Labor. Congress established the agency under the Occupational Safety and Health Act, which President Richard M. Nixon signed into law on December 29, 1970. OSHA's mission is to "assure safe and healthy working conditions for working men and women by setting and enforcing standards and by providing training, outreach, education and assistance". The agency is also charged with enforcing a variety of whistleblower statutes and regulations. OSHA is currently headed by Acting Assistant Secretary of Labor Loren Sweatt. OSHA's workplace safety inspections have been shown to reduce injury rates and injury costs without adverse effects to employment, sales, credit ratings, or firm survival.

Exam Probability: **High**

32. *Answer choices:*

(see index for correct answer)

- a. functional perspective
- b. hierarchical perspective
- c. Occupational Safety and Health Administration
- d. co-culture

Guidance: level 1

:: Advertising techniques ::

The _____ is a story from the Trojan War about the subterfuge that the Greeks used to enter the independent city of Troy and win the war. In the canonical version, after a fruitless 10-year siege, the Greeks constructed a huge wooden horse, and hid a select force of men inside including Odysseus. The Greeks pretended to sail away, and the Trojans pulled the horse into their city as a victory trophy. That night the Greek force crept out of the horse and opened the gates for the rest of the Greek army, which had sailed back under cover of night. The Greeks entered and destroyed the city of Troy, ending the war.

Exam Probability: **High**

33. *Answer choices:*

(see index for correct answer)

- a. Roll-in
- b. Trojan horse
- c. FAST marketing
- d. Below the line

Guidance: level 1

:: Electronic waste ::

_____ or e-waste describes discarded electrical or electronic devices. Used electronics which are destined for refurbishment, reuse, resale, salvage, recycling through material recovery, or disposal are also considered e-waste. Informal processing of e-waste in developing countries can lead to adverse human health effects and environmental pollution.

Exam Probability: **Low**

34. *Answer choices:*

(see index for correct answer)

- a. Computer liquidator
- b. Electronic waste
- c. World Reuse, Repair and Recycling Association
- d. ReGlobe

Guidance: level 1

:: ::

_____ refers to a business initiative to increase the access between a company and their current and potential customers through the use of the Internet. The Internet allows the company to market themselves and attract new customers to their website where they can provide product information and better customer service. Customers can place orders electronically, therefore reducing expensive long distant phone calls and postage costs of placing orders, while saving time on behalf of the customer and company.

Exam Probability: **Medium**

35. *Answer choices:*

(see index for correct answer)

- a. hierarchical perspective

- b. process perspective
- c. Global reach
- d. Sarbanes-Oxley act of 2002

Guidance: level 1

:: ::

The _____ of 1977 is a United States federal law known primarily for two of its main provisions: one that addresses accounting transparency requirements under the Securities Exchange Act of 1934 and another concerning bribery of foreign officials. The Act was amended in 1988 and in 1998, and has been subject to continued congressional concerns, namely whether its enforcement discourages U.S. companies from investing abroad.

Exam Probability: **Medium**

36. *Answer choices:*

(see index for correct answer)

- a. information systems assessment
- b. hierarchical
- c. personal values
- d. Foreign Corrupt Practices Act

Guidance: level 1

:: Water law ::

The _____ is the primary federal law in the United States governing water pollution. Its objective is to restore and maintain the chemical, physical, and biological integrity of the nation's waters; recognizing the responsibilities of the states in addressing pollution and providing assistance to states to do so, including funding for publicly owned treatment works for the improvement of wastewater treatment; and maintaining the integrity of wetlands. It is one of the United States' first and most influential modern environmental laws. As with many other major U.S. federal environmental statutes, it is administered by the U.S. Environmental Protection Agency , in coordination with state governments. Its implementing regulations are codified at 40 C.F.R. Subchapters D, N, and O .

Exam Probability: **High**

37. *Answer choices:*

(see index for correct answer)

- a. Water law
- b. Return flow
- c. Water quality law
- d. Clean Water Act

Guidance: level 1

:: ::

A _____ is an astronomical body orbiting a star or stellar remnant that is massive enough to be rounded by its own gravity, is not massive enough to cause thermonuclear fusion, and has cleared its neighbouring region of _____ esimals.

Exam Probability: **Low**

38. *Answer choices:*
(see index for correct answer)

- a. Character
- b. Planet
- c. corporate values
- d. deep-level diversity

Guidance: level 1

:: Parental leave ::

_____, or family leave, is an employee benefit available in almost all countries. The term "_____" may include maternity, paternity, and adoption leave; or may be used distinctively from "maternity leave" and "paternity leave" to describe separate family leave available to either parent to care for small children. In some countries and jurisdictions, "family leave" also includes leave provided to care for ill family members. Often, the minimum benefits and eligibility requirements are stipulated by law.

Exam Probability: **Medium**

39. *Answer choices:*

(see index for correct answer)

- a. Parental leave
- b. Geduldig v. Aiello
- c. Parental leave economics
- d. Pregnant Workers Directive

Guidance: level 1

:: Dutch inventions ::

The Fairtrade certification initiative was created to form a new method for economic trade. This method takes an ethical standpoint, and considers the producers first.

Exam Probability: **Medium**

40. *Answer choices:*

(see index for correct answer)

- a. Dijkstra's algorithm
- b. Fair Trade Certified

Guidance: level 1

:: Leadership ::

_____ is leadership that is directed by respect for ethical beliefs and values and for the dignity and rights of others. It is thus related to concepts such as trust, honesty, consideration, charisma, and fairness.

Exam Probability: **Medium**

41. *Answer choices:*

(see index for correct answer)

- a. Evolutionary leadership theory
- b. Motivational Leadership
- c. Ethical leadership
- d. Situational leadership theory

Guidance: level 1

:: Offshoring ::

A _____ is the temporary suspension or permanent termination of employment of an employee or, more commonly, a group of employees for business reasons, such as personnel management or downsizing an organization. Originally, _____ referred exclusively to a temporary interruption in work, or employment but this has evolved to a permanent elimination of a position in both British and US English, requiring the addition of "temporary" to specify the original meaning of the word. A _____ is not to be confused with wrongful termination. Laid off workers or displaced workers are workers who have lost or left their jobs because their employer has closed or moved, there was insufficient work for them to do, or their position or shift was abolished. Downsizing in a company is defined to involve the reduction of employees in a workforce. Downsizing in companies became a popular practice in the 1980s and early 1990s as it was seen as a way to deliver better shareholder value as it helps to reduce the costs of employers. Indeed, recent research on downsizing in the U.S., UK, and Japan suggests that downsizing is being regarded by management as one of the preferred routes to help declining organizations, cutting unnecessary costs, and improve organizational performance. Usually a _____ occurs as a cost cutting measure.

Exam Probability: **High**

42. *Answer choices:*

(see index for correct answer)

- a. Offshore custom software development
- b. Layoff
- c. Global labor arbitrage
- d. Sourcing advisory

Guidance: level 1

:: United States federal trade legislation ::

The _____ of 1914 established the Federal Trade Commission. The Act, signed into law by Woodrow Wilson in 1914, outlaws unfair methods of competition and outlaws unfair acts or practices that affect commerce.

Exam Probability: **High**

43. *Answer choices:*

(see index for correct answer)

- a. Non-Intercourse Act
- b. Act to Protect the Commerce of the United States and Punish the Crime of Piracy
- c. Bell Trade Act
- d. Federal Trade Commission Act

Guidance: level 1

:: ::

_____ is the introduction of contaminants into the natural environment that cause adverse change. _____ can take the form of chemical substances or energy, such as noise, heat or light. Pollutants, the components of _____ , can be either foreign substances/energies or naturally occurring contaminants. _____ is often classed as point source or nonpoint source _____ .In 2015, _____ killed 9 million people in the world.

Exam Probability: **Low**

44. *Answer choices:*

(see index for correct answer)

- a. deep-level diversity
- b. Pollution
- c. surface-level diversity
- d. process perspective

Guidance: level 1

:: Television terminology ::

A _____ organization, also known as a non-business entity, not-for-profit organization, or _____ institution, is dedicated to furthering a particular social cause or advocating for a shared point of view. In economic terms, it is an organization that uses its surplus of the revenues to further achieve its ultimate objective, rather than distributing its income to the organization's shareholders, leaders, or members. _____ s are tax exempt or charitable, meaning they do not pay income tax on the money that they receive for their organization. They can operate in religious, scientific, research, or educational settings.

Exam Probability: **Low**

45. *Answer choices:*

(see index for correct answer)

- a. Satellite television
- b. not-for-profit
- c. distance learning
- d. multiplexing

Guidance: level 1

:: Waste ::

_____ is any unwanted material in all forms that can cause harm. Many of today's household products such as televisions, computers and phones contain toxic chemicals that can pollute the air and contaminate soil and water. Disposing of such waste is a major public health issue.

Exam Probability: **Low**

46. *Answer choices:*

(see index for correct answer)

- a. Toxic waste
- b. Abandoned footwear
- c. Metabolic waste
- d. Green waste

Guidance: level 1

:: ::

A _____ is the ability to carry out a task with determined results often within a given amount of time, energy, or both. _____ s can often be divided into domain-general and domain-specific _____ s. For example, in the domain of work, some general _____ s would include time management, teamwork and leadership, self-motivation and others, whereas domain-specific _____ s would be used only for a certain job. _____ usually requires certain environmental stimuli and situations to assess the level of _____ being shown and used.

Exam Probability: **Medium**

47. *Answer choices:*

(see index for correct answer)

- a. cultural
- b. imperative
- c. Skill
- d. similarity-attraction theory

Guidance: level 1

:: Corporate governance ::

_____ refers to the practice of members of a corporate board of directors serving on the boards of multiple corporations. A person that sits on multiple boards is known as a multiple director. Two firms have a direct interlock if a director or executive of one firm is also a director of the other, and an indirect interlock if a director of each sits on the board of a third firm. This practice, although widespread and lawful, raises questions about the quality and independence of board decisions.

Exam Probability: **Low**

48. *Answer choices:*

(see index for correct answer)

- a. The Samuel and Ronnie Heyman Center on Corporate Governance
- b. Digital strategy manager
- c. Interlocking directorate
- d. Compliance Ireland

Guidance: level 1

:: ::

_____ is the collection of mechanisms, processes and relations by which corporations are controlled and operated. Governance structures and principles identify the distribution of rights and responsibilities among different participants in the corporation and include the rules and procedures for making decisions in corporate affairs. _____ is necessary because of the possibility of conflicts of interests between stakeholders, primarily between shareholders and upper management or among shareholders.

49. *Answer choices:*

(see index for correct answer)

- a. Corporate governance
- b. co-culture
- c. levels of analysis
- d. similarity-attraction theory

Guidance: level 1

:: Reputation management ::

_____ or image of a social entity is an opinion about that entity, typically as a result of social evaluation on a set of criteria.

Exam Probability: **Medium**

50. *Answer choices:*

(see index for correct answer)

- a. Yasni
- b. Reputation
- c. Advogato
- d. Get Satisfaction

Guidance: level 1

:: Workplace ::

In business management, _____ is a management style whereby a manager closely observes and/or controls the work of his/her subordinates or employees.

Exam Probability: **Low**

51. *Answer choices:*
(see index for correct answer)

- a. Micromanagement
- b. Workplace wellness
- c. Rat race
- d. Feminisation of the workplace

Guidance: level 1

:: Social philosophy ::

The "_____" is a method of determining the morality of issues. It asks a decision-maker to make a choice about a social or moral issue, and assumes that they have enough information to know the consequences of their possible decisions for everyone but would not know, or would not take into account, which person he or she is. The theory contends that not knowing one's ultimate position in society would lead to the creation of a just system, as the decision-maker would not want to make decisions which benefit a certain group at the expense of another, because the decision-maker could theoretically end up in either group. The idea has been present in moral philosophy at least since the eighteenth century. The _____ is part of a long tradition of thinking in terms of a social contract that includes the writings of Immanuel Kant, Thomas Hobbes, John Locke, Jean Jacques Rousseau, and Thomas Jefferson. Prominent modern names attached to it are John Harsanyi and John Rawls.

Exam Probability: **High**

52. *Answer choices:*

(see index for correct answer)

- a. vacancy chain
- b. Societal attitudes towards abortion
- c. Veil of ignorance
- d. Freedom to contract

Guidance: level 1

_____ generally refers to a focus on the needs or desires of one's self. A number of philosophical, psychological, and economic theories examine the role of _____ in motivating human action.

Exam Probability: **High**

53. *Answer choices:*

(see index for correct answer)

- a. Character
- b. personal values
- c. Self-interest
- d. functional perspective

Guidance: level 1

:: ::

Competition law is a law that promotes or seeks to maintain market competition by regulating anti-competitive conduct by companies. Competition law is implemented through public and private enforcement. Competition law is known as "_____ law" in the United States for historical reasons, and as "anti-monopoly law" in China and Russia. In previous years it has been known as trade practices law in the United Kingdom and Australia. In the European Union, it is referred to as both _____ and competition law.

Exam Probability: **Low**

54. Answer choices:

(see index for correct answer)

- a. Antitrust
- b. imperative
- c. levels of analysis
- d. hierarchical

Guidance: level 1

:: Natural gas ::

_____ is a naturally occurring hydrocarbon gas mixture consisting primarily of methane, but commonly including varying amounts of other higher alkanes, and sometimes a small percentage of carbon dioxide, nitrogen, hydrogen sulfide, or helium. It is formed when layers of decomposing plant and animal matter are exposed to intense heat and pressure under the surface of the Earth over millions of years. The energy that the plants originally obtained from the sun is stored in the form of chemical bonds in the gas.

Exam Probability: **Low**

55. Answer choices:

(see index for correct answer)

- a. Renewable natural gas
- b. Wet gas
- c. Retrograde condensation

- d. Associated petroleum gas

Guidance: level 1

:: Socialism ::

_____ is a label used to define the first currents of modern socialist thought as exemplified by the work of Henri de Saint-Simon, Charles Fourier, Étienne Cabet and Robert Owen.

Exam Probability: **Medium**

56. *Answer choices:*

(see index for correct answer)

- a. Utopian socialism
- b. Production for use
- c. Socialization
- d. Kim Se-jin

Guidance: level 1

:: Culture ::

_____ is a society which is characterized by individualism, which is the prioritization or emphasis, of the individual over the entire group. _____ s are oriented around the self, being independent instead of identifying with a group mentality. They see each other as only loosely linked, and value personal goals over group interests. _____ s tend to have a more diverse population and are characterized with emphasis on personal achievements, and a rational assessment of both the beneficial and detrimental aspects of relationships with others. _____ s have such unique aspects of communication as being a low power-distance culture and having a low-context communication style. The United States, Australia, Great Britain, Canada, the Netherlands, and New Zealand have been identified as highly _____ s.

Exam Probability: **High**

57. *Answer choices:*
(see index for correct answer)

- a. Low-context culture
- b. cultural framework
- c. Intracultural
- d. High-context

Guidance: level 1

:: Financial regulatory authorities of the United States ::

The _____ is an agency of the United States government responsible for consumer protection in the financial sector. CFPB's jurisdiction includes banks, credit unions, securities firms, payday lenders, mortgage-servicing operations, foreclosure relief services, debt collectors and other financial companies operating in the United States.

Exam Probability: **Low**

58. *Answer choices:*

(see index for correct answer)

- a. Consumer Financial Protection Bureau
- b. Commodity Futures Trading Commission
- c. Federal Reserve Board
- d. Operation Choke Point

Guidance: level 1

:: Trade unions ::

A _____ was a group formed of private citizens to administer law and order where they considered governmental structures to be inadequate. The term is commonly associated with the frontier areas of the American West in the mid-19th century, where groups attacked cattle rustlers and gangs, and people at gold mining claims. As non-state organizations no functioning checks existed to protect against excessive force or safeguard due process from the committees. In the years prior to the Civil War, some committees worked to free slaves and transport them to freedom.

Exam Probability: **High**

59. *Answer choices:*

(see index for correct answer)

- a. Vigilance committee
- b. LabourStart
- c. Service model
- d. Local union

Guidance: level 1

Accounting

Accounting or accountancy is the measurement, processing, and communication of financial information about economic entities such as businesses and corporations. The modern field was established by the Italian mathematician Luca Pacioli in 1494. Accounting, which has been called the "language of business", measures the results of an organization's economic activities and conveys this information to a variety of users, including investors, creditors, management, and regulators.

:: Management accounting ::

_____ is a managerial accounting cost concept. Under this method, manufacturing overhead is incurred in the period that a product is produced. This addresses the issue of absorption costing that allows income to rise as production rises. Under an absorption cost method, management can push forward costs to the next period when products are sold. This artificially inflates profits in the period of production by incurring less cost than would be incurred under a _____ system. _____ is generally not used for external reporting purposes. Under the Tax Reform Act of 1986, income statements must use absorption costing to comply with GAAP.

Exam Probability: **High**

1. *Answer choices:*

(see index for correct answer)

- a. Fixed assets management
- b. Dual overhead rate
- c. Investment center
- d. Variable Costing

Guidance: level 1

_____ or accountancy is the measurement, processing, and communication of financial information about economic entities such as businesses and corporations. The modern field was established by the Italian mathematician Luca Pacioli in 1494. _____ , which has been called the "language of business", measures the results of an organization's economic activities and conveys this information to a variety of users, including investors, creditors, management, and regulators. Practitioners of _____ are known as accountants. The terms "_____" and "financial reporting" are often used as synonyms.

Exam Probability: **Medium**

2. *Answer choices:*

(see index for correct answer)

- a. Accounting
- b. personal values
- c. Sarbanes-Oxley act of 2002
- d. functional perspective

Guidance: level 1

:: Credit cards ::

The _____ Company, also known as Amex, is an American multinational financial services corporation headquartered in Three World Financial Center in New York City. The company was founded in 1850 and is one of the 30 components of the Dow Jones Industrial Average. The company is best known for its charge card, credit card, and traveler's cheque businesses.

Exam Probability: **High**

3. *Answer choices:*

(see index for correct answer)

- a. NexG PrePaid
- b. American Express
- c. Palladium Card
- d. Japan Credit Bureau

Guidance: level 1

:: Accounting in the United States ::

The _____ is a private-sector, nonprofit corporation created by the Sarbanes–Oxley Act of 2002 to oversee the audits of public companies and other issuers in order to protect the interests of investors and further the public interest in the preparation of informative, accurate and independent audit reports. The PCAOB also oversees the audits of broker-dealers, including compliance reports filed pursuant to federal securities laws, to promote investor protection. All PCAOB rules and standards must be approved by the U.S. Securities and Exchange Commission .

Exam Probability: **Low**

4. *Answer choices:*

(see index for correct answer)

- a. Comprehensive Performance Assessment
- b. International Qualification Examination
- c. Adjusted basis
- d. Accounting Today

Guidance: level 1

:: Finance ::

_____, in finance and accounting, means stated value or face value. From this come the expressions at par, over par and under par.

Exam Probability: **High**

5. *Answer choices:*
(see index for correct answer)

- a. Par value
- b. Fixed liability
- c. Nanex
- d. Pecking order

Guidance: level 1

:: Debt ::

A _____ is a monetary amount owed to a creditor that is unlikely to be paid and, or which the creditor is not willing to take action to collect for various reasons, often due to the debtor not having the money to pay, for example due to a company going into liquidation or insolvency. There are various technical definitions of what constitutes a _____ , depending on accounting conventions, regulatory treatment and the institution provisioning. In the USA, bank loans with more than ninety days` arrears become "problem loans". Accounting sources advise that the full amount of a _____ be written off to the profit and loss account or a provision for _____ s as soon as it is foreseen.

Exam Probability: **Low**

6. *Answer choices:*

(see index for correct answer)

- a. Vulture fund
- b. Crown debt
- c. Bad debt
- d. Rule of 72

Guidance: level 1

:: Management accounting ::

An _____ allows a company to provide a monetary value for items that make up their inventory. Inventories are usually the largest current asset of a business, and proper measurement of them is necessary to assure accurate financial statements. If inventory is not properly measured, expenses and revenues cannot be properly matched and a company could make poor business decisions.

Exam Probability: **Medium**

7. *Answer choices:*

(see index for correct answer)

- a. Inventory valuation
- b. Target costing
- c. Overhead
- d. Average per-bit delivery cost

Guidance: level 1

:: Management ::

Business _____ is a discipline in operations management in which people use various methods to discover, model, analyze, measure, improve, optimize, and automate business processes. BPM focuses on improving corporate performance by managing business processes. Any combination of methods used to manage a company's business processes is BPM. Processes can be structured and repeatable or unstructured and variable. Though not required, enabling technologies are often used with BPM.

Exam Probability: **Medium**

8. *Answer choices:*

(see index for correct answer)

- a. IT performance management
- b. Process Management
- c. Project management information system
- d. Business chess

Guidance: level 1

:: Financial ratios ::

_____ is the difference between revenue and cost of goods sold divided by revenue. _____ is expressed as a percentage. Generally, it is calculated as the selling price of an item, less the cost of goods sold .
_____ is often used interchangeably with Gross Profit, but the terms are different. When speaking about a monetary amount, it is technically correct to use the term Gross Profit; when referring to a percentage or ratio, it is correct to use _____ . In other words, _____ is a percentage value, while Gross Profit is a monetary value.

Exam Probability: **High**

9. *Answer choices:*

(see index for correct answer)

- a. Dividend yield
- b. Operating margin
- c. DuPont analysis
- d. Gross margin

Guidance: level 1

:: ::

_____ is the income that is gained by governments through taxation. Taxation is the primary source of income for a state. Revenue may be extracted from sources such as individuals, public enterprises, trade, royalties on natural resources and/or foreign aid. An inefficient collection of taxes is greater in countries characterized by poverty, a large agricultural sector and large amounts of foreign aid.

Exam Probability: **Low**

10. *Answer choices:*
(see index for correct answer)

- a. Sarbanes-Oxley act of 2002
- b. process perspective
- c. Tax revenue
- d. interpersonal communication

Guidance: level 1

:: Accounting source documents ::

An _____, bill or tab is a commercial document issued by a seller to a buyer, relating to a sale transaction and indicating the products, quantities, and agreed prices for products or services the seller had provided the buyer.

Exam Probability: **Low**

11. *Answer choices:*
(see index for correct answer)

- a. Parcel audit
- b. Purchase order
- c. Air waybill
- d. Bank statement

Guidance: level 1

:: Business models ::

A _____ is a company that owns enough voting stock in another firm to control management and operation by influencing or electing its board of directors. The company is deemed a subsidiary of the _____ .

Exam Probability: **Low**

12. Answer choices:

(see index for correct answer)

- a. Very small business
- b. Business Model Canvas
- c. Dependent growth business model
- d. Parent company

Guidance: level 1

:: Management accounting ::

A _____ is a cost that differs between alternatives being considered. In order for a cost to be a _____ it must be.

Exam Probability: **High**

13. Answer choices:

(see index for correct answer)

- a. Pre-determined overhead rate
- b. Entity-level controls
- c. Relevant cost
- d. Environmental full-cost accounting

Guidance: level 1

:: ::

From an accounting perspective, _____ is crucial because _____ and _____ taxes considerably affect the net income of most companies and because they are subject to laws and regulations.

Exam Probability: **Medium**

14. *Answer choices:*

(see index for correct answer)

- a. Payroll
- b. imperative
- c. levels of analysis
- d. process perspective

Guidance: level 1

:: Real estate valuation ::

_____ or OMV is the price at which an asset would trade in a competitive auction setting. _____ is often used interchangeably with open _____, fair value or fair _____, although these terms have distinct definitions in different standards, and may or may not differ in some circumstances.

Exam Probability: **Low**

15. *Answer choices:*

(see index for correct answer)

- a. Days on market
- b. E.surv
- c. Market value
- d. Broker%27s Price Opinion

Guidance: level 1

:: ::

In production, research, retail, and accounting, a _____ is the value of money that has been used up to produce something or deliver a service, and hence is not available for use anymore. In business, the _____ may be one of acquisition, in which case the amount of money expended to acquire it is counted as _____ . In this case, money is the input that is gone in order to acquire the thing. This acquisition _____ may be the sum of the _____ of production as incurred by the original producer, and further _____ s of transaction as incurred by the acquirer over and above the price paid to the producer. Usually, the price also includes a mark-up for profit over the _____ of production.

Exam Probability: **High**

16. *Answer choices:*

(see index for correct answer)

- a. Cost
- b. deep-level diversity
- c. process perspective
- d. hierarchical perspective

Guidance: level 1

:: Taxation ::

_____ refers to the base upon which an income tax system imposes tax. Generally, it includes some or all items of income and is reduced by expenses and other deductions. The amounts included as income, expenses, and other deductions vary by country or system. Many systems provide that some types of income are not taxable and some expenditures not deductible in computing _____. Some systems base tax on _____ of the current period, and some on prior periods. _____ may refer to the income of any taxpayer, including individuals and corporations, as well as entities that themselves do not pay tax, such as partnerships, in which case it may be called "net profit".

Exam Probability: **Medium**

17. *Answer choices:*

(see index for correct answer)

- a. Virtual tax
- b. Tax cut
- c. Sales tax token
- d. Hotchpot

Guidance: level 1

:: Corporate governance ::

The _____ is the officer of a company that has primary responsibility for managing the company's finances, including financial planning, management of financial risks, record-keeping, and financial reporting. In some sectors, the CFO is also responsible for analysis of data. Some CFOs have the title CFOO for chief financial and operating officer. In the United Kingdom, the typical term for a CFO is finance director . The CFO typically reports to the chief executive officer and the board of directors and may additionally have a seat on the board. The CFO supervises the finance unit and is the chief financial spokesperson for the organization. The CFO directly assists the chief operating officer on all strategic and tactical matters relating to budget management, cost–benefit analysis, forecasting needs, and securing of new funding.

Exam Probability: **High**

18. *Answer choices:*

(see index for correct answer)

- a. Yasser Akkaoui
- b. Proxy firm
- c. Chief financial officer
- d. Partnership limited by shares

Guidance: level 1

:: Business law ::

The expression " _____ " is somewhat confusing as it has a different meaning based on the context that is under consideration. From a product characteristic stand point, this type of a lease, as distinguished from a finance lease, is one where the lessor takes residual risk. As such, the lease is non full payout. From an accounting stand point, this type of lease results in off balance sheet financing.

Exam Probability: **Low**

19. *Answer choices:*

(see index for correct answer)

- a. Complex structured finance transactions
- b. Arbitration clause
- c. Single business enterprise
- d. Companies Acts

Guidance: level 1

:: Accounting in the United States ::

The _____ is the source of generally accepted accounting principles used by state and local governments in the United States. As with most of the entities involved in creating GAAP in the United States, it is a private, non-governmental organization.

Exam Probability: **Medium**

20. *Answer choices:*

(see index for correct answer)

- a. The Wheat Committee
- b. Public Company Accounting Oversight Board
- c. Variable interest entity
- d. Governmental Accounting Standards Board

Guidance: level 1

:: Legal terms ::

An _____ is an action which is inaccurate or incorrect. In some usages, an _____ is synonymous with a mistake. In statistics, "_____" refers to the difference between the value which has been computed and the correct value. An _____ could result in failure or in a deviation from the intended performance or behaviour.

Exam Probability: **Low**

21. *Answer choices:*

(see index for correct answer)

- a. Condonation
- b. Judicial opinion

- c. Error
- d. Good conduct time

Guidance: level 1

:: Business economics ::

_____ is one of the constituents of a leasing calculus or operation. It describes the future value of a good in terms of absolute value in monetary terms and it is sometimes abbreviated into a percentage of the initial price when the item was new.

Exam Probability: **High**

22. *Answer choices:*
(see index for correct answer)

- a. Vendor finance
- b. Inorganic growth
- c. Residual value
- d. Center for Business and Economic Research

Guidance: level 1

:: Marketing ::

_____ or stock is the goods and materials that a business holds for the ultimate goal of resale.

Exam Probability: **Medium**

23. *Answer choices:*

(see index for correct answer)

- a. Back to school
- b. Earned media
- c. Inventory
- d. Customer acquisition management

Guidance: level 1

:: Accounting in the United States ::

_____ refers to a Memorandum of Understanding signed in September 2002 between the Financial Accounting Standards Board, the US standard setter, and the International Accounting Standards Board. The agreement is so called as it was reached in Norwalk.

Exam Probability: **Low**

24. *Answer choices:*

(see index for correct answer)

- a. Certified Public Accountant
- b. Cotton Plantation Record and Account Book
- c. Norwalk Agreement
- d. Certified Government Financial Manager

Guidance: level 1

:: ::

_____ are electronic transfer of money from one bank account to another, either within a single financial institution or across multiple institutions, via computer-based systems, without the direct intervention of bank staff.

Exam Probability: **Low**

25. *Answer choices:*
(see index for correct answer)

- a. process perspective
- b. Electronic funds transfer
- c. interpersonal communication
- d. personal values

Guidance: level 1

:: Financial accounting ::

_____ in accounting is the process of treating investments in associate companies. Equity accounting is usually applied where an investor entity holds 20–50% of the voting stock of the associate company. The investor records such investments as an asset on its balance sheet. The investor's proportional share of the associate company's net income increases the investment, and proportional payments of dividends decrease it. In the investor's income statement, the proportional share of the investor's net income or net loss is reported as a single-line item.

Exam Probability: **Low**

26. *Answer choices:*
(see index for correct answer)

- a. Money measurement
- b. Financial Condition Report
- c. Hidden asset
- d. Equity method

Guidance: level 1

:: Management accounting ::

_____, or dollar contribution per unit, is the selling price per unit minus the variable cost per unit. "Contribution" represents the portion of sales revenue that is not consumed by variable costs and so contributes to the coverage of fixed costs. This concept is one of the key building blocks of break-even analysis.

Exam Probability: **High**

27. *Answer choices:*

(see index for correct answer)

- a. Certified Management Accountant
- b. Certified Management Accountants of Canada
- c. Average per-bit delivery cost
- d. Corporate travel management

Guidance: level 1

:: Finance ::

The _____ of a corporation is the accumulated net income of the corporation that is retained by the corporation at a particular point of time, such as at the end of the reporting period. At the end of that period, the net income at that point is transferred from the Profit and Loss Account to the _____ account. If the balance of the _____ account is negative it may be called accumulated losses, retained losses or accumulated deficit, or similar terminology.

Exam Probability: **Medium**

28. *Answer choices:*

(see index for correct answer)

- a. Real-time energy trader
- b. Performance attribution
- c. Retained earnings
- d. Undervalued stock

Guidance: level 1

:: Accounting terminology ::

_____ is a legally enforceable claim for payment held by a business for goods supplied and/or services rendered that customers/clients have ordered but not paid for. These are generally in the form of invoices raised by a business and delivered to the customer for payment within an agreed time frame. _____ is shown in a balance sheet as an asset. It is one of a series of accounting transactions dealing with the billing of a customer for goods and services that the customer has ordered. These may be distinguished from notes receivable, which are debts created through formal legal instruments called promissory notes.

Exam Probability: **Low**

29. *Answer choices:*

(see index for correct answer)

- a. revenue recognition principle
- b. Absorption costing
- c. Accounts receivable
- d. Internal auditing

Guidance: level 1

:: ::

In the field of analysis of algorithms in computer science, the _____ is a method of amortized analysis based on accounting. The _____ often gives a more intuitive account of the amortized cost of an operation than either aggregate analysis or the potential method. Note, however, that this does not guarantee such analysis will be immediately obvious; often, choosing the correct parameters for the _____ requires as much knowledge of the problem and the complexity bounds one is attempting to prove as the other two methods.

Exam Probability: **High**

30. *Answer choices:*

(see index for correct answer)

- a. deep-level diversity
- b. open system
- c. surface-level diversity
- d. Accounting method

Guidance: level 1

:: Management accounting ::

_____s are costs that change as the quantity of the good or service that a business produces changes. _____s are the sum of marginal costs over all units produced. They can also be considered normal costs. Fixed costs and _____s make up the two components of total cost. Direct costs are costs that can easily be associated with a particular cost object. However, not all _____s are direct costs. For example, variable manufacturing overhead costs are _____s that are indirect costs, not direct costs. _____s are sometimes called unit-level costs as they vary with the number of units produced.

Exam Probability: **High**

31. *Answer choices:*
(see index for correct answer)

- a. Variable cost
- b. Accounting management
- c. Extended cost
- d. Operating profit margin

Guidance: level 1

:: Income taxes ::

An _____ is a tax imposed on individuals or entities that varies with respective income or profits . _____ generally is computed as the product of a tax rate times taxable income. Taxation rates may vary by type or characteristics of the taxpayer.

Exam Probability: **High**

32. *Answer choices:*

(see index for correct answer)

- a. Income and Corporation Taxes Act 1988
- b. Income splitting
- c. Income Tax Assessment Act 1936
- d. Income tax

Guidance: level 1

:: Generally Accepted Accounting Principles ::

A _____ or reacquired stock is stock which is bought back by the issuing company, reducing the amount of outstanding stock on the open market .

Exam Probability: **Medium**

33. *Answer choices:*

(see index for correct answer)

- a. Treasury stock
- b. Generally accepted accounting principles
- c. Earnings before interest, taxes, depreciation, and amortization
- d. Cost pool

Guidance: level 1

:: Business models ::

A _____, _____ company or daughter company is a company that is owned or controlled by another company, which is called the parent company, parent, or holding company. The _____ can be a company, corporation, or limited liability company. In some cases it is a government or state-owned enterprise. In some cases, particularly in the music and book publishing industries, subsidiaries are referred to as imprints.

Exam Probability: **High**

34. *Answer choices:*

(see index for correct answer)

- a. Lemonade stand
- b. Premium business model
- c. Subsidiary
- d. Microfranchising

Guidance: level 1

:: Accounting source documents ::

A _____ is a commercial document and first official offer issued by a buyer to a seller indicating types, quantities, and agreed prices for products or services. It is used to control the purchasing of products and services from external suppliers. _____ s can be an essential part of enterprise resource planning system orders.

Exam Probability: **Low**

35. *Answer choices:*
(see index for correct answer)

- a. Superbill
- b. Parcel audit
- c. Remittance advice
- d. Credit memo

Guidance: level 1

:: Debt ::

A _____ is a party that has a claim on the services of a second party. It is a person or institution to whom money is owed. The first party, in general, has provided some property or service to the second party under the assumption that the second party will return an equivalent property and service. The second party is frequently called a debtor or borrower. The first party is called the _____ , which is the lender of property, service, or money.

Exam Probability: **High**

36. *Answer choices:*

(see index for correct answer)

- a. Vulture fund
- b. Legal liability
- c. Creditor
- d. Debt wall

Guidance: level 1

:: ::

The _____ of 1938 29 U.S.C. § 203 is a United States labor law that creates the right to a minimum wage, and "time-and-a-half" overtime pay when people work over forty hours a week. It also prohibits most employment of minors in "oppressive child labor". It applies to employees engaged in interstate commerce or employed by an enterprise engaged in commerce or in the production of goods for commerce, unless the employer can claim an exemption from coverage.

Exam Probability: **Medium**

37. *Answer choices:*

(see index for correct answer)

- a. Fair Labor Standards Act
- b. process perspective
- c. co-culture
- d. levels of analysis

Guidance: level 1

:: Financial accounting ::

A _____ is an ownership interest in a corporation with enough voting stock shares to prevail in any stockholders' motion. A majority of voting shares is always a _____ . When a party holds less than the majority of the voting shares, other present circumstances can be considered to determine whether that party is still considered to hold a controlling ownership interest.

Exam Probability: **Medium**

38. *Answer choices:*

(see index for correct answer)

- a. SEC filing
- b. Associate company

- c. Authorised capital
- d. Money measurement

Guidance: level 1

:: International Financial Reporting Standards ::

_____ , usually called IFRS, are standards issued by the IFRS Foundation and the International Accounting Standards Board to provide a common global language for business affairs so that company accounts are understandable and comparable across international boundaries. They are a consequence of growing international shareholding and trade and are particularly important for companies that have dealings in several countries. They are progressively replacing the many different national accounting standards. They are the rules to be followed by accountants to maintain books of accounts which are comparable, understandable, reliable and relevant as per the users internal or external. IFRS, with the exception of IAS 29 Financial Reporting in Hyperinflationary Economies and IFRIC 7 Applying the Restatement Approach under IAS 29, are authorized in terms of the historical cost paradigm. IAS 29 and IFRIC 7 are authorized in terms of the units of constant purchasing power paradigm.IAS 2 is related to inventories in this standard we talk about the stock its production process etcIFRS began as an attempt to harmonize accounting across the European Union but the value of harmonization quickly made the concept attractive around the world. However, it has been debated whether or not de facto harmonization has occurred. Standards that were issued by IASC are still within use today and go by the name International Accounting Standards , while standards issued by IASB are called IFRS. IAS were issued between 1973 and 2001 by the Board of the International Accounting Standards Committee . On 1 April 2001, the new International Accounting Standards Board took over from the IASC the responsibility for setting International Accounting Standards. During its first meeting the new Board adopted existing IAS and Standing Interpretations Committee standards . The IASB has continued to develop standards calling the new standards " _____ ".

Exam Probability: **Medium**

39. *Answer choices:*

(see index for correct answer)

- a. IFRS 5
- b. International Financial Reporting Standards
- c. International Public Sector Accounting Standards
- d. IFRS Foundation

Guidance: level 1

:: Commerce ::

A _____ , is a document acknowledging that a person has received money or property in payment following a sale or other transfer of goods or provision of a service. All _____ s must have the date of purchase on them. If the recipient of the payment is legally required to collect sales tax or VAT from the customer, the amount would be added to the _____ and the collection would be deemed to have been on behalf of the relevant tax authority. In many countries, a retailer is required to include the sales tax or VAT in the displayed price of goods sold, from which the tax amount would be calculated at point of sale and remitted to the tax authorities in due course. Similarly, amounts may be deducted from amounts payable, as in the case of wage withholding taxes. On the other hand, tips or other gratuities given by a customer, for example in a restaurant, would not form part of the payment amount or appear on the _____ .

Exam Probability: **High**

40. *Answer choices:*

(see index for correct answer)

- a. Card association
- b. Receipt
- c. Group buying
- d. Bidding

Guidance: level 1

:: Finance ::

_____ is the ability of a bank customer in the United States and Canada to deposit a check into a bank account from a remote location, such as an office or home, without having to physically deliver the check to the bank. This is typically accomplished by scanning a digital image of a check into a computer, then transmitting that image to the bank. The practice became legal in the United States in 2004 when the Check Clearing for the 21st Century Act took effect, though not all banks have implemented the system.

Exam Probability: **Medium**

41. *Answer choices:*

(see index for correct answer)

- a. SONIA
- b. Quantum finance
- c. Ultra high-net-worth individual

- d. Remote deposit

Guidance: level 1

:: Accounting in the United States ::

_____ were documents issued by the Committee on Accounting Procedure between 1938 and 1959 on various accounting problems. They were discontinued with the dissolution of the Committee in 1959 under a recommendation from the Special Committee on Research Program. In all, 17 bulletins were issued; however, the lack of binding authority over AICPA`s membership reduced the influence of, and compliance with the content of the bulletins. The _____ have all been superseded by the Accounting Standards Codification .

Exam Probability: **Low**

42. *Answer choices:*
(see index for correct answer)

- a. Accounting Research Bulletins
- b. Institute of Internal Auditors
- c. Uniform Certified Public Accountant Examination
- d. Public Company Accounting Oversight Board

Guidance: level 1

:: Accounting terminology ::

In management accounting or _____ , managers use the provisions of accounting information in order to better inform themselves before they decide matters within their organizations, which aids their management and performance of control functions.

Exam Probability: **High**

43. *Answer choices:*

(see index for correct answer)

- a. Accounting equation
- b. Share premium
- c. Managerial accounting
- d. Double-entry accounting

Guidance: level 1

:: Accounting systems ::

In accounting, the controlling account is an account in the general ledger for which a corresponding subsidiary ledger has been created. The subsidiary ledger allows for tracking transactions within the controlling account in more detail. Individual transactions are posted both to the controlling account and the corresponding subsidiary ledger, and the totals for both are compared when preparing a trial balance to ensure accuracy.

Exam Probability: **High**

44. Answer choices:

(see index for correct answer)

- a. Bookkeeping association
- b. Control account
- c. Dome Publishing
- d. Bank reconciliation

Guidance: level 1

:: Taxation ::

A _____ is a person or organization subject to pay a tax. _____s have an Identification Number, a reference number issued by a government to its citizens.

Exam Probability: **Low**

45. Answer choices:

(see index for correct answer)

- a. Taxpayer
- b. Per unit tax
- c. Tax deferral
- d. Lindahl tax

Guidance: level 1

:: Stock market ::

A _____ , securities exchange or bourse, is a facility where stock brokers and traders can buy and sell securities, such as shares of stock and bonds and other financial instruments. _____ s may also provide for facilities the issue and redemption of such securities and instruments and capital events including the payment of income and dividends. Securities traded on a _____ include stock issued by listed companies, unit trusts, derivatives, pooled investment products and bonds. _____ s often function as "continuous auction" markets with buyers and sellers consummating transactions via open outcry at a central location such as the floor of the exchange or by using an electronic trading platform.

Exam Probability: **Medium**

46. *Answer choices:*
(see index for correct answer)

- a. Immediate or cancel
- b. stock price
- c. Initial public offering
- d. Stock Exchange

Guidance: level 1

:: Bank regulation ::

_____ is a measure implemented in many countries to protect bank depositors, in full or in part, from losses caused by a bank's inability to pay its debts when due. _____ systems are one component of a financial system safety net that promotes financial stability.

Exam Probability: **Medium**

47. *Answer choices:*

(see index for correct answer)

- a. Exposure at default
- b. Bank regulation
- c. Deposit insurance
- d. Financial Consumer Agency of Canada

Guidance: level 1

:: ::

A _____, in the word's original meaning, is a sheet of paper on which one performs work. They come in many forms, most commonly associated with children's school work assignments, tax forms, and accounting or other business environments. Software is increasingly taking over the paper-based _____.

Exam Probability: **Medium**

48. *Answer choices:*

(see index for correct answer)

- a. personal values
- b. process perspective
- c. Worksheet
- d. co-culture

Guidance: level 1

:: Management accounting ::

A _____ is an organizational unit headed by a manager, who is responsible for its activities and results. In responsibility accounting, revenues and cost information are collected and reported on by _____ s.

Exam Probability: **Low**

49. *Answer choices:*

(see index for correct answer)

- a. Extended cost
- b. Responsibility center
- c. Net present value
- d. Corporate travel management

Guidance: level 1

:: Real property law ::

_____ is the judicial process whereby a will is "proved" in a court of law and accepted as a valid public document that is the true last testament of the deceased, or whereby the estate is settled according to the laws of intestacy in the state of residence [or real property] of the deceased at time of death in the absence of a legal will.

Exam Probability: **Low**

50. *Answer choices:*
(see index for correct answer)

- a. Solar easement
- b. Probate
- c. Purveyance
- d. Buyer listing

Guidance: level 1

:: Management accounting ::

_____ are costs that are not directly accountable to a cost object. _____ may be either fixed or variable. _____ include administration, personnel and security costs. These are those costs which are not directly related to production. Some _____ may be overhead. But some overhead costs can be directly attributed to a project and are direct costs.

Exam Probability: **Low**

51. Answer choices:

(see index for correct answer)

- a. Variable Costing
- b. Construction accounting
- c. Indirect costs
- d. Notional profit

Guidance: level 1

:: Free accounting software ::

A _____ is the principal book or computer file for recording and totaling economic transactions measured in terms of a monetary unit of account by account type, with debits and credits in separate columns and a beginning monetary balance and ending monetary balance for each account.

Exam Probability: **High**

52. Answer choices:

(see index for correct answer)

- a. Ledger
- b. SQL-Ledger
- c. JGnash

- d. HomeBank

Guidance: level 1

:: Management accounting ::

_____ is the process of recording, classifying, analyzing, summarizing, and allocating costs associated with a process, after that developing various courses of action to control the costs. Its goal is to advise the management on how to optimize business practices and processes based on cost efficiency and capability. _____ provides the detailed cost information that management needs to control current operations and plan for the future.

Exam Probability: **Medium**

53. *Answer choices:*

(see index for correct answer)

- a. Semi-variable cost
- b. Invested capital
- c. Fixed assets management
- d. RCA open-source application

Guidance: level 1

:: ::

The _____ is an American stock exchange located at 11 Wall Street, Lower Manhattan, New York City, New York. It is by far the world's largest stock exchange by market capitalization of its listed companies at US$30.1 trillion as of February 2018. The average daily trading value was approximately US$169 billion in 2013. The NYSE trading floor is located at 11 Wall Street and is composed of 21 rooms used for the facilitation of trading. A fifth trading room, located at 30 Broad Street, was closed in February 2007. The main building and the 11 Wall Street building were designated National Historic Landmarks in 1978.

Exam Probability: **High**

54. *Answer choices:*

(see index for correct answer)

- a. empathy
- b. imperative
- c. New York Stock Exchange
- d. information systems assessment

Guidance: level 1

:: Budgets ::

An _____ is the annual budget of an activity stated in terms of Budget Classification Code, functional/subfunctional categories and cost accounts. It contains estimates of the total value of resources required for the performance of the operation including reimbursable work or services for others. It also includes estimates of workload in terms of total work units identified by cost accounts.

Exam Probability: **Medium**

55. *Answer choices:*

(see index for correct answer)

- a. Personal budget
- b. Budget
- c. Operating budget
- d. Marginal budgeting for bottlenecks

Guidance: level 1

:: Taxation ::

In a tax system, the _____ is the ratio at which a business or person is taxed. There are several methods used to present a _____ : statutory, average, marginal, and effective. These rates can also be presented using different definitions applied to a tax base: inclusive and exclusive.

Exam Probability: **High**

56. *Answer choices:*

(see index for correct answer)

- a. Tax rate
- b. Steuerberater
- c. Inflation tax
- d. Taxpayer

Guidance: level 1

:: Data security ::

_____ is the concept of having more than one person required to complete a task. In business the separation by sharing of more than one individual in one single task is an internal control intended to prevent fraud and error. The concept is alternatively called segregation of duties or, in the political realm, separation of powers. In democracies, the separation of legislation from administration serves a similar purpose. The concept is addressed in technical systems and in information technology equivalently and generally addressed as redundancy.

Exam Probability: **Medium**

57. *Answer choices:*

(see index for correct answer)

- a. Defense in depth
- b. Multi-party authorization

- c. Separation of duties
- d. Backup

Guidance: level 1

:: Generally Accepted Accounting Principles ::

In business and accounting, _____ is an entity's income minus cost of goods sold, expenses and taxes for an accounting period. It is computed as the residual of all revenues and gains over all expenses and losses for the period, and has also been defined as the net increase in shareholders' equity that results from a company's operations. In the context of the presentation of financial statements, the IFRS Foundation defines _____ as synonymous with profit and loss. The difference between revenue and the cost of making a product or providing a service, before deducting overheads, payroll, taxation, and interest payments. This is different from operating income .

Exam Probability: **Medium**

58. *Answer choices:*

(see index for correct answer)

- a. Gross income
- b. Net income
- c. Long-term liabilities
- d. Trial balance

Guidance: level 1

:: Pricing ::

_____ is the difference between a lower selling price and a higher purchase price, resulting in a financial loss for the seller.

Exam Probability: **Medium**

59. *Answer choices:*

(see index for correct answer)

- a. Expected marginal seat revenue
- b. No-bid contract
- c. Nonlinear pricing
- d. Fire sale

Guidance: level 1

INDEX: Correct Answers

Foundations of Business

1. a: Insurance

2. : Competitor

3. : Life

4. d: E-commerce

5. a: Free trade

6. : Entrepreneur

7. : Planning

8. : Brainstorming

9. d: Advertising

10. c: Property

11. c: Meeting

12. b: Corporate governance

13. : Tariff

14. a: Logistics

15. b: Financial crisis

16. b: Employment

17. c: Business process

18. a: Market segmentation

19. c: Performance

20. b: Stock

21. : Labor relations

22. b: Marketing strategy

23. : Foreign direct investment

24. d: Common stock

25. : Document

26. : Cash flow

27. c: Interest

28. c: Schedule

29. a: Customs

30. : Consumer Protection

31. : Interest rate

32. d: Market research

33. c: Corporation

34. b: Economies of scale

35. c: Market value

36. a: Copyright

37. : Ownership

38. : Bias

39. a: Demand

40. d: Good

41. c: Trade

42. a: Case study

43. : Procurement

44. : Mission statement

45. b: Firm

46. c: Stock market

47. b: Supply chain

48. a: Outsourcing

49. b: Retail

50. b: Information

51. b: Stock exchange

52. a: Size

53. a: Pattern

54. d: Gross domestic product

55. : Brand

56. b: Budget

57. d: Opportunity cost

58. : Limited liability

59. b: Cooperative

Management

1. : Glass ceiling

2. b: Career

3. c: Resource management

4. c: Scientific management

5. c: Feedback

6. : Employee stock

7. d: Ambiguity

8. c: Leadership style

9. : Statistical process control

10. d: Expatriate

11. d: Hotel

12. b: Scheduling

13. c: Trade

14. c: Compromise

15. d: Tariff

16. : Assembly line

17. a: Incentive

18. b: Emotional intelligence

19. b: Transactional leadership

20. d: Law

21. c: Social loafing

22. : Transformational leadership

23. : Problem solving

24. b: Sharing

25. a: Enabling

26. a: Human resource management

27. d: Project team

28. a: Leadership development

29. c: Code

30. a: Decision tree

31. d: Industrial Revolution

32. d: Organization chart

33. b: Organizational commitment

34. c: Political risk

35. d: Risk management

36. c: Organizational learning

37. d: Business plan

38. b: Affirmative action

39. a: Statistic

40. d: Empowerment

41. a: Ownership

42. b: Questionnaire

43. d: Procurement

44. b: Training

45. b: Crisis

46. a: Lead

47. a: Creativity

48. a: Choice

49. b: Job enlargement

50. d: Human capital

51. b: Market research

52. : International trade

53. : 360-degree feedback

54. b: Enron

55. a: Good

56. c: Argument

57. a: Supervisor

58. d: Total quality management

59. : Quality control

Business law

1. b: Merger

2. b: Shareholder

3. d: Verdict

4. a: World Trade Organization

5. : Procedural law

6. : Statute

7. c: Economic espionage

8. b: Hearing

9. b: Sherman Act

10. d: Firm offer

11. a: Supreme Court

12. : Appellate Court

13. a: Sherman Antitrust

14. c: False imprisonment

15. d: Antitrust

16. d: Appeal

17. a: Parol evidence

18. b: Cause of action

19. b: Cooperative

20. a: Testimony

21. : Delegation

22. c: Offeree

23. d: Contract

24. b: Revenue

25. : Surety

26. : Good faith

27. d: Consumer Good

28. c: Operating agreement

29. a: Fair use

30. a: Contract Clause

31. : Contributory negligence

32. : Real estate

33. a: Corporation

34. : Certiorari

35. b: Statute of frauds

36. b: Identity theft

37. c: Lanham Act

38. a: Liquidated damages

39. c: Common carrier

40. a: Ratification

41. a: Collective bargaining

42. c: Trustee

43. d: Sole proprietorship

44. b: Industry

45. b: Adverse possession

46. c: Constitutional law

47. c: Promissory note

48. : Secured transaction

49. c: Assumption of risk

50. c: Employment discrimination

51. : Offeror

52. d: Inventory

53. d: Federal government

54. a: Consideration

55. : Holder in due course

56. d: Prohibition

57. c: Welfare

58. d: Economic Espionage Act

59. a: Credit

Finance

1. a: Intangible asset

2. b: Copyright

3. a: Earnings per share

4. a: Variable Costing

5. a: Preferred stock

6. d: Liquidation

7. a: Sole proprietorship

8. b: Asset turnover

9. : Sales

10. c: Fixed asset

11. b: Money market

12. b: Shares

13. : Deferral

14. c: Capital expenditure

15. : Contract

16. d: Firm

17. a: Monetary policy

18. b: Secondary market

19. b: Trade

20. c: Book value

21. a: Fraud

22. a: Current asset

23. b: Total cost

24. : Callable bond

25. d: Cash flow

26. b: Issuer

27. d: Purchasing

28. a: Net present value

29. c: Bank statement

30. b: Chief financial officer

31. a: Property

32. b: Cost of goods sold

33. b: Need

34. c: Fiscal year

35. : Interest rate

36. b: Mortgage

37. : Merger

38. a: Variable cost

39. : Currency

40. d: Stock split

41. : Loan

42. : Inventory

43. : Payroll

44. d: Income

45. : Rate of return

46. d: Income tax

47. a: Indenture

48. b: Petty cash

49. a: Break-even

50. d: Return on assets

51. d: Derivative

52. c: Credit card

53. : Cost driver

54. d: Common stock

55. d: Demand

56. d: Treasury stock

57. a: Risk management

58. b: Bankruptcy

59. b: Fixed cost

Human resource management

1. c: Employee retention

2. a: Performance

3. d: Sweatshop

4. a: Authoritarianism

5. d: Cost leadership

6. a: Social contract

7. c: Strategic management

8. d: Resource management

9. a: Bargaining unit

10. b: On-the-job training

11. d: Sexual orientation

12. b: Exit interview

13. d: Psychological contract

14. c: Employee benefit

15. d: Reinforcement

16. a: Love contract

17. d: Open shop

18. b: Piece rate

19. c: Analysis

20. a: Employee Free Choice Act

21. c: Career development

22. : Ingratiation

23. : Internship

24. c: Bureau of Labor Statistics

25. d: Glass ceiling

26. b: Independent contractor

27. c: Job enlargement

28. : Centralization

29. a: Aggression

30. c: National Labor Relations Act

31. b: American Federation of Government Employees

32. c: Restricted stock

33. b: Closed shop

34. b: Cultural intelligence

35. c: Social network

36. b: Telecommuting

37. d: Retirement

38. b: Balance sheet

39. d: Picketing

40. : Total Quality Management

41. d: Expatriate

42. b: Vesting

43. b: Cafeteria plan

44. d: Transformational leadership

45. b: Job satisfaction

46. c: Trade union

47. d: Job evaluation

48. b: Coaching

49. d: Compa-ratio

50. c: Parental leave

51. b: Human capital

52. a: Questionnaire

53. b: Minimum wage

54. a: Construct validity

55. d: Salary

56. b: Progressive discipline

57. c: Right to work

58. d: Knowledge management

59. c: Bottom line

Information systems

1. a: Wiki

2. d: Data model

3. a: YouTube

4. b: Semantic Web

5. d: Global Positioning System

6. d: Supply chain

7. a: Software as a service

8. c: Non-repudiation

9. : Click-through rate

10. d: Google Calendar

11. a: Metadata

12. d: Business rule

13. b: Information technology

14. b: Network interface card

15. c: Competitive intelligence

16. b: Expert system

17. b: Pop-up ad

18. c: Privacy policy

19. a: Drill down

20. d: ICANN

21. a: Mobile computing

22. c: Groupware

23. a: Utility computing

24. b: Questionnaire

25. a: Input device

26. c: Resource management

27. d: Worm

28. a: Domain Name System

29. b: Google

30. : Social shopping

31. a: Click fraud

32. d: Credit card

33. b: World Wide Web

34. a: Chief information officer

35. d: Interactivity

36. c: Interaction

37. b: Online analytical processing

38. c: Information silo

39. a: Text mining

40. c: Manifesto

41. a: Peer production

42. b: Web server

43. a: Help desk

44. b: Data warehouse

45. c: Data governance

46. : COBIT

47. c: Social network

48. : Telnet

49. b: Total cost

50. d: Electronic funds transfer

51. a: Personalization

52. c: Executive information system

53. d: Change control

54. b: Authentication

55. c: Fraud

56. b: Computer-aided manufacturing

57. c: Joint application design

58. : Information management

59. : Bit rate

Marketing

1. c: Aid

2. d: Investment

3. a: Advertising campaign

4. b: General Motors

5. : Merchant

6. c: Early adopter

7. : Loyalty program

8. d: Merchandising

9. d: Direct selling

10. d: Household

11. a: Testimonial

12. a: Strategic planning

13. d: Mission statement

14. a: Global marketing

15. d: Viral marketing

16. d: Globalization

17. c: Brand loyalty

18. : Customer retention

19. : Marketing mix

20. d: Consumerism

21. a: Brainstorming

22. c: Raw material

23. b: Derived demand

24. : Social media

25. a: Planning

26. b: Marketing research

27. c: Preference

28. b: Business Week

29. d: Project

30. a: Demand

31. d: Questionnaire

32. a: Return on investment

33. : Attention

34. a: Cost-plus pricing

35. b: Data warehouse

36. d: Situation analysis

37. c: Authority

38. d: Code

39. b: Direct mail

40. a: Corporation

41. a: Microsoft

42. c: Business model

43. a: Organizational structure

44. d: Health

45. d: Sales

46. c: Utility

47. d: Social networking

48. b: Electronic data interchange

49. a: New product development

50. c: Google

51. b: Dimension

52. : Quantitative research

53. c: Industry

54. : Concept testing

55. b: Interactive marketing

56. d: Technology

57. d: Manager

58. a: Primary data

59. d: Inflation

Manufacturing

1. a: EFQM

2. : Reorder point

3. c: Average cost

4. c: Reflux

5. : Sharing

6. : Bill of materials

7. a: Purchasing manager

8. a: Economies of scope

9. a: Bullwhip effect

10. c: Process capability

11. b: Business process

12. b: Concurrent engineering

13. a: Sony

14. : Perfect competition

15. : Service level

16. d: Indirect costs

17. b: Reboiler

18. : Property

19. a: Ball

20. b: Value engineering

21. : Downtime

22. : Thomas Register

23. b: Milestone

24. c: Control limits

25. b: Stakeholder management

26. d: Consortium

27. a: Service quality

28. d: Furnace

29. : Zero Defects

30. d: Goal

31. d: Original equipment manufacturer

32. a: Process flow diagram

33. d: Vendor relationship management

34. b: Project

35. a: Knowledge management

36. : Voice of the customer

37. b: Sunk costs

38. : Minitab

39. b: Total cost

40. : Strategic planning

41. b: Control chart

42. d: Total productive maintenance

43. a: Forecasting

44. d: E-procurement

45. a: Cost

46. c: Pattern

47. d: Estimation

48. c: Gantt chart

49. d: Metal

50. : Capacity planning

51. b: Financial plan

52. b: Manufacturing

53. a: Check sheet

54. b: Licensed production

55. c: Cost estimate

56. a: Process control

57. a: Histogram

58. : Joint Commission

59. : Change management

Commerce

1. : Sexual harassment

2. a: Buyer

3. b: Mass production

4. b: Consortium

5. b: Argument

6. a: Competitive advantage

7. b: Public policy

8. d: Advertising

9. : Economic regulation

10. : Americans with Disabilities Act

11. : Total revenue

12. d: Collaborative filtering

13. : E-procurement

14. d: Bank

15. a: York

16. a: Pop-up ad

17. a: Jury

18. a: Customer service

19. d: Federal government

20. b: Strategic alliance

21. b: Marketing strategy

22. d: Complaint

23. b: Economic development

24. : Logistics

25. a: Optimum

26. c: Recruitment

27. c: WebSphere Commerce

28. a: Transaction cost

29. : Total cost

30. c: Regulatory agency

31. b: Disintermediation

32. c: Publicity

33. c: Marketing mix

34. : Product line

35. a: Bottom line

36. : Overtime

37. : Automation

38. d: Industry

39. d: Minimum wage

40. d: Business-to-business

41. b: Level of service

42. d: Electronic funds transfer

43. c: Economics

44. b: Bankruptcy

45. c: Trade show

46. a: Phishing

47. c: Fixed cost

48. a: Chief executive officer

49. b: Lease

50. : Commerce

51. d: Personnel

52. : Wage

53. c: PayPal

54. : Warehouse

55. a: Mining

56. d: English auction

57. : General manager

58. d: Market research

59. d: Consideration

Business ethics

1. : Retaliation

2. b: Lanham Act

3. : Locus of control

4. b: Marijuana

5. a: White-collar crime

6. a: Junk bond

7. a: Kyoto Protocol

8. : United Farm Workers

9. c: East India

10. : Sullivan principles

11. c: Medicaid

12. b: Communist Manifesto

13. : Empowerment

14. c: Capitalism

15. : Hedonism

16. a: Edgewood College

17. d: Fraud

18. b: Public relations

19. : Pure Food and Drug Act

20. b: Enron

21. : Employee Polygraph Protection Act

22. d: Whistleblower

23. c: Habitat

24. : Principal Financial

25. d: Pyramid scheme

26. c: Madoff

27. : Oil spill

28. d: Transformational leadership

29. c: Volcker Rule

30. a: Corporate social responsibility

31. a: Solar power

32. c: Occupational Safety and Health Administration

33. b: Trojan horse

34. b: Electronic waste

35. c: Global reach

36. d: Foreign Corrupt Practices Act

37. d: Clean Water Act

38. b: Planet

39. a: Parental leave

40. b: Fair Trade Certified

41. c: Ethical leadership

42. b: Layoff

43. d: Federal Trade Commission Act

44. b: Pollution

45. : Nonprofit

46. a: Toxic waste

47. c: Skill

48. c: Interlocking directorate

49. a: Corporate governance

50. b: Reputation

51. a: Micromanagement

52. c: Veil of ignorance

53. c: Self-interest

54. a: Antitrust

55. : Natural gas

56. a: Utopian socialism

57. : Individualistic culture

58. a: Consumer Financial Protection Bureau

59. a: Vigilance committee

Accounting

1. d: Variable Costing

2. a: Accounting

3. b: American Express

4. : Public Company Accounting Oversight Board

5. a: Par value

6. c: Bad debt

7. a: Inventory valuation

8. b: Process Management

9. d: Gross margin

10. c: Tax revenue

11. : Invoice

12. d: Parent company

13. c: Relevant cost

14. a: Payroll

15. c: Market value

16. a: Cost

17. : Taxable income

18. c: Chief financial officer

19. : Operating lease

20. d: Governmental Accounting Standards Board

21. c: Error

22. c: Residual value

23. c: Inventory

24. c: Norwalk Agreement

25. b: Electronic funds transfer

26. d: Equity method

27. : Contribution margin

28. c: Retained earnings

29. c: Accounts receivable

30. d: Accounting method

31. a: Variable cost

32. d: Income tax

33. a: Treasury stock

34. c: Subsidiary

35. : Purchase order

36. c: Creditor

37. a: Fair Labor Standards Act

38. : Controlling interest

39. b: International Financial Reporting Standards

40. b: Receipt

41. d: Remote deposit

42. a: Accounting Research Bulletins

43. c: Managerial accounting

44. b: Control account

45. a: Taxpayer

46. d: Stock Exchange

47. c: Deposit insurance

48. c: Worksheet

49. b: Responsibility center

50. b: Probate

51. c: Indirect costs

52. a: Ledger

53. : Cost accounting

54. c: New York Stock Exchange

55. c: Operating budget

56. a: Tax rate

57. c: Separation of duties

58. b: Net income

59. : Capital loss

CPSIA information can be obtained
at www.ICGtesting.com
Printed in the USA
LVHW011543301019
635718LV00004B/393/P